HISTORICIZING FEAR

Historicizing Fear

IGNORANCE, VILIFICATION, AND OTHERING

edited by
Travis D. Boyce and Winsome M. Chunnu

University Press of Colorado
Louisville

Published by University Press of Colorado
245 Century Circle, Suite 202
Louisville, Colorado 80027

ASSOCIATION of UNIVERSITY PRESSES   The University Press of Colorado is a proud member of
the Association of University Presses.

The University Press of Colorado is a cooperative publishing enterprise supported, in part, by
Adams State University, Colorado State University, Fort Lewis College, Metropolitan State
University of Denver, Regis University, University of Colorado, University of Northern Colorado,
University of Wyoming, Utah State University, and Western Colorado University.

ISBN:978- 1-60732-813-1(cloth)
ISBN:978- 1-64642-001-8(paperback)
ISBN:978- 1-64642-002-5 (open-accessPDF)
ISBN:978- 1-64642-003-2 (open-accessePUB)
https://doi.org/10.5876/9781646420025

Library of Congress Cataloging-in-Publication Data

Names: Boyce, Travis D., editor. | Chunnu, Winsome M., editor.
Title: Historicizing fear : ignorance, vilification, and othering / edited by Travis D. Boyce and
   Winsome M. Chunnu.
Description: Louisville : University Press of Colorado, [2019] | Includes bibliographical references
   and index.
Identifiers: LCCN 2019035864 (print) | LCCN 2019035865 (ebook) | ISBN 9781607328131 (cloth)
|
   ISBN 9781646420025 (ebook)
Subjects: LCSH: Fear—Political aspects—History. | Fear—Social aspects—History. | Political
   persecution—Psychological aspects—History.
Classification: LCC BF575.F2 H57 2019 (print) | LCC BF575.F2 (ebook) | DDC 305.8— dc23
LC record available at https://lccn.loc.gov/2019035864
LC ebook record available at https://lccn.loc.gov/2019035865

An electronic version of this book is freely available, thanks to the support of libraries
working with Knowledge Unlatched. KU is a collaborative initiative designed to make
high-quality books open access for the public good. More information about the initiative and links to the open-access versions can be found at www.knowledgeunlatched.org.

Contents

HOW FEAR, ONCE CREATED AND SPREAD, IS USED FOR POLITICAL ENDS

HISTORICIZING FEAR

"I Want to Get Rid of My Fear"

An Introduction

Travis D. Boyce and Winsome M. Chunnu

> Fear of unconformity, fear of race, fear of disease, fear of touch, fear of blood, fear of non-straight sex, fear of workers, fear of desire, fear of women, fear of subaltern rage, fear of color, fear of desire, fear of crime, fear of "illegals," and the fear of uprising: Fear is both the metanarrative that drives the disciplinary apparatus of the nation-state (police, Immigration and Naturalization Services [INS], military, schools) and the intended effects on the body politic.
> —ARTURO J. ALDAMA (*VIOLENCE AND THE BODY: RACE, GENDER, AND THE STATE*, 1–2).

This edited volume examines the use of fear and "Othering." Certainly, we'll show how fear is used within contemporary political events. But this book goes deeper, searching many historical cultures and societies. We believe historians are crucial to the understanding today of how fear is used as a tool. This volume vigorously tackles how the "Other" is defined, how fear of the Other is reinforced and spread, and its use for political gain.

Throughout this volume, the reader will get a clear view of how individuals and groups are oppressed and marginalized. When we look at the past, we can better understand how fear is used now and how it could be used in the future. Fearful framing is ever-present in our society, as can be easily seen in modern life. For example, on July 21, 2016, Donald J. Trump officially accepted the nomination to become the Republican Party's candidate for president of the United States. Once

DOI: 10.5876/9781646420025.c000

considered a long shot because of his lack of political experience, circus-like persona, and bombastic and divisive rhetoric, Trump successfully secured the nomination by exploiting and exaggerating his "liabilities." Trump emerged from a crowded field of candidates during the primaries that included Texas senator Ted Cruz and the initial favorite, former governor of Florida Jeb (John Ellis) Bush, among others. Trump ran a presidential primary campaign featuring rhetoric centered on nationalism, ethnocentrism, and fear—most notably connecting Mexican immigrants to drugs and violent crimes such as rape. He even promised to build a wall along the US–Mexican border.[1] In his nomination acceptance speech, Trump played on the fears of white Americans, a demographic that has historically controlled the political economy in the United States but that is now in decline and projected to become a minority racial group by 2042.[2]

Covertly calling for white unity in his campaign slogan "Let's Make America Great Again," Trump painted a bleak picture of the state of domestic affairs in the United States. He implicitly indicted people of color (African Americans) and Mexican immigrants for the "rise" of violent crimes (under the administration of this nation's first African American president). He noted:

> Decades of progress made in bringing down crime are now being reversed by this Administration's rollback of criminal enforcement. Homicides last year increased by 17% in America's fifty largest cities. That's the largest increase in 25 years. In our nation's capital, killings have risen by 50 percent. They are up nearly 60% in nearby Baltimore. In the President's hometown of Chicago, more than 2,000 have been the victims of shootings this year alone. And more than 3,600 have been killed in the Chicago area since he took office. The number of police officers killed in the line of duty has risen by almost 50% compared to this point last year. Nearly 180,000 illegal immigrants with criminal records, ordered deported from our country, are tonight roaming free to threaten peaceful citizens.[3]

Framing himself as the "law and order" candidate, Trump relished delivering a convention speech that emphasized supporting the police force, ignoring the fact that these institutions have historically had a troubled and violent relationship with communities of color. While offering his sympathies to officers wounded or killed by black assailants in the recent shootings in Dallas, Texas, and Baton Rouge, Louisiana, respectively, he remained silent on the murders of Alton Sterling and Philando Castile, among others, by police—thus essentially endorsing the narrative, as noted by ethnic studies professor Arturo J. Aldama, that state violence against the Other (people of color) is acceptable:[4]

> America was shocked to its core when our police officers in Dallas were brutally executed. In the days after Dallas, we have seen continued threats and violence

against our law enforcement officials. Law officers have been shot or killed in recent days in Georgia, Missouri, Wisconsin, Kansas, Michigan, and Tennessee.

On Sunday, more police were gunned down in Baton Rouge, Louisiana. Three were killed, and four were badly injured. An attack on law enforcement is an attack on all Americans. I have a message to every last person threatening the peace on our streets and the safety of our police: when I take the oath of office next year, I will restore law and order in our country.[5]

Instead of extolling national unity, Trump promoted division. Instead of offering ideas for reconciliation, Trump conjured up reasons for agitation. Instead of providing reassurance, Trump preached "fear of the Other." His convention speech and rhetoric during the 2016 presidential primary and general election campaign reflected these issues, especially fear of the Other.

The election of Barack Obama in 2008 as this nation's first African American president was a signal to white America that they would no longer be the numerical majority in the coming years. Political science professors Christopher Parker and Matt Barreto argue that an Obama presidency signaled to a conservative white America "the erosion of their position in America."[6] Moreover, Algernon Austin, an economist, notes that the white, conservative populous who hates and fears an Obama presidency translates to a sector of the population that harbors xenophobic, racist, and Islamophobic feelings.[7] Trump successfully tapped into these anxieties to assemble a political base. He won the support of prominent white nationalists such as David Duke and other members of the extreme right (colloquially, "Alternative Right" or "Alt Right") by carefully portraying people of color, immigrants, and Muslims as the Other (pathologically dangerous, a burden on the economy, and so forth) and thus a group to be feared.

Trump's creation of the intimidating and even monstrous Other is not a single or isolated event but instead mirrors what is happening around the world, particularly in western and central Europe where majority white populations are told by right-wing politicians that their way of life is threatened by immigrants and non-whites. Nigel Farage, former leader of the far-right United Kingdom Independence Party (UKIP), rose to political prominence on right-wing ideologies, most notably his anti-immigration stance. He has especially opposed Muslim immigration; in addition, in 2014, he smeared Romanian immigrants as criminals. Farage's racist campaign was controversial but still succeeded in propagating negative stereotypes of Eastern European immigrants. He increased the tension between white people born in Britain and communities of refugees and others seeking a place in UK society.[8] Moreover, in the spring of 2016, during Austrian presidential elections, Nobert Hofer of the far-right and anti-immigrant Freedom Party, captured 35 percent of the popular vote in the first round of voting. Although Hofer did not win in the runoff, his anti-immigrant platform won a considerable amount of the votes and even won heavy support in areas that were historically left-leaning. Hermine Löffler, a fifty-seven-year-old Austrian retiree and a supporter of Hofer and the Freedom Party, was asked why she supported this politician's political party with its anti-immigrant platform. She replied simply, "I want to get rid of my fear."[9]

While xenophobia is propagated in many western and central European nations in an attempt to get far-right candidates into office, such efforts have recently proven most successful in the United Kingdom. On June 23, 2016, approximately a month prior to Trump accepting the presidential nomination, the United Kingdom voted to leave the European Union. This referendum, popularly known as Brexit, was marketed to British, Scottish, and Irish voters with a shrewd combination of messages springing from racial hatred and xenophobia.[10] These feelings were fundamentally grounded in working-class anxieties about losing jobs to immigrants. Exaggerated stories about the benefits available to people coming to the United Kingdom from other countries were also circulated. These myths about the effects of immigration are commonly held all over western and central Europe.[11] Three years prior to the Brexit vote, exit polls from the May 2013 elections indicated that 45 percent of those who voted for the UK Independence Party agreed that the whole of Europe should put a freeze on immigration.[12] Boris Johnson, London's former mayor and prominent Brexit supporter (and a member of the UKIP), campaigned heavily under the slogan "Let's take back control." Johnson's simplistic slogan's nationalist, xenophobic flavor can easily be identified as being of one piece with Trump's catchphrase "Let's make America great again."

Brexit supporters came to believe they were no longer bound by the moderate immigrant policies designated by the European Union. They began to act out their extremist and even violent anti-immigrant sentiments in the newly independent United Kingdom. While policies regarding immigration actually require a long legislative process to alter, there has been immediate backlash at the street level against non-whites and immigrants in the United Kingdom. Xenophobic violence, discrimination, and harassment toward immigrants and non-whites as a result of the fear rhetoric increased sharply.[13] In the weeks leading up to and following the historic Brexit vote, hate crimes increased by a whopping 42 percent.[14] In late August 2016, Polish immigrant Arek Jozwik, age forty, was hit in the head by a gang of British teenagers because he was overheard speaking in Polish.[15] Jozwik died.

Examining fear and "Othering" within the framework of contemporary political events is an important and significant issue in history. But this volume seeks to do more—to broaden the context of how fear of the "Other" can used as a propaganda tool. The authors of this book examine many cultures and societies to see how fear is historicized. How is fear used to construct laws? How can fear help to devise policies of oppression? We decided that a collection of original essays examining the use of fear as a tool was a much-needed narrative after we coauthored a chapter titled "Fear Factor: When Black Equality Is Framed as Militant," which is included in Novotny Lawrence's 2014 book, *Documenting the Black Experience*. This chapter shows how "fear of the Other" has been used historically as a propaganda tool against African Americans seeking equality.[16]

This volume, *Historicizing Fear*, is grounded on the theory of "Othering," which was coined in 1948 by French philosopher Emmanuel Levinas.[17] This theory has received an incredible amount of attention as a theoretical framework explaining oppression. While a significant body of literature examines the concept of the Other, this book provides a global perspective. This book is motivated by historian Peter Stearns's assessment in 2006 that historians should be part of the discourse with regard to fear and contemporary history.[18] Further, this volume looks at examples of the use of fear as a tool *to prevent groups or individuals from gaining equality*.

Perhaps one of the best ways to understand the concept of Othering is to examine the institution of slavery and justifications for its existence. Orlando Patterson's 1982 *Slavery and Social Death* is a helpful, comparative examination of slavery.[19] Drawing from various societies in human history that treated human beings as property, Patterson's premise is simple: human and social relationships have a power dynamic. The framing of one who is enslaved correlates to the notion of powerlessness and therefore the Other.

There is a range of literature that also provides a background in the Other concept. For example, Saidiya Hartman's 1997 *Scenes of Subjection* reinforces the narrative of the Other within the context of slavery.[20] Unlike Patterson, who examines slavery from various societies in world history, Hartman specifically examines slavery through the lens of the development of black identity, as a result of Otherness in nineteenth-century US history (antebellum to the end of the Reconstruction era). Examining Otherness within the context of postcolonial/post-emancipation periods is also important. For example, Columbia University philosopher Gayatri Spivak's essay and best-known 1988 work, "Can the Subaltern Speak," tackles the issue of Otherness from the perspective of postcolonial India.[21] What is most universally understood about her essay are the problems, ethical issues, and misinterpretations that may occur when one examines a culture based on stereotypes and universal understandings of that culture.

W.E.B. Du Bois's *The Souls of Black Folk* (1903) and Franz Fanon's *Black Skin, White Masks* (1952) embody a universal narrative of how the dominant society's narrative of the Other can have a negative psychological impact on the Othered.[22]

Du Bois framed it (coining the term *double consciousness* from the experiences of African American life during the early twentieth century). For Fanon, the cultural lens that resonated for him was the racism experienced by blacks in colonial French Caribbean society. Sociologist Simone Brown's 2015 book appears to carry on the spirit of Franz Fanon. In *Dark Matters: On the Surveillance of Blackness*, she examines how the notion of surveillance and systemic Othering has perpetuated anti-black racism and reinforced white supremacy since the founding of this nation.[23] Historian Kahlil Gibran Muhammad argues that black Americans have historically been defined as criminals and pathological. Consequently, the white power structure has used this narrative to justify racial segregation, discriminatory treatment, and racial violence.[24]

Michael Waltman, an associate professor of communication, critiques popular and seminal right-wing literature (such as Ayn Rand's 1957 *Atlas Shrugged* and Kyle Bristow's 2010 *White Apocalypse*). His 2014 book theorizes that right-wing discourse in the United States is shaped by the basic concept of fear of white extinction and the Othering of communities of color.[25] Inspired and motivated by Fanon's 1961 work *The Wretched of the Earth*, ethnic studies scholar Arturo J. Aldama provides an edited volume that examines the Otherization of physical bodies (as seen through the lens of colonialism, the US–Mexico borderland, and Latin American studies). Aldama elucidates how physical and material violence reinforces social norms in that respective society.[26] Historian Clive Webb provides an interesting perspective on the American Civil Rights movement by examining the rhetoric and activism of five far-right grassroots activists who effectively peddled fear of racial integration in the wake of the 1954 *Brown v. Board of Education* decision by Othering African Americans, communists, and so on.[27] What is unique about Webb's 2010 work in the broader context is that (1) it specifically examines fear and Othering at the grass-roots level, and (2) the rhetoric and activism of the five activists in the book can easily be applied to any society (in terms of their techniques).

In José Esteban Muñoz's 1999 *Disidentifications*, the author examines the performances of queer communities of color through the old white and hetero-normative context.[28] While these members of society are Othered, Muñoz suggests that the performance of queer communities of color works within societal norms but at the same time redefines or challenges social norms.

Our volume, *Historicizing Fear*, consists of ten chapters, carefully organized in three sections:

1. Defining the "Other"/Pathologizing Differences
2. Reinforcing or Spreading Fear of the "Other"
3. How Fear, Once Created and Spread, Is Used for Political Ends

These sections provide an unflinching look at racism, fearful framing, oppression, and marginalization.

DEFINING THE "OTHER"/PATHOLOGIZING DIFFERENCES

In chapter 1, Quaylan Allen and Henry Santos Metcalf have provided a stellar look at masculinity. They identify the race-gendered discourse about black male identity, showing that it reflects the discursive practices of a racially hegemonic society. Black male performances (what black men do) are often viewed or defined through a lens of pathology. In this narrow view, black men are assumed to be intellectually and morally inferior to white men—but also inherently deviant, dangerous, and a threat to society. How is the fear of black masculinities constructed? How is this fear propagated? Allen and Metcalf walk us through various social institutions that facilitate this fear, including the media, schools, and social policy. The authors take on the controversy of race-gendered profiling, which is evident in a legal system in which black men are disproportionately arrested and disciplined more harshly than their white male counterparts for committing the same offenses. The chapter gives us a close-up look at a tragedy: the 2013 killing of a seventeen-year-old black male, Trayvon Martin, and the subsequent acquittal of his killer, George Zimmerman. The event mimics the verdict of the infamous 1955 killing of teen Emmett Till and as such re-ignited a national debate over the racial profiling of black men. The authors detail how the assumption of black male deviancy may have implicated Martin in his own death.

In chapter 2, Adam Fong moves us to ancient China. In this chapter we learn about the attitudes of Chinese elites during the Tang dynasty toward their newly re-conquered regions of the West River basin. They had gained what today are the Guangdong and Hainan Provinces and the Guangxi Zhuang Ethnicity Autonomous Region of the People's Republic of China. The author tells us that the Tang dynasty was a period of reunification and then expansion for the Chinese empire. Tang elite classes were forced to grapple with how and to what extent these newly conquered (or re-conquered) peoples would be incorporated into their empire. The elites viewed the southernmost parts of the Tang, the West River basin, as a wild frontier area full of manifold and hidden dangers, many leading to sudden death. To them, to be sent to this region was to be exiled from civilization, a fate that was only partially offset by the possibility of becoming rich along the frontier. These fears worked to marginalize the inhabitants of the south, who were dismissed as subhuman savages. The fear also strengthened notions of what "Chinese" civilization was by comparing it to an exotic, southern "Other."

Chapter 3 concludes this section. In this chapter, Melanie Armstrong dissects the materiality of unseen, living, mutating microbes. Armstrong explores how the discovery of an environment teeming with microscopic life re-made fears of nature and, in turn, how this knowledge transformed people's lives. The author shows us how the fear of germs enabled racialized political practices. The people in power found that they could manage citizens through the management of microbes. Armstrong examines images and descriptions of microbes in science reporting during the late nineteenth century, when people were "taught" to fear germs. She also considers how locating germs outside the human body created the belief that specific diseases could be controlled, even eradicated. Racialized representations of the smallpox virus during the global smallpox eradication campaign of the mid-twentieth century illustrate how fear of disease revives colonial narratives and rationalizes militant acts on the part of the state. In this history of microbial fear, Armstrong shows how biology became entwined with security. The author illuminates the present moment, when microbes are taking on new meanings through biotechnology. She calls our attention to the mechanisms of governance rooted in moral panics over the belief that human life is at risk from unseen microbes.

REINFORCING OR SPREADING FEAR OF THE "OTHER"

Kirsten Dyck reveals, in chapter 4, the contemporary scene of today's white-power musicians. These artists use their music to promote overtly racist white-power and/or neo-Nazi goals. According to this rhetoric, "enemies" of the white race (such as Jews, Muslims, people of African descent, and multicultural Western governments) are working to introduce people of non-European descent into geographic areas previously controlled by whites, hoping to "race-mix" whites out of existence. For white-power musicians and their fans, this purported threat justifies not only violent propaganda but also, occasionally, actual violence as well. Dyck illustrates how these lyrics not only update old racist constructs from eras such as the US Civil War and the Third Reich but also offer new ones (such as the Zionist Occupation Government Jewish conspiracy theory). Dyck explains why some individuals of European descent believe in white-power racism and the fear of miscegenation, despite the fact that *overt* racism has become a taboo in most Western countries.

In chapter 5, Guy Lancaster takes the reader to Arkansas in the late nineteenth and early twentieth centuries. This was a time of terror, in which both vigilantes and state authorities carried out racial cleansing by the expulsion of African Americans. To make their point even clearer, they created exclusively white communities dubbed "sundown towns" (no African Americans, not even those employed as servants, were allowed to remain within their boundaries after sundown). This chapter is grounded in the work of philosopher Claudia Card as well as that of anthropologists Andrew Strathern and Pamela J. Stewart, who observe that terror is "based on an interlocking feedback between memory and anticipation."[29] Lancaster shows how state authorities helped to promote fear, usually directed at white audiences. Racial-cleansing violence was rarely deadly, but it proved effective at altering the demography of entire geographic regions because it was explicitly couched in terror directed at an entire community. Thus there was no realistic expectation that the violence might subside when a particular alleged wrongdoer was apprehended and eliminated, as in the horrific but time-limited mob violence that led to a lynching.

Julie M. Powell, in chapter 6, reassesses the meaning of the first Red Scare and early domestic anticommunism through the lens of racial theory. This theory questions old notions of a grassroots hysteria by positing that Red Scare domestic anticommunism (what became an expression of racist nativism) was deliberately used by white business interests to cripple unionized labor. Souring American citizens on working-class solidarity, even if it was against their own interests, required an appeal to fear—not of the dangers of an intangible ideology but of the threat of the not-quite-white racial outsider. In 1919, elites (and those people with business interests) inaugurated a project of racializing communism. They capitalized on the rampant nativism of early twentieth-century Americans and a new racial hierarchy to ensure that communistic ideology and its attendant union collectivism gained no ground stateside. Ultimately, what elites needed to maintain the capitalist class system was a closed chain of signification that equated unionized labor with the alien, not-quite-white Other and the vague specter of communism.

Powell shows us how this emerged during the Red Scare of 1919–1920. Political cartoons from the Red Scare era serve as extant links in this chain—evidence of the pedagogical racialization of communism. *Pro*scriptive cartoons, which instructed citizens to fear and hate the Other, racialized the communist as a menacing, savage outsider, un-American in origin, appearance, and comportment. *Pre*scriptive cartoons supplemented such notions, calling on Americans to remedy the invasion by rejecting communism through racially charged calls for deportation and violent reprisal. This racial project inaugurated a shift in the nature of American anticommunism, in which conservative opposition gained ground not on the basis of any broad-based ideological aversion to liberalism but on the fear and hatred of a racialized Other.

Chapter 7 concludes this section. In this chapter, we explore how the plot, select scenes, and political messages from D. W. Griffith's controversial film *The Birth of a Nation* (1915) left a lasting legacy of institutional racism, fear of equality, and Othering of African Americans. Both implicitly and explicitly, millions of white viewers in 1915 were reminded by *Birth* that black equality was to be feared. The idea that equality would be a disaster was framed in the context of the vulnerability of white womanhood, the possibility of black-on-white violence, and the probable ineptitude of black elected officials. Subsequent generations received the message that blacks were rapists and fundamentally violent and that they needed to stay in their place (and certainly out of politics).

Clearly, throughout the twentieth and early twenty-first centuries, African Americans have made significant achievements with regard to racial equality. By the twenty-first century, an African American was elected to the presidency of the United States. Thus the nation should be moving toward a post-racial society. We argue that to the contrary, the United States has experienced a "rebirth" as a polarized, racialized nation, grounded on white anxiety and fear of black equality. To what extent is US society still mired in the message of D. W. Griffith's film? Readers will explore three historical/contemporary issues related to themes presented in Griffith's film in which blacks who sought equality were Othered and vilified as rapists—violent, untrustworthy, lustful, and incapable of self-rule.

HOW FEAR, ONCE CREATED AND SPREAD, IS USED FOR POLITICAL ENDS

The Vietnam War is sometimes referred to as the first "pharmacological war" because the consumption of drugs by those in the service assumed alarming proportions, consequently resulting in a perfect example of how fear can be used to achieve political ends. In chapter 8, Łukasz Kamieński reveals that massive and habitual consumption of drugs during the war was contextual and usually did not continue after these soldiers returned home. But some media, politicians, and intellectuals (notably John Steinbeck IV) created the myth of the "addicted army." For what purpose? The author shows that those people exploited the myth to blame soldiers for the nation's inability to win the war. The Vietnam veterans were victimized; the public began recognizing them as dangerous "Others," as junkies who would spread an epidemic of narcotic use across the United States. What is more, the image of the druggie veteran created a moral panic that was used to introduce and justify national anti-narcotic measures. One example is the launch of the War on Drugs in 1971 by then-president Richard Nixon. Thus the fear of the drug-crazed veteran was, in fact, politically constructed.

In chapter 9, Jelle Versieren and Brecht De Smet offer the fascinating story of the Belgian and Dutch organized workers' movement. The authors transport us to the third quarter of the nineteenth century, when the Belgian and Dutch organized workers' movement came into being. Why did the workers organize? The movement was a result of a series of local labor conflicts combined with the mass-movement politics of hitherto isolated socialist initiatives. Between 1780 and 1880, early industrialists used several social-economic tactics (as well as techniques of micro-physical power) to discipline the impoverished urban craftsmen and the influx of proletarianized rural laborers. The factory owners legitimized their practices of fear and discipline through a heterodox discursive strategy. First, there was a patriarchal call for obedience and also for the conceptualization of the factory floor as a natural chain of command. Second, there was the concept of individual prudence, which followed from a sense of duty of both capitalist and worker.

Only after the introduction of the economics of scale and an intensive socialization of production could the socialist movement link the economic-corporate interests of each group of workers with a political program. The factory owners tried to turn the tide by waging a propaganda war in widely read conservative newspapers.

The broadly anti-radical and specifically anti-Jewish hysteria of World War I is exposed by Jeffery A. Johnson. His chapter 10 concludes this section. He argues that anti-radical sentiments were largely subtexts of ethnic and religious discrimination. The most commonly persecuted and discriminated group was leftist Jewish Americans. Leftist (specifically Jewish) agitators during World War I spoke bravely against US intervention in the affairs of Europe. Jewish antiwar dissent (and fear of "alien radicals") was greeted with a firm, negative response by the anxious average citizen. This seems ironic given the length of time it took America to enter the war and widespread separatist sentiments throughout the United States that held Europe responsible for settling its own political problems. But consistency has never been an obstacle to racist stereotypes or legislation. The darkest moment came with the passage of the 1917 Espionage Act and the 1918 Sedition Act, both of which drastically restricted free-speech rights and other civil liberties. As wartime paranoia reached its apex, two Jewish leftists, socialists Victor Berger and Louis Waldman, were actually refused their democratically elected seats in the US House of Representatives and the New York State Assembly, respectively. Few people today remember this incredibly high-handed refusal to seat a duly elected representative of the voters. The Red Scare of 1919–1920 culminated in hundreds of deportations. This culture of fear had profound implications for the political left. The mood of anti-radicalism and anti-Semitism offers powerful lessons about racism, discrimination, and unfounded alarm. This chapter suggests just how quickly and easily fear can drive political reactions that restrict prized freedoms.

College history instructors and students will find much of what is offered here to be thought-provoking. But all readers, especially in divisive political climates around the world where nationalism, ethnocentrism, xenophobia, and fear of the Other are on the rise, will discover something of interest in this book because of its interdisciplinary spirit and wide range of eras covered. For example, there is much in this book that will interest people who study popular culture, critical race issues, social justice, ethnicity, and contemporary history. It is our hope that this book represents the first in a series that discusses how fear and Othering from a historical context can provide a better understanding of how power and oppression are used in the present day.

NOTES

1. Beinart, "The Republican Party's White Strategy."
2. NPR Staff, "US Will Have Minority Whites Sooner, Says Demographer."
3. Trump, "Republican Nomination Presidential Acceptance Speech."
4. Aldama, "Violence, Bodies, and the Color of Fear," 3.
5. Trump, "Republican Nomination Presidential Acceptance Speech."
6. Parker and Barreto, *Change They Can't Believe In*, 100.
7. Austin, *America Is Not Post-Racial*, xii.
8. Beauchamp, "Brexit Isn't about Economics." Also see, BBC Staff, "Nigel Farage Attacked over Romanian 'Slur.'"
9. Troianovski, "Europe's Populist Politicians Tap into Deep-Seated Frustration."
10. Aziz, "Brexit Wasn't about Economics."
11. Betz, *Radical Right-Wing Populism in Western Europe*, 69–106.
12. Flamini, "The UK Independence Party," 37.
13. *Al Jazerra*, "Brexit: Increase in Racist Attacks after EU Referendum." Also see de Freytas-Tamura, "After 'Brexit' Vote, Immigrants Feel a Town Turn against Them."
14. Dewan, "Hate Crime Reports Surge in Britain in Weeks around 'Brexit.'"
15. Bilefsky. "Fatal Beating of Polish Man."
16. Chunnu-Brayda and Boyce, "Fear Factor."
17. Levinas. *Le Temps et l'Autre*. Also see Levinas, *Totalité et Infini*.
18. Stearns, "Fear and Contemporary History," 483.
19. Patterson, *Slavery and Social Death*.
20. Hartman, *Scenes of Subjection*.
21. Spivak, "Can the Subaltern Speak," 271–313.
22. Du Bois, *The Souls of Black Folk*. Also see Fanon, *Black Skin, White Masks*.
23. Brown, *Dark Matters*.
24. Muhammad, *The Condemnation of Blackness*, 1–4.
25. Waltman, *Hate on the Right*.
26. Aldama, *Violence and the Body*.
27. Webb, *Rabble Rousers*.
28. Muñoz, *Disidentifications*.
29. Strathern and Stewart, "Introduction," 3.

BIBLIOGRAPHY

Aldama, Arturo J. "Violence, Bodies, and the Color of Fear: An Introduction." In *Violence and the Body: Race, Gender and the State*, ed. Arturo J. Aldama, 1–16. Bloomington: Indiana University Press, 2003.

Al Jazerra. "Brexit: Increase in Racist Attacks after EU Referendum." *Al Jazerra*, June 28, 2016. http://www.aljazeera.com/news/2016/06/brexit-increase-racist-attacks-eu -referendum-160628045317215.html.

Austin, Algernon. *America Is Not Post-Racial: Xenophobia, Islamophobia, Racism, and the 44th President*. Santa Barbara, CA: Praeger, 2015.

Aziz, Omer. "Brexit Wasn't about Economics, It Was about Racial Hatred." *Huffington Post*, June 29, 2016. http://www.huffingtonpost.com/entry/brexit-wasnt-about-economics-it -was-about-racial_us_5773b50be4b0d24f8fb51d03?section.

BBC Staff. "Nigel Farage Attacked over Romanian 'Slur.'" *BBC.com*, May 18, 2014. http:// www.bbc.com/news/uk-27459923.

Beauchamp, Zack. "Brexit Isn't about Economics, It's about Xenophobia." *VOX*, June 24, 2016. http://www.vox.com/2016/6/23/12005814/brexit-eu-referendum-immigrants.

Beinart, Peter. "The Republican Party's White Strategy." *The Atlantic*, July–August 2016. http://www.theatlantic.com/magazine/archive/2016/07/the-white-strategy/485612/.

Betz, Hans-Georg. *Radical Right-Wing Populism in Western Europe*. New York: St. Martin's, 1993.

Bilefsky, Dan. "Fatal Beating of Polish Man Fuels Debate over Xenophobia in Britain." *New York Times*, September 1, 2016.

Brown, Simone. *Dark Matters: On the Surveillance of Blackness*. Durham, NC: Duke University Press, 2015.

Chunnu-Brayda, Winsome, and Travis D. Boyce. "Fear Factor: When Black Equality Is Framed as Militant." In *Documenting the Black Experience: Essays on African American History, Culture, and Identity in Nonfiction Films*, ed. Novotny Lawrence, 57–73. Jefferson, NC: McFarland, 2014.

de Freytas-Tamura, Kimiko. "After 'Brexit' Vote, Immigrants Feel a Town Turn against Them." *New York Times*, July 9, 2016. http://www.nytimes.com/2016/07/10/world /europe/ brexit-immigrants-great-britain-eu.html?_r=0.

Dewan, Angela. "Hate Crime Reports Surge in Britain in Weeks around 'Brexit.'" *CNN*, July 8, 2016.

Du Bois, W.E.B. *The Souls of Black Folk*. Chicago: A. C. McClurg, 1903; New York: Bartleby.com, 1999.

Fanon, Franz. *Black Skin, White Masks*. Paris: Éditions du Seuil, 1952.

Flamini, Roland. "The UK Independence Party: Euroskeptics Rattle Cameron." *World Affairs* 176, no. 2 (2013): 35–41.

Hartman, Saidiya. *Scenes of Subjection: Terror, Slavery, and Self-Making in Nineteenth-Century America*. New York: Oxford University Press, 1997.

Levinas, Emmanuel. *Le Temps et l'Autre* [*Time and the Other*]. Lectures in Paris at the College Philosophique, 1946–1947, trans. Richard A. Cohen. Pittsburgh, PA: Duquesne University Press, 1990.

Levinas, Emmanuel. *Totalité et Infini* [*Totality and Infinity*], trans. Alphonso Lingis. The Hague, Netherlands: Martinus Nijhoff, 1961 (in French); Pittsburgh, PA: Duquesne University Press, 1969 (in English).

Muhammad, Kahlil Gibran. *The Condemnation of Blackness: Race, Crime, and the Making of Modern Urban America*. Cambridge, MA: Harvard University Press, 2010.

Muñoz, José Esteban. *Disidentifications: Queers of Color and the Performance of Politics*. Minneapolis: University of Minnesota Press, 1999.

NPR Staff. "US Will Have Minority Whites Sooner, Says Demographer." *NPR*, June 27, 2011. http://www.npr.org/2011/06/27/137448906/us-will-have-minority-whites-sooner -says-demographer.

Parker, Christopher S., and Matt A. Barreto. *Change They Can't Believe In: The Tea Party and Reactionary Politics in America*. Princeton, NJ: Princeton University Press, 2013.

Patterson, Orlando. *Slavery and Social Death: A Comparative Study*. Cambridge, MA: Harvard University Press, 1982.

Spivak, Gayatri Chakravorty. "Can the Subaltern Speak?" In *Marxism and the Interpretation of Culture*, ed. Cary Nelson and Lawrence Grossberg, 271–331. Urbana: University of Illinois Press, 1988.

Stearns, Peter N. "Fear and Contemporary History: A Review Essay." *Journal of Social History* 40, no. 2 (Winter 2006): 477–484.

Strathern, Andrew, and Pamela J. Stewart. "Introduction: Terror, the Imagination, and Cosmology." In *Terror and Violence: Imagination and the Unimaginable*, ed. Andrew Strathern, Pamela J. Stewart, and Neil L. Whitehead, 1–3. Ann Arbor, MI: Pluto, 2006.

Troianovski, Anton. "Europe's Populist Politicians Tap into Deep-Seated Frustration." *Wall Street Journal*, May 19, 2016. http://www.wsj.com/articles/europes-populist -politicians-win-voters-hearts-1463689360.

Trump, Donald. J. "Republican Nomination Presidential Acceptance Speech." Cleveland, OH, July 21, 2016. *Washington Post*, https://www.washingtonpost.com/news/the-fix /wp/2016/07/21/full-text-donald-trumps-prepared-remarks-accepting-the-republican -nomination/.

Waltman, Michael. *Hate on the Right: Right-Wing Political Groups and Hate Speech*. New York: Peter Lang, 2014.

Webb, Clive. *Rabble Rousers: The American Far Right in the Civil Rights Era*. Athens: University of Georgia Press, 2010.

Defining the "Other"/Pathologizing Differences

1

"Up to No Good"

The Intersection of Race, Gender, and Fear of Black Men in US Society

Quaylan Allen and Henry Santos Metcalf

George Stinney Jr. became the youngest person (at fourteen years old) executed in the United States in the twentieth century, by electric chair in Alcolu, South Carolina. He had been accused and convicted of brutally murdering two young white girls in a nearby meadow. Records of this case indicate that proceedings were questionable. The fact that Stinney was a black youth in the South suggests that he was at a disadvantage in a predominantly white justice system. All-white mobs demanded retaliation. Within three months of the girls' murders, he was accused, tried by an all-white jury, convicted, and executed. Evidence was vague, witnesses were absent, and his "confession" (after an interrogation by white officers) was the primary argument incriminating him.[1] This case demonstrates a severe instance in which a black youth was seen as criminal, absent evidence. It typifies the historical stigmatization and normalization of young black men in a negative light. It is this view that directly influences dominant attitudes of fear and oppression that persist today.

A modern-day illustration was seen on February 26, 2012, on a rainy Sunday evening in central Florida. A seventeen-year-old black male, Trayvon Martin, was walking home through a gated community after purchasing an Arizona iced tea and a bag of Skittles from a local 7-Eleven store. During the walk home, Martin was followed by twenty-eight-year-old George Zimmerman, an armed, white, neighborhood-watch volunteer. Zimmerman viewed Martin as suspicious and (in Zimmerman's words) "up to no good." The resulting encounter between the two ended with Zimmerman fatally shooting Martin. Zimmerman's story was that the

DOI: 10.5876/9781646420025.c001

seventeen-year-old Martin had attacked him. Zimmerman was acquitted of murder on the premise of self-defense. (He was not acquitted by Florida's Stand Your Ground law, which is commonly mis-cited as the reason.) This event sparked a national discussion regarding racial profiling and the killing of black men and was the genesis of the #BlackLivesMatter movement.

The murder of Trayvon also points to how race and gender intersect for black men in the United States. The logic Zimmerman used to pursue Martin draws on a long-standing public assumption of black male deviancy. In this sense, the fear of black masculinity is a socially constructed ideology that implies wrongdoing by black males (such as Trayvon Martin and countless others), resulting in their surveillance, discipline, and (in many cases) death.

This chapter shows how fear is part of society's view of black masculinity. In particular, the chapter will reveal how the fear of black men is constructed and propagated through various social institutions (including the media and social policy). The chapter looks closely at the Trayvon Martin case, among other examples, to highlight how dominant ontologies are mapped onto the black male body. We describe how these ontologies are used to subjugate black men through particular forms of surveillance, discipline, marginalization, and exploitation. First, the social construction of black masculinities is described. Then the chapter goes further to examine how media representation, surveillance, and discipline policies all serve as powerful ideological and repressive institutions that reproduce the fear of black masculinities.

BLACK MASCULINITIES

An exploration of the history of fear of black men begins with the social construction of black masculinity. Historically, black men have been perceived and treated by whites as an inferior race, as if they were an un-evolved form of masculinity. Because both race and gender are socially constructed identities informed by and through relationships of power in a white, patriarchal, capitalist society, black masculinities have been largely interpreted in relationship to white, hegemonic masculinity. Thus black masculinities have largely been developed through xenophobia of the black male body. Ironically, black men are seen as both a threat and a commodity by the white, patriarchal, capitalist society. As such, black masculinities might be understood to be a collection of practices constructed through social anxiety and fear of black men. This fear is then mediated by the state through particular hegemonic, discursive, and repressive practices.[2]

For example, early theories on black masculinity (fueled by what is now known as racist and flawed science) described black men as intellectually and morally inferior to white men.[3] Black men were assumed to be uneducable yet physically superior or hyper-masculine, making them dangerous and needing to be controlled by white patriarchs.[4] The overemphasis on the physicality of the black body and concomitant under-emphasis on intellectual capacities seems to serve the corporate interests of a white, capitalist class reliant on maintaining systems of worker exploitation (such as slavery, sharecropping, low-wage employment, and so forth).[5]

A discourse of fear of black male physicality similarly exploits black male sexuality. White America's fascination with black sexual practices equated black men's presumed sexual prowess with animalistic desires.[6] Black men were and continue to be viewed as hyper-sexual and sexually aggressive, lacking the capacity to control their sexual urges and conform to Victorian notions of middle-class sexual decency. White women in particular were assumed to be the ultimate sexual conquest of black men and warranted the need for white men to protect white racial and sexual purity. This was largely done through the regulation (e.g., miscegenation laws) and punishment (e.g., lynching) of the black body. The quest to regulate racial purity is likely part of the Stinney case. The black teen had apparently "confessed" to wanting to have sexual relations with the two white girls who had been murdered, though evidence did not demonstrate that the deceased had been sexually assaulted. His execution could be interpreted as white men protecting the white female body.

In this sense, in a white, patriarchal, capitalist regime, both black men and white women were seen as property of white men. In this regime, white women needed protection and black men needed regulation. One illustration is the well-known 1955 case of Emmett Till. Till, a fourteen-year-old boy visiting family in Money, Mississippi, was accused of breaking cultural mores by interacting with a white woman. Subsequently, the teen was brutally beaten and killed by the accuser's husband and brother-in-law. Situated in a discourse of fear of miscegenation, as in Till's case, black male sexuality is regulated to protect the property value of white women.[7]

Popular conceptions and fear of black male sexuality are largely mediated by mass communications. The next section explains how popular media representations perpetuate a stigmatized construction of black masculinities.

POPULAR REPRESENTATION IN MEDIA

Popular representations of black men, particularly through mass media, have been influential in propagating fear of black masculinities. Black men—particularly men living in urban communities—are regularly depicted as violent, angry, prone to criminal behavior, and hyper-sexual.[8] Although former president Barack Obama, the first black male president of the United States, is currently a habituated image of black masculinity, the most commonly consumed images of black men in contemporary times are of the athlete, the gangster rapper, and the criminal. Each of these images is celebrated and appropriated while concomitantly loathed and feared.[9] As John Hoberman explains, "The merger of the athlete, the gangster rapper, and the criminal into a single black male persona" has created a dominant black masculinity that supersedes other masculinities and confirms white fears.[10] On the occasions where middle-class black men are represented, they often appear assimilated into dominant cultural norms, emasculated, or asexual, safe, and appeasing white fears.[11] This situation has led to a somewhat bipolar representation of black masculinity, where black men are constructed as either "good" or "bad" depending on how much their behaviors either appease or create anxiety among gazing whites.[12]

For instance, local and network news programming regularly associates black men with crime, making criminality the most common stereotype of black masculinity in the media.[13] Black men are disproportionately portrayed in scowling mug shots or in handcuffs.[14] In examining negative media messages about blacks, Lanier Frush Holt describes how media communications set a primer for racial perceptions that influence the general public.[15] Priming is defined as the process by which certain aspects of an issue are made more salient by the media and, in turn, influence a person's perception or understanding. Thus when media portrayals constantly show black men as participants in criminal activity, "this overexposure has the dual effect of causing many whites to conflate violence with being black and increasing the belief that committing crime is a natural tendency for blacks."[16] People with limited or minimal interactions with black men may draw upon what they infer from the media's priming, which inherently invokes fear and distrust. The cognitive effect of racial priming on public perceptions contributes to how black males are monitored and judged based on whether their masculine behaviors confirm or contradict preconceived notions of black male deviancy.[17] Furthermore, media-propagated racial stereotypes play a significant role in inducing and perpetuating viewers' beliefs that black men are more likely than white men to commit a crime. If so, white people might reason, black men are thus deserving of differential racial profiling, convictions, sentencing, and even death.[18]

The case of Trayvon Martin presents a complex example of media representation. The media started out with one narrative, but then moved to another. For instance, initial pictures of both Martin and George Zimmerman were polarizing. A photo provided by the Martin family pictured Trayvon as a young, innocent-looking teen, wearing a black Hollister T-shirt and smiling into the camera. This particular picture was taken roughly four years before Martin's death. That photo of the teen was often presented alongside a mug shot of Zimmerman, taken roughly six years earlier when he had been arrested for assaulting an officer. (The charges filed against Zimmerman for this incident were later dropped.) When shown side by side, the two photos constructed an initial narrative of an innocent child gunned down by a vigilante who "had it in for" black male youth. This visual story drew upon a long history of black male witchhunts at the hands of white male aggressors. The nature of Martin's death was often compared to that of Emmett Till over half a century earlier. In the public's eye, Martin's innocence and Zimmerman's guilt were initially presumed.

The narrative shifted as other images and reports of Martin surfaced. Photographs emerged showing him with gold fronts on his teeth, wearing pants that were sagged, and "flipping off" the camera. Such images countered the previous images of youthful innocence. The more recent Martin photos were placed alongside new images of Zimmerman wearing a suit and smiling. Reports of Martin's disciplinary record in school, which included suspensions for being tardy, writing graffiti, and possessing remnants of marijuana, were used by media in conjunction with the new images to paint Martin as a "thug" with disciplinary issues.

Of course, teens of all racial backgrounds stylize their bodies and engage in self-representations of resistance in ways consistent with what they might see in the media.[19] Youth today often wear saggy pants, have tattoos and piercings, and dress in Goth style. And it is not uncommon to find teens who have been suspended for nonviolent offenses such as truancy or willful defiance (the latter a highly subjective and broadly defined infraction that might include rolling one's eyes at a teacher or refusing to have a cell phone confiscated). Trayvon's disciplinary record was hardly an indicator of a future criminal and more that of an average American high school teenager.

Nevertheless, media's *re*-presentation of Martin as a "thug" and the downplaying of earlier images of him as innocent more closely mirror the dominant racial prime used by the media: the view of black men as deviant. There had been a shift in the narrative about both Zimmerman and Martin, where Zimmerman was seen less as a racist vigilante and more as a protector of private property holding the right to defend himself against a supposed black male attacker. Likewise, images of Martin's masculine posturing were, for many, affirmation that Martin, like most black men, was prone to criminal behavior and thus deserving of harsh discipline—despite the fact that Martin's posturing was but one of many ways he might have shown masculinity. Smith College researcher Ann Ferguson studied the ways young black youth are viewed by their teachers. Ferguson's assertion about how black boys are perceived in school is equally applicable to Martin, in that even teens who pose no real threat can easily be relabeled as "troublemakers" if their masculine performances affirm preconceived racist notions of black male deviance.[20]

Today, media offer up sensationalized, narrow representations of certain black male performances over others. Despite this fact, black masculinities are diverse and complex, and in most cases they diverge from the dominant narrative presented through the media. To take no notice of black men's uniqueness is to discount the freedom of black men to make their own race-gendered identity, including the way black boys and men may conceptualize manhood and perform different masculinities across time and space.[21]

Furthermore, negative and stereotypical representations of black masculinity are not reflective of the history of black men. One must take into consideration the hegemonic and structural practices that marginalize and oppress black males in particular ways.[22] As mentioned, the public infatuation with certain black masculinities over others subjects the black male body to particular types of labor exploitation and commodification. Though the gender performances of black men are varied and diverse, the most commercial images in popular media are the thug, gangster, athlete, and criminal. Thus men who fit these identities (such as Lil Wayne and those in the movie *Training Day*) can generate more revenue than the black male scholar. In a capitalist economy, black men performing these essentialized masculine roles are both capital and labor, used as entertainment and marketing tools. Perhaps the successful labor exploitation of particular black masculinities is not only dependent on a general fear of black men but also simultaneously reproduces fear among viewers. This economically motivated and socially constructed fear of black men through popular media appears to be a hegemonic narrative that subjects the black male body to a particular set of material, ideological, and repressive tools of surveillance and discipline.

SURVEILLANCE AND DISCIPLINE

The fear of black men constructed through the media in part informs and is informed by the particular modes of surveillance and discipline black men face in the larger society. As Robert Entman and others have shown, the media—particularly national news broadcasts—is more likely to represent black men as criminals than as lawyers, police officers, or other positive professional images.[23] The dilemma with these racial stereotypes is that while the labels narrowly frame the performances of black men, they are based, though rather uncritically, in the reality that black men are disproportionately represented in the criminal justice system. Though black males make up less than 10 percent of the national population, they are overrepresented in the judicial system, experiencing disproportionate arrests and conviction rates compared to their white male counterparts.[24] Within their lifetimes, black men are seven times more likely to be arrested than their white counterparts.

The reality is that though black males are disproportionately represented in the criminal justice system relative to their overall national population, it is actually whites who make up the majority of prison convicts.[25] Thus it is more likely that a white male will commit a crime than that a black male will do so. Nevertheless, popular racial theories and frames of deviance are more persuasive than actual data in dominant discourse. Research has shown that whites regularly characterize black men as aggressive, deviant, and more prone than whites to violence and criminal behavior.[26] Whites tend to associate street crime with black men, and whites assume that black males account for more crime than statistics actually indicate.[27] To many people, the framing of black men in the media and the overestimation of black criminality justifies the surveillance and excessive discipline of black males.[28]

RACIAL PROFILING

As a surveillance technique, the practice of racial profiling by police officers plays on both the dominant narrative of deviance and the overestimation of black male criminality—a reflection of white anxiety and fear of black masculinities.[29] Racial profiling is the use of race as a major factor in engaging in law enforcement activity with citizens. Thus in this practice, an individual's perceived racial identity is the most salient reason for police-initiated action, more so than the actual behavior of the individual.[30] Any black man in a public or private space at a given time (or whose behaviors are interpreted as "suspicious") is subject to this particular type of surveillance.

Racial profiling disproportionately impacts black men more than other racial groups. The assumption that black men will commit the most crimes contributes to the disproportionate surveillance and encounters with law enforcement. For instance, stop-and-frisk practices in cities such as New York and Philadelphia empower law enforcement officer to target black males deemed suspicious. In addition, the notion of "driving while black" is the experience wherein black men are pulled over by police simply because they are black rather than for a substantive driving infraction.

The fear of black masculinities used in racial profiling extends to other forms of surveillance and discipline. Because racial profiling is used by police in pre-arrest contacts, the practice of profiling is an entrance point into the criminal justice system for many black men.[31] The current trend is that one in three black men will be arrested during his lifetime. When convicted of a crime, black men will likely experience a longer sentence relative to their white counterparts.[32] Considering the way black masculinity is constructed (through a discourse of violence and criminality), it appears that a fear of black men pervades the political ideologies, decision-making processes, and procedures of the law enforcement and criminal justice systems in ways that perpetuate higher conviction rates and longer sentences for black men.[33]

The frequency and duration of black male discipline, in addition to racial profiling practices by law enforcement, mean that many black men will spend their lives under constant surveillance. Considering these realities, racial profiling exemplifies how race and gender intersect in particular ways for black men. Neither black women nor white men are racially profiled to the same degree as black men. Racial profiling is unique to black men in that they are profiled because they are both black *and* male and are criminalized in ways unique to the intersection of their race-gendered identity.

Of course, racial profiling is not unique to law enforcement. The public draws on dominant stereotypes in its observations of black men. Trayvon Martin, as a race-gendered teen navigating a gated community, was considered suspicious and out of place by George Zimmerman and was thus subject to surveillance. Black thieves had recently hit the area, proclaimed Zimmerman and his defense team. They offered this background fact consistently, both in court and during media sessions, as if to legitimize Zimmerman's profiling. Thus, they claimed, when Zimmerman identified Martin, he did so assuming that Martin might be a burglar. As Zimmerman explained to the police dispatcher, "Hey, we've had some break-ins in my neighborhood, and there's a real suspicious guy . . ." To a degree, Zimmerman may have been justified in his concern for neighborhood safety, given recent events in the community. However, the only commonalities Martin had with the previous culprits were his race and gender. Still, Zimmerman and his defense team regularly cited previous burglaries by black men as justification for Zimmerman viewing Martin suspiciously.

Being racially profiled led Martin to his unfortunate death. Subsequently, there was a seemingly poor investigation by law enforcement. Though Martin was killed less than a few hundred feet from his father's fiancée's house (where he was headed home), law enforcement officials never knocked on doors to see if anyone in the community could identify his body. Both Zimmerman and law enforcement apparently assumed that the teen did not belong in the community. Furthermore, Zimmerman's forty-four-day–delayed arrest suggests that law enforcement uncritically took his claim of killing an unarmed black male out of self-defense as the only truth. It would appear that Martin was a victim of "walking while black" in a space where his race-gender evoked fear. His death was initially trivialized by law enforcement as signifying simply one less black criminal.

If Martin had been a black female or a white male, would the series of events have been different? Perhaps a teen of a different race or gender would not have been deemed suspicious or out of place, let alone under surveillance and aggressively confronted. The same question could be applied to George Stinney Jr.'s situation. Had he been white, would he have been the primary suspect, enduring unlawful due

process? The likely answer is no, but the question exemplifies the nature of historical racial profiling and its particular impact on black males today.

<h2 style="text-align:center">Trayvon Martin as Racial Hoax</h2>

Black men are particularly susceptible to the racial hoax, which is a false accusation
of criminal activity. In the hoax, a person frames someone of another race as the per-
petuator to deflect attention away from the actual criminal. A well-known case is the
racial hoax committed by Susan Smith in 1994. Smith, who is white, reported that a
black man had kidnapped her two sons by carjacking her vehicle. She said the boys
were in the car, and the man drove away with them.[34] It was later discovered that she
had murdered her sons by making her car roll into a nearby lake, causing their deaths
by drowning. In another example, in 1996, Robert Harris, who is white, claimed that
he and his fiancée, Teresa McLeod, had been shot and robbed by a black man. Harris
would later confess to having hired a hit man to shoot and rob McLeod.

Because a racial hoax is meant to make a black man at fault for a murder committed by a white person, the Martin case could be considered a hoax. Numerous
people, including journalist Geraldo Rivera, proposed that Martin *caused himself
to be killed* by wearing a hoodie and baggy pants. His masculinity was blamed as
the reason for his death. If Martin hadn't worn a hoodie and looked dangerous to a
white observer, he might still be alive. This naive assumption seems to be the crux of
racial hoaxes. In this case, the public fear of black men (even unarmed teenage boys)
and the ease of black male criminalization in public discourse ("blame the black
guy") have implicated Martin in his own murder. This type of racial hoax can also
be seen in the more recent killings of Jordan Davis, Jonathan Ferrell, and Michael
Brown, among others, each gunned down because he was falsely accused of posing
a threat to his killer.

These cases, as well as others (such as the Scottsboro Boys in 1931 and the Central
Park Five in 1989), are only possible in a society in which particular black masculinities are feared. It is possible that the fear of black men accounts for many of the
racial hoaxes and false accusations of black male criminality, especially considering
that over half of exonerations involve wrongly accused black men.[35]

In a white, patriarchal, capitalist society, black men are perceived as threats
to the interests and property of the ruling class and thus are subject to particular forms of surveillance, discipline, and punishment.[36] The ways black men are
disciplined and punished are then reused as powerful forms of representation
through various types of media. The media's sensationalism of certain black male
performances reaffirms a hegemonic regime of truth. But the media ignores that
which constitutes reality for the majority of black men, which is inconsistent with

the dominant narrative on black masculinity. The reality is that most black men are not in prison. Many have experienced moderate to great success in life. Most are employed and principled, and most perform masculinities that contradict the meta-narrative of black male deviancy.[37]

CONCLUSION

Black masculinities have been historically constructed and contemporarily regulated through a social discourse of fear and anxiety. Through mass-media representations, surveillance, and discipline policies, black male sexuality and gender performances are stigmatized in ways that have material, economic, physical, social, and psychological implications for black males in the United States.

Certainly, each of these institutions informs the others. Media representation is reflective of and reproduces a dominant racial ontology that is mapped onto the black male body. For instance, nationwide television network news stations report on black crimes such as drug use almost twice as much as they report on similar white crimes, demonstrating that black deviancy is more "newsworthy" than white deviancy.[38] These dominant ideologies and discourses about black male criminality are then used to inform public policy, including racial profiling and discipline practices. The outcome of disproportionate representation in the criminal justice system is then used to reaffirm a dominant racial ontology—which is then constructed, sold, and consumed through mass media. Though race and gender are socially constructed categories, fear plays a crucial role in the reproduction of black masculinities through particular discursive and structural practices.

NOTES

1. Jones. *South Carolina Killers*.

2. Marriott, "Reading Black Masculinities"; Foucault, *Discipline and Punish*; Foucault, "On Governmentality"; Hall et al., *Policing the Crisis*.

3. Mahalik et al., "The Effects of Racism"; Saint-Aubin, "A Grammar of Black Masculinity."

4. Saint-Aubin, "A Grammar of Black Masculinity"; Fanon, *Black Skin, White Masks*.

5. Du Bois, *The Souls of Black Folk*; Fredrickson, *The Black Image in the White Mind*; Gregory et al., "The Achievement Gap and the Discipline Gap."

6. Haller, *Outcasts from Evolution*; Howard, "The Negro as a Distinct Ethnic Factor in Civilization"; Talbot, *Degeneracy*.

7. Myrdal, *An American Dilemma*; Harris, *Boys, Boyz, Bois*.

8. Cureton, "Something Wicked This Way Comes," 347; Littlefield, "The Media as a System of Racialization"; Holtzman, "Stories of Race in Popular Culture."

9. Fiske et al., "Images of Black Americans"; Boyd, *Young, Black, Rich, and Famous*; Hoberman, *Darwin's Athletes*; Collins, *Black Sexual Politics*.

10. Hoberman, *Darwin's Athletes*, xviii.

11. Collins, *Black Sexual Politics*.

12. Cooper, "Against Bipolar Black Masculinity"; Ferber, "The Construction of Black Masculinity"; Leonard, "The Next M.J. or the Next O.J."

13. Entman and Rojecki, *The Black Image in the White Mind*; Dixon, "Network News and Racial Beliefs"; Chiricos and Eschholz, "The Racial and Ethnic Typification of Crime," 400.

14. Entman and Rojecki, The Black Image in the White Mind, 321–337; Chiricos and Eschholz, "The Racial and Ethnic Typification of Crime," 400; Surette, *Media, Crime, and Criminal Justice*.

15. Holt, "Writing the Wrong," 108.

16. Holt, "Writing the Wrong," 108.

17. Devine at al., "The Regulation of Explicit and Implicit Race Bias," 835; Ward, "Wading through the Stereotypes"; Fujioka, "Television Portrayals and African-American Stereotypes."

18. Peffley et al., "The Intersection of Race and Crime in Television News Stories," 309.

19. Littlefield, "The Media as a System of Racialization."

20. Ferguson, *Bad Boys*.

21. Mutua, *Progressive Black Masculinities*; Hunter and Davis, "Constructing Gender"; Dancy, *The Brother Code*.

22. Ramaswamy, "Progressive Paths to Masculinity."

23. Reid-Brinkley, "Ghetto Kids Gone Good"; Covington, *Crime and Racial Constructions*; Entman and Gross, "Race to Judgment."

24. Bureau of Justice Statistics, *Prison and Jail Inmates at Midyear*.

25. Bureau of Justice Statistics, Prison and Jail Inmates at Midyear.

26. Davis and Smith, *General Social Surveys, 1972–1996*; Hurwitz and Peffley, *Perception and Prejudice*.

27. Chiricos and Eschholz, "The Racial and Ethic Typification of Crime," 400.

28. Weitzer, "Racialized Policing."

29. Bass, "Policing Space, Policing Race."

30. Ramirez et al., *A Resource Guide on Racial Profiling Data Collection Systems*.

31. Glover, *Racial Profiling*.

32. United States Sentencing Commission, *Report on the Continuing Impact of "United States v. Booker" on Federal Sentencing*; Mustard, "Racial, Ethnic, and Gender Disparities in Sentencing."

33. Bushway and Piehl, "Judging Judicial Discretion"; Higginbotham, "Unequal Justice."

34. Russell-Brown, *The Color of Crime.*

35. Registry, Exonerations in 2013.

36. Mahalik, "The Effects of Racism"; Saint-Aubin, "A Grammar of Black Masculinity."

37. Hout, "Occupational Mobility of Black Men"; Lacy, *Blue-Chip Black*; Pattillo-McCoy, *Black Picket Fences.*

38. Bjornstrom et al. "Race and Ethnic Representations of Lawbreakers and Victims in Crime News"; Entman and Rojecki, The Black Image in the White Mind.

BIBLIOGRAPHY

Bass, Sandra. "Policing Space, Policing Race: Social Control Imperatives and Police Discretionary Decisions." *Social Justice* 1 (2009): 156–176.

Bjornstrom, Eileen E.S., Robert L. Kaufman, Ruth D. Peterson, and Michael D. Slater. "Race and Ethnic Representations of Lawbreakers and Victims in Crime News: A National Study of Television Coverage." *Social Problems* 57, no. 2 (2010): 269–293.

Boyd, Todd. *Young, Black, Rich, and Famous: The Rise of the NBA, the Hip Hop Invasion, and the Transformation of American Culture.* New York: Doubleday, 2001.

Bureau of Justice Statistics. *Prison and Jail Inmates at Midyear.* Washington, DC: US Department of Justice, 2012.

Bushway, Shawn D., and Anne Morrison Piehl. "Judging Judicial Discretion: Legal Factors and Racial Discrimination in Sentencing." *Law and Society Review* 35, no. 4 (2001): 733–764.

Chiricos, Ted, and Sarah Eschholz. "The Racial and Ethnic Typification of Crime and the Criminal Typification of Race and Ethnicity in Local Television News (Abstract)." *Journal of Research in Crime and Delinquency* 4 (2002): 400–420.

Collins, Patricia Hill. *Black Sexual Politics: African-Americans, Gender, and the New Racism.* New York: Routledge, 2004.

Cooper, Frank Rudy. "Against Bipolar Black Masculinity: Intersectionality, Assimilation, Identity Performance, and Hierarchy." *UC Davis Law Review* 39 (2006): 853–904.

Covington, Jeanette. *Crime and Racial Constructions: Cultural Misinformation about African Americans in Media and Academia.* Lanham, MD: Lexington Books, 2010.

Cureton, Steven R. "Something Wicked This Way Comes: A Historical Account of Black Gangsterism Offers Wisdom and Warning for African American Leadership." *Journal of Black Studies* 2 (2009): 347–361. doi: 10.2307/40282639.

Dancy II, T. Elon E. *The Brother Code: Manhood and Masculinity among African American Males in College.* Charlotte, NC: Information Age Publishing, 2012.

Davis, James Allan, and Tom W. Smith. *General Social Surveys, 1972–1996, National Data Program for the Social Sciences Series, no. 15*. Chicago: National Opinion Research Center [producer]. Storrs, CT: Roper Public Opinion Research Center, 1996.

Devine, Patricia G., E. Ashby Plant, David M. Amodio, Eddie Harmon-Jones, and Stephanie L. Vance. "The Regulation of Explicit and Implicit Race Bias: The Role of Motivations to Respond without Prejudice (Abstract)." *Journal of Personality and Social Psychology* 5 (2002): 835–848.

Dixon, Travis L. "Network News and Racial Beliefs: Exploring the Connection between National Television News Exposure and Stereotypical Perceptions of African Americans." *Journal of Communication* 58, no. 2 (2008): 321–337. doi: 10.1111/j.1460-2466.2008.00387.x.

Du Bois, W.E.B. *The Souls of Black Folk*. Chicago: A. C. McClurg, 1903.

Entman, Robert, and Kimberly A. Gross. "Race to Judgment: Stereotyping Media and Criminal Defendants." *Law and Contemporary Problems* 71 (Autumn 2008): 93–133.

Entman, Robert, and Andrew Rojecki. *The Black Image in the White Mind: Media and Race in America*. Chicago: University of Chicago Press, 2000.

Fanon, Frantz. *Black Skin, White Masks*. New York: Grove, 1967.

Ferber, Abby L. "The Construction of Black Masculinity: White Supremacy Now and Then." *Journal of Sport and Social Issues* 31, no. 1 (2007): 11–24.

Ferguson, Ann Arnett. *Bad Boys: Public School in the Making of Black Masculinity*. Ann Arbor: University of Michigan Press, 2000.

Fiske, Susan T., Hilary B. Bergsieker, Ann Marie Russell, and Lyle Williams. "Images of Black Americans." *Du Bois Review: Social Science Research on Race* 6, no. 1 (2009): 83–101. doi: doi:10.1017/S1742058X0909002X.

Foucault, Michel. *Discipline and Punish*, trans. Alan Sheridan. New York: Vintage, 1979.

Foucault, Michel. "On Governmentality." *Ideology and Consciousness* 6 (1979): 5–22.

Fredrickson, George M. *The Black Image in the White Mind: The Debate on Afro-American Character and Destiny, 1817–1914*. New York, Harper and Row, 1971.

Fujioka, Yuki. "Television Portrayals and African-American Stereotypes: Examination of Television Effects When Direct Contacts Is Lacking." *Journalism and Mass Communication Quarterly* 76, no. 1 (1999): 52–75.

Glover, Karen S. *Racial Profiling: Research, Racism, and Resistance: Issues in Crime and Justice*: Lanham, MD: Rowman and Littlefield, 2009.

Gregory, Anne, Russell Skiba, and Pedro Noguera. "The Achievement Gap and the Discipline Gap: Two Sides of the Same Coin?" *Educational Researcher* 39, no. 1 (2009): 59–68.

Hall, Stuart, Charles Critcher, Tony Jefferson, John Clarke, and Brian Robert. *Policing the Crisis: Mugging, the State, and Law and Order*. London: Macmillan, 1978.

Haller, John S., Jr. *Outcasts from Evolution: Scientific Attitudes of Racial Inferiority, 1859–1900*. Urbana: University of Illinois Press, 1971.

Harris, Cheryl I. "Whiteness as Property." *Harvard Law Review* 106, no. 8 (1993): 1707–1791.

Harris, Keith M. *Boys, Boyz, Bois: An Ethics of Black Masculinity in Film and Popular Media*. New York: Routledge, 2006.

Higginbotham, A. Leon, Jr. "Unequal Justice in the State Criminal Justice System." In *African American Classics in Criminology and Criminal Justice*, ed. Shaun L. Gabbidon, Helen Taylor Greene, and Vernetta D. Young, 137–158. Thousand Oaks, CA: Sage, 2002.

Hoberman, John. *Darwin's Athletes: How Sport Has Damaged Black America and Preserved the Myth of Race*. New York: Mariner Books, 1997.

Holt, Lanier Frush. "Writing the Wrong: Can Counter-stereotypes Offset Negative Media Messages about African Americans?" *Journalism and Mass Communication Quarterly* 1 (2013): 108–125.

Holtzman, Linda. "Stories of Race in Popular Culture." In *Media Messages: What Film, Television, and Popular Music Teach Us about Race, Class, Gender, and Sexual Orientation*, ed. Leon Sharpe and Linda Holtzman, 209–254. Armonk, NY: M. E. Sharpe, 2000.

Hout, Mochael. "Occupational Mobility of Black Men: 1962–1973." *American Sociological Review* 49 (1984): 308–322.

Howard, William. Lee. "The Negro as a Distinct Ethnic Factor in Civilization." *Medicine* 10 (1903): 420–433.

Hunter, Andrea, and James Earl Davis. "Constructing Gender: An Exploration of Afro-American Men's Conceptualization of Manhood." *Gender and Society* 6, no. 3 (1992): 464–479.

Hurwitz, Jon, and Mark Peffley. *Perception and Prejudice: Race and Politics in the United States*. New Haven, CT: Yale University Press, 1998.

Jones, Mark. *South Carolina Killers: Crimes of Passion*. Charleston, SC: History Press, 2007.

Lacy, Karyn R. *Blue-Chip Black: Race, Class, and Status in the New Black Middle Class*. Berkeley: University of California Press, 2007.

Leonard, David J. "The Next M.J. or the Next O.J.? Kobe Bryant, Race, and the Absurdity of Colorblind Rhetoric." *Journal of Sport and Social Issues* 28, no. 3 (2004): 284–313.

Littlefield, Marci Bounds. "The Media as a System of Racialization: Exploring Images of African American Women and the New Racism." *American Behavioral Scientist* 51, no. 5 (2008): 675–685.

Mahalik, James R., Martin R. Pierre, and Malcolm H. Woodland. "The Effects of Racism, African Self-Consciousness, and Psychological Functioning on Black Masculinity: A

Historical and Social Adaption Framework." *Journal of African American Men* 6, no. 2 (2001): 19–39.

Marriott, David. "Reading Black Masculinities." In *Understanding Masculinities*, ed. Máirtín Mac an Ghaill, 185–201. Buckingham, UK: Open University, 1996.

Mustard, David B. "Racial, Ethnic, and Gender Disparities in Sentencing: Evidence from the US Federal Courts." *Journal of Law and Economics* 44, no. 1 (2001): 285–314.

Mutua, Athena D., ed. *Progressive Black Masculinities*. New York: Routledge, 2006.

Myrdal, Gunnar. *An American Dilemma: The Negro Problem and Modern Democracy*. New York: Harper and Brothers, 1963.

Pattillo-McCoy, Mary. *Black Picket Fences: Privilege and Peril among the Black Middle Class*. Chicago: University of Chicago Press, 1999.

Peffley, Mark, Todd Shields, and Bruce Williams. "The Intersection of Race and Crime in Television News Stories: An Experimental Study." *Political Communication* 3 (1996): 309–327.

Ramaswamy, Megha. "Progressive Paths to Masculinity for Young Black and Latino Men in an Urban Alternatives-to-Incarceration Program." *Western Journal of Black Studies* 34, no. 4 (2010): 412–424.

Ramirez, Deborah, Jack McDevitt, and Amy Farrell. *A Resource Guide on Racial Profiling Data Collection Systems: Promising Practices and Lessons Learned*. Washington, DC: US Department of Justice, 2000.

Registry. Exonerations in 2013. http://www.law.umich.edu/special/exoneration/Pages/.

Reid-Brinkley, Shanara Rose. "Ghetto Kids Gone Good: Race, Representation, and Authority in the Scripting of Inner-City Youths in the Urban Debate League." *Argumentation and Advocacy* 49, no. 2 (2012): 77–99.

Romer, Daniel, Kathleen H. Jamieson, and Nicole J. de Coteau. "The Treatment of Persons of Color in Local Television News: Ethnic Blame Discourse or Realistic Group Conflict?" *Communication Research* 3 (1998): 286–305.

Russell-Brown, Katheryn. *The Color of Crime: Racial Hoaxes, White Fear, Black Protectionism, Police Harassment, and Other Macroaggressions*. New York: New York University Press, 1998.

Saint-Aubin, Arthur F. "A Grammar of Black Masculinity: A Body of Science." *Journal of Men's Studies* 10, no. 3 (2002): 247–270.

Saint-Aubin, Arthur F. "Testeria: The Dis-ease of Black Men in White Supremacist, Patriarchal Culture." *Callaloo* 17, no. 4 (1994): 1054–1073.

Surette, Ray. *Media, Crime, and Criminal Justice: Images, Realities, and Policies*, 3rd ed. Belmont, CA: Thomson/Wadsworth, 2007.

Talbot, Eugene S. *The Contemporary Science Series*, vol. 5: *Degeneracy: Its Causes, Signs, and Results*. London: Scott, 1898.

United States Sentencing Commission. *Report on the Continuing Impact of "United States v. Booker" on Federal Sentencing.* Washington, DC: United States Sentencing Commission, 2012.

Ward, L. Monique. "Wading through the Stereotypes: Positive and Negative Associations between Media Use and Black Adolescents' Conceptions of Self." *Developmental Psychology* 40, no. 4 (2004): 284–294.

Weitzer, Ronald. "Racialized Policing: Residents' Perceptions in Three Neighborhoods." *Law and Society Review* 34, no. 1 (2000): 129–155.

2

Southern Perils

Chinese Views of Their Southern Territories during the Tang Dynasty (618–907 CE)

Adam C. Fong

In 717 CE, a bear was found entering the walled city of Guangzhou during the day, and the animal even entered the gate of the area commander. The soldiers chased it for ten *li* (5 kilometers) and then killed it. After more than a month, the area commander, Li Chujian, died. When the head commissioner, Zhu Sixian, was assigned to take Li Chujian's place, he strongly opposed the assignment and delayed going for half a year. When he finally went to Guangzhou, he, too, died. Afterward, both the celebrated soldier Sima Song and the head commissioner, Dou Chongjia, went south to Guangzhou and died in succession.[1] This fictional story represents one way the elites of the Tang dynasty viewed the southern parts of their empire. The story is structured so that the death of the bear is the necessary and sufficient cause for the subsequent untimely deaths of officials sent to Guangzhou. These deaths have a supernatural cause in the story that cannot be avoided or counteracted—the mere act of going to the south caused the three officials to die. However, behind this proximate cause lies the historical reality of a subtropical Guangzhou rife with diseases to which northern officials had no immunity. This view exhibits the deep fears Tang elites had of their southern territories and evokes the strong sense that anything could happen in such a dangerous environment.

During the Tang dynasty (618–907 CE), most of the territories that now comprise the People's Republic of China were united in a strong and flourishing empire. Many of the institutions that are credited with encouraging centralized authority—such as the civil service examinations to enter government service—were adopted during

DOI: 10.5876/9781646420025.c002

the Tang dynasty. However, the Tang elites, drawing on the experiences of previous generations, viewed the southern part of their empire as a wild and dangerous place, and they considered the indigenous peoples of that region to be almost subhuman worshippers of demonic forces. A long period of contact between Tang elites and the southern region, particularly in the city of Guangzhou, helped some Tang elites to move past the fears and *Othering* that were evident in earlier writings. The fears of the Tang elites reflected not just cross-cultural anxieties or simply the unease of a smaller conquering group ruling over a large subordinate population. Their views of a southern Other reveal a struggle over the definition of which groups could and could not be considered "Chinese." Over the course of the Tang dynasty, elites gradually came to accept the south, reconciling their fears and moving southerners out of the category of Other and into the category of Chinese. This historical example from the Tang dynasty illustrates that East Asian and pre-modern societies grappled with fears of the Other; the example also illustrates the way one society moved past such fears of the Other.

BACKGROUND

Geographically, the West River (Xi Jiang) basin, which comprised the southernmost region of the Tang realm, was very different from the temperate zone Yellow River valley that was the center of the Tang dynasty's imperial culture. The climate and soils of the south were very well suited for agriculture, so much so that it was possible to harvest two rice crops per year and six or more vegetable crops.[2] This region is separated from the Yangzi River basin and the rest of China by the Nanling range, which has an average elevation of about 3,000 feet above sea level, with some peaks rising to 6,000 feet above sea level. The entire area south of the Nanling range has been referred to as *Lingnan*, meaning "south of the mountains," since early imperial times.[3] Lingnan encompasses most of the Pearl River basin and the modern-day units of Guangdong and Hainan Provinces, the Guangxi Zhuang Ethnicity Autonomous Region, and sometimes northern Vietnam.

Scholars have largely ignored Lingnan when studying the expansion of the Han Chinese cultural sphere, preferring instead to study regions where the distinction between Han Chinese and the "Other" clearly stands out in the historical documents. A large body of scholarship has focused on the relationship between Han Chinese and their nomadic neighbors to the north, for example, or on the era of imperial expansion in the early modern period.[4] This body of research, while not directly related to the study of the southern frontiers of Han Chinese expansion, reveals that the relations between cultures in East Asia frequently used the same techniques found in European history of knowledge production and narrative building to create unequal power relations between the "us" society and the "them" societies. In some cases, these narratives created connections across cultures while still maintaining the superiority of the "us" society. But in many other cases, the narratives served to objectify the "them" societies as different and inferior.

The southward movement of Han Chinese over the centuries of "China's march to the tropics" has been characterized as involving two aspects: (1) Han technological and cultural superiority versus its southern neighbors and (2) the flight, assimilation, or extinction of the indigenous southern peoples. Early scholarship on this issue stated that because of the difference in environments, the move southward by the Han Chinese was limited more by disease than by the indigenous people. These people, despite their efforts of resistance, were eventually overwhelmed by the waves of immigrants from the north.[5] The frontier thus created was that of an unequal clash between the civilized Han invaders/immigrants and the unsophisticated indigenous groups, with the struggle inevitably resulting in Han success and indigenous sinification.

This simple model of the frontier has been altered by Richard Von Glahn, who has divided the frontier process in Song dynasty Sichuan into three non-linear stages: borderlands, peripheries, and hinterlands. In this model, the borderland represents the period when extraction by the imperial metropole is hampered by a lack of manpower. The periphery indicates that while the majority of the population is still non-Han Chinese, the central government has enough operatives in place for large-scale exploitation of the locality. Being a hinterland signifies that the majority of the population, regardless of ethnicity, has accepted the cultural norms of Han Chinese culture, with correspondingly strong links between the region and the metropole further supporting the economic integration of the region into the empire.[6] When this model is applied to an earlier period of Chinese history, then Lingnan (as constituted during the Tang dynasty) moves from a periphery to a hinterland. As a consequence, attitudes about the region shift from unfamiliarity and fear to acceptability and tolerance.

To combat the conquest/submission characterization of frontier zones, recent scholars have applied the concept of a "middle ground," which was first used to examine borderlands in US history.[7] Brett Walker applies this "middle ground" theory to East Asian history. The middle ground is "a place where the local context and historical moment shape cultural and political interaction among diverse groups of people."[8] The value of this approach is that it puts the focus on "how the middle ground arose from ethnic and cultural interaction between people and the natural world. In other words, with the focus now on place rather than exclusively on process, borderland history is no longer simply the tale of the conquerors."[9] Lingnan during the Tang dynasty fits the definition of a middle ground, a place containing diverse groups of people interacting with each other and with the natural environment. As in other pre-modern settings, the employment of symbols, myths, and communication allows for the eventual incorporation of Lingnan into a Han Chinese identity.[10]

Scholarly themes that have been explored in other fields of history involving the conquest and assimilation of people have largely been missing from scholarly explorations of the southern expansion of the Chinese empire. In particular, the biased production of knowledge and the creation of an "Other," as detailed by Edward Said, have rarely been mentioned in works researching the history of southern China.[11] Said's research actually focused on a much later period of history. But he made important observations about a culture's production of knowledge regarding other societies. This knowledge can give that culture a certain power over those societies. Said's theory of power from knowledge has strong parallels to the historical experiences found in the southward expansion of Chinese civilization. For example, fear has been theorized as working in two main ways in modern societies—as either a top-down projection from political leaders or as a consequence of the social, political, and economic divisions within a specific society. This model can work well for pre-modern societies as well.[12] Although fear and the projections of that fear onto an "Other" can readily be found in pre-modern Chinese texts, these subjects have not yet been explored in detail, nor have they been compared to similar moments in world history.

PERCEPTIONS AND FEARS OF THE SOUTH

The incorporation of the Yangzi and Pearl River basins into the Chinese political and cultural spheres has had tremendous consequences for Chinese history. One of those consequences is that it took many centuries before the southern lands were viewed as anything other than a wild frontier area. This perception of the south existed long before the unification of China into a single empire in 221 BCE; as the borders of the empire moved farther south, the old perceptions spread to cover the newer territories, too.[13] By the start of the Tang dynasty, the Yangzi River basin was no longer considered wild or a frontier; those qualities had been transferred to the Lingnan region. Building on the legacy of previous dynasties, the Tang dynasty elites looked on the Lingnan region and its capital, Guangzhou, as a dangerous frontier zone. Lingnan threatened the northerners both physically (with an unfamiliar environment full of hostile indigenous peoples) and spiritually (by offering the corrupting temptation of easy riches that only the most virtuous could resist). Many Tang writings continued to reflect such fears, with tales that painted the south as an area of physical and supernatural dangers. Other writings exist that demonstrate a way to move beyond those fears, however.

As the elites from the north moved into Lingnan to administer the region for the imperial center, the chief distinction they made between north and south was an ethnic one. The history of the Liu Song, which ruled the south during the fifth century CE, states that "in all the mountains of Guangzhou there are the Li and the Liao, of many varieties; in all places, time and again, they engage in violent invasions, bringing bitter misfortune to the successive generations."[14] This source describes the indigenous peoples of Lingnan as an undifferentiated mass of violent and unreasonable savages, whose actions caused endless trouble for everyone. Although definitions for "non-Chinese" tribes change over time, Liao "referred to inhabitants of the southern mountains," while Li stood for "non-Chinese peoples leading a settled existence in the lowlands."[15] Not only were these people "Others," they were violent Others who destabilized Han Chinese society. As imperial elites had done with other ethnicities, the names they used for the southerners implied a subhuman nature. *Man*, a common name for southern ethnicities, indicated insect or reptilian qualities, whereas *Liao* indicated a close relationship to dogs or other beasts.[16] This naming was a direct form of creating a subordinate Other; while the people may have looked human, in all written works the association of these groups with animals was preserved. These cultural attitudes survived into the Tang period, and the demonization worked to disadvantage southerners in many ways in Tang society. In a well-known story from the *Platform Sutra*, the Fifth Patriarch of Zen Buddhism asked his future successor, "You are a southerner, and an aborigine; how can you be a buddha?"[17] Though the question—asked when the Sixth Patriarch of Zen was first seeking admittance as a Buddhist disciple—may have been apocryphal, the attitude behind it was not. Association with the Lingnan region in Tang times not only made a person different; it also made one inferior.

Another characteristic of the south that separated it from the civilized lands of the Yellow River basin was its vast wealth, which often led to corruption and decadence. Confucian ideals included a deep distrust of merchants and those people who sought wealth, who were seen as only interested in profits to the detriment of the overall society.[18] A description from the third century CE states, "Guangzhou is surrounded by the mountains and sea; of the rare things that come out of there, one trunk's worth of treasure is able to enrich many."[19] The Spring of Avarice at Stone Gate was a famous landmark just north of Guangzhou whose water—first recorded in a poem written by Wu Yin of the Western Jin dynasty—was supposed to be the cause of new administrators to Guangzhou turning into rapacious officials.[20] This supernatural reason for corrupt officials—a reason that was reiterated and recorded by Tang elites as well—underlines the historical reality that despite their Confucian training, many elites who went south as administrators became prime examples of greedy and corrupt officials. Lingnan's reputation for easy riches lasted through succeeding dynasties. According to one text, "The lands of the south are truly fertile, the officials often rule in great wealth, so that people say: The magistrate of Guangzhou has only to pass through the city gates once, in order to earn 30,000,000 [cash]."[21] In the sixth century CE, the Sui conquerors of the south noted that "from the beginning of the Liang dynasty, only the capital and the areas of San Wu, Jing, Ying, Jiang, Xiang, Liang, and Yi used coinage. The rest of the counties and prefectures used a combination of cowrie shells and silk. The cities of Jiao and Guang all used gold and silver for commodities."[22] In other words, most of the south still used a mixture of bartering, with silk, and shells for money. Certain prosperous regions of the Yangzi River basin used minted coins; however, Guangzhou and Jiaozhou, because of the volume of maritime trade, could use gold and silver as money.[23] This wealth in the far south made the south categorically different from the agrarian and austere ideals of the orthodox Confucian areas of the Yellow River valley.

Merchants from beyond the empire, moving in and out of Guangzhou, further established Lingnan as a strange and alien place. A number of these merchants came to Guangzhou as part of an official tributary mission; twenty-three different states sent such missions to the Tang dynasty in their first 140 years of rule.[24] This foreign community resorted to violence on occasions when confronted with what they considered to be unfair treatment, as seen by the assassination of the imperial governor in 684 CE and the sacking of Guangzhou by foreigners in 758 CE.[25] Violence from foreigners, though, was less frequent than violence from the indigenous southerners.

DANGERS OF THE SOUTH

Tang elites feared the south and its peoples because many of the local non-Han people—elites as well as common folk—continued to actively resist imperial rule from the north during the almost 300-year period of the Tang dynasty. Although only one of these native insurrections may have threatened the city of Guangzhou, the hinterlands of the city were most definitely not filled with happy indigenous peasants laboring peacefully to support their Tang overlords.[26] Forty-six separate rebellions led by the indigenous peoples of Lingnan are found in existing records.[27] The areas most prone to rebellion were the prefectures located along the coast, west of Guangzhou and south of the West River (Xi Jiang) but northeast of Jiaozhou.[28] Thus although the indigenous people of Lingnan may not have left many written records of their incorporation into the Chinese imperium, their actions stand as a strong record of resistance.

In fiction, southerners could express their resistance in other ways, employing supernatural forces to do so. In one story, the people of Zhenzhou worked to grow rich from maritime trade, but not in the usual ways. Zhenzhou, which corresponds to the modern-day area around Sanya on Hainan Island, was along the coastal route to Guangzhou; however, it was not a place where merchants normally stopped. So the people of Zhenzhou used sorcery to bring the merchants close to shore and strand them on the beach. As a result of these beachings, local leaders accumulated several warehouses full of the riches of maritime trade—rhinoceros horn, ivory, and tortoiseshell are specifically mentioned—and they used this wealth to try to bribe their way out of imperial sanction but were ultimately unsuccessful.[29] This story confirms the elite's fears about the dangerousness of southerners; the southerners' greed and supernatural powers, it was feared, made them destabilizing forces within the Tang empire. The inhabitants of Zhenzhou were seen as pirates with the terrifying ability to control the weather. They were thought to evade punishment through bribery, which reaffirmed their corrupt nature.

Guangzhou during the Tang dynasty could be a dangerous assignment for officials even without the threats of local insurrections, piracy, or foreign invasion. As the bear story from the *Taiping Guangji* indicates, mortality rates of officials in the city could be very high. Elites credited the environment with the ability to reverse civilization, as seen in the recurring legend of the Spring of Avarice. But beyond supernatural/miasmal afflictions, Lingnan had a more direct way to affect and eliminate northerners: *gu* poison.

Gu poison in Tang times came in many forms, according to written sources. But Tang elites and the imperial government always interpreted the poison as sorcery used to harm others. The indigenous peoples of Lingnan produced this poison from venomous creatures through secret rituals.[30] This poison not only produced death but also caused those who were poisoned to want to poison others as well. In some cases, the poison could be used as a love charm because it was associated with extremely strong sexual desire. *Gu* poison also came from the environment.[31] The government listed *gu* poison as one of the Ten Abominations. Those who were caught producing it were sentenced to death by strangulation.[32] These fears of the disruptive power of the south through sorcery served to regularize harsh treatment against anything that could be considered to be *gu* poison. Because the only definitive thing about *gu* poison was its southern origin, the flexibility of its application meant that many aspects of southern culture could be legally proscribed. In many cases, the power to make the poison was associated with indigenous deities; the Tang dynasty made several efforts to stamp out these "illicit cults."

FEARS OF THE DEMONIC

Tang elites also feared the indigenous religions of the south, branding the majority of them as "illicit cults," and they did their best to repress these religions. Religion in this period of imperial Chinese history represented more than just spirituality; religiously inspired uprisings had seriously weakened and even destroyed a number of previous dynasties. One of the most famous officials of the Tang dynasty was the upright and righteous official Di Renjie, popularly known in English as "Judge/ Detective Dee." While his work to ensure the continuation of the Tang dynasty during the reign of Wu Zetian has been considered his chief historical accomplishment, he also toured the southern territories of the empire to purge illicit cults and establish correct belief. In the official history of the Tang dynasty, Di Renjie was made a district magistrate in Ningzhou, which is in modern-day Gansu Province. There, he "supported harmony and lowered weapons, allowing them joyful hearts; so the people of the region put up a monument to praise him."[33] After paying his respects to the other officials of the area, he went on a tour of the Jiangnan Circuit, along the Yangzi River valley. At this time, "[The regions of] Wu and Chu commonly had many illicit temples. [Di] Renjie prohibited this practice, burning one thousand seven hundred buildings in all. He allowed four cults to continue: Xia Yu, Wu Taibai, Li Ji, and Wu Yuan."[34] Another official from later in the Tang, Li Deyu, would also work to eliminate illicit cults in the same area, which attests not only to the strong support such cults had among the local people but also to the strong desire of the government to control religious practices.[35]

Di Renjie's purge of religious cults is depicted in fictional stories of the time as well as in the historical records. In one story, a particular "southern barbarian god" was famous for killing all officials who entered his temple. Di Renjie was able to burn down the temple after recruiting local people who used his authority as a representative of the emperor to defeat the deity. After returning north, a fortune-teller told Di Renjie he had an angry southern spirit following him that was saying, "He burned my house, I want revenge." However, this spirit and the more than twenty other evicted gods following Di Renjie could not act against him because of his official position, so they eventually all returned to the south.[36] This story supports the established theme of the south being a supernaturally hostile region; however, it also points to the superior nature of imperial power to defeat these southern dangers. This confidence in the ability of the Tang imperium to successfully subdue the south moves beyond fears and Othering, which then allows for incorporating Lingnan and its peoples as proper Tang subjects.

BEYOND FEAR?

Economic integration and the increased interactions it required were other important factors in moving the Tang elites beyond their fears of the south. With regard to maritime commerce during the Tang period, the city of Guangzhou was the major port of trade for most of the dynasty. This flow of revenue into the empire was not always the most important source of imperial revenue; but as the expansion of the early Tang period slowed (and then reversed), commercial revenues from maritime trade suddenly became an imperial priority.[37] Following the An Lushan Rebellion (755–763 CE), the revenue from this maritime trade was vital for the survival of the dynasty.[38] At this time, the overland trade routes were only tenuously open to the Tang empire; therefore, any threat to control of maritime routes had to be countered immediately.[39] The importance of this source of revenue had been recognized even before the An Lushan Rebellion. Around 714 CE, the imperial court created the office of Superintendent of Trade, ostensibly to make sure commerce was carried out fairly in Guangzhou; however, this official's main duty consisted of making sure the profits from international trade went directly into the imperial treasury.[40] As a result of the establishment of this important official post, many prominent members of the Tang elite lived and worked in Guangzhou for parts of their careers, which served to increase the number of contacts between the imperial center and the Lingnan region. Increased contact pushed knowledge of the Lingnan region into the mainstream consciousness of imperial culture, as many elites either had been to the region themselves or knew many who had gone there. Lingnan became more than just a fearfully strange wild frontier; with so many elites having experienced the area, the region could instead be subsumed within regular Tang society.

The nature of Tang incorporation of the Lingnan region into mainstream imperial culture can be seen in the story of a man called Cui Wei who lived in Guangzhou during the Zhenyuan period (785–805 CE). He was the son of an official who was stationed in Guangzhou and was famous for his poetry. He was a smart person, but he was not interested in the family business. Instead, according to the text, he preferred stories of great heroes. Within a few years, he had spent all his money, and for a while he lived in a Buddhist establishment. On the day of the Zhongyuan Festival, which is the fifteenth day of the seventh month, the people of Guangzhou set up and displayed rare and strange things at the Buddhist temples, and they gathered for 100 plays at the Kaiyuan Monastery, according to the text of the story.[41]

It is at this festival that Cui Wei started off on his real adventures. He helped a strange woman, who did not appear grateful at the time. But later she gave him a potent herb that can cure various illnesses. He used it to heal a man, who decided to sacrifice Cui to a household demon; luckily, Cui was saved by the man's daughter, and he escaped into a forest. While fleeing, he fell into a pit, where he met a big white snake with a tumor on its lip. Cui healed the snake, who then took him to a fabulous underground palace. Inside the palace, he met several women. They treated him very well but spoke in cryptic messages. They gave him a great treasure, the Solar Igniting Pearl. They told him he was being treated well because of the good deeds of one of his ancestors, and they sent him back to Guangzhou on a white ram. On his return, Cui discovered that he had been gone for three years, which he confirmed by noting the change in prefects since he was last in Guangzhou.[42]

Thereupon, he arrived at the Persian market to secretly sell the pearl. At the market, there was an old foreign man. With one glance, the old man recognized the pearl as an item buried with an ancient king of the region, a man named Zhao Tuo. The pearl was used to cover Zhao Tuo when he was buried. Cui sold the pearl for 100,000 strings of cash and asked the foreigner how he recognized the treasure. The foreigner replied that the Solar Igniting Pearl was an ancient treasure from his homeland of Arabia; he later took a boat and returned to the Middle East. When visiting the City God temple on business, Cui recognized the statue within and saw that the words above the brush of the god were identical to those he had seen in the underground palace. He then realized that the "City of Rams" he had heard about in the underground palace was Guangzhou, and he saw five rams in the temple.[43]

This story contains several important themes that point to a less divisive understanding of the Lingnan region by the literate elites of the Tang. Even though the hero starts out by losing all his money in Guangzhou, by the end of the story he has once again become wealthy. Guangzhou is thus confirmed as a place to make money—but because of the hero's travails, it is money made from his virtuous behavior and not from exploiting others. In this way, the wealth associated with Guangzhou can be transformed from a corrupting influence into a reward for virtue. The hero is the son of a northern immigrant, but along the way he meets some unsavory local people who consort with demons. This scene refers to the frontier nature of the city and to the strange local cults of the indigenous people. Human sacrifice was a mark of savagery, confirming that dangerous elements are still active in the south. The history of the region is fully exploited; although it is mysterious to the hero, this history would have been instantly recognizable to the readers of the story. Bringing the historical past into the story is important because it validates and normalizes the city, referencing an ancient and famous ruler known to the imperial elites of the Tang. This brings Guangzhou to a similar level of civilization as cities in the Yellow and Yangzi River basins of the north. Buddhist institutions exist in the city to take care of the indigent, as they did in all other important cities of the Tang, and Guangzhou is mentioned as having a City God temple, which is a feature of all good Tang cities at the time.[44] In addition, the foreign settlement in Guangzhou plays a crucial role in the story, as that place is not only where the hero regains his wealth but is also where the hero learns where he has been and the significance of his supernatural encounters. The foreigner in this story is also assigned positive characteristics; he is knowledgeable, honest, and generous—as opposed to the more "Confucian" characterization of merchants as greedy and exploitative or the characterization of foreigners as uncivilized and ignorant.

The story of Cui Wei represents a shift in Tang dynasty discourse about the southern territories or at least a shift in discourse about Guangzhou. Its main characteristics—wealth, dangerousness, and multi-ethnicity—had been transformed or supplanted so that these factors now supported imperial cultural values rather than challenged them. Wealth rewarded virtue rather than corrupted the virtuous. Even if the indigenous southerner wanted to sacrifice someone to a household demon (which officials feared illicit cults would encourage), someone else in the family would provide an escape route. Foreigners were wise and generous instead of threatening and greedy. The differences between Guangzhou and other parts of the empire remained, as the story points out in several distinct incidents customs or situations specific to the city. However, those differences did not separate Guangzhou into an "Other," as many story elements, such as the shared historical background and the cult of City God, continued to connect the city with Tang elite expectations.

In another example of Tang accommodation and acculturation of southern culture, some local deities could receive the approval of government officials and become officially sanctioned gods. The clearest example of this is the God of the Southern Sea, a local deity from the city of Guangzhou. During the Kaiyuan period (713–741) of the Tang dynasty, this deity was honored with the title "King of Vast Benefit."[45] Imperial officials actively promoted the worship of this deity, associated as he was with the maritime trade that directly benefited the imperial throne. Near the end of the Early Tang period, Li Yong wrote an inscription at the temple of the God of the Southern Sea titled *Ce Ji Nanhai Shen Ji Bei*. He states in the inscription, "The god's principle is bent on sacrificial offerings, weary for one hundred blessings and it will reach his ears; the emperor's [the God of the Southern Sea's] way answers promptly forever, he looks out at the nine oceans and all is regulated, of all the oceans, what does he not yet begin to have?"[46] The official approval of this southern god occurred at the same time the imperial government found it necessary to create the office of Superintendent of Trade; southern gods who supported the imperial project were suitable allies and treated as such.

Worship of the sea god continued throughout the Tang dynasty. Han Yu, the famous writer and thinker of the Late Tang period, also wrote an inscription at the temple of the God of the Southern Sea titled the *Nanhai Shen Guangli Wang Miao Bei*. In it he states that "because of this appointment respecting the Southern Sea God to be the King of Vast Benefit, pray and call upon him with sacrifices and reverence, and following it will be entirely peaceful."[47] The god also responded to his promotion with blessings for the city: "Therefore, this old temple, changed and its new, at present Guangzhou controls its east and south, the sea direction is eighty *li* [40 km], its port is Fuxu, its bay is the Huangmu."⁴⁸ Describing another beneficiary of this god, Han Yu wrote "[Kong Kui] was fair and upright with a severe demeanor, in his heart he was happy and simple. He was respectful and careful regarding his duty; ruling the people he used understanding, concerning the god he used sincerity."⁴⁹ These inscriptions reinforce the connection of the god with bestowing favors and controlling the oceans. When approached correctly and with sincerity, the god was eager to show his benevolence, much like the idealized Confucian official. Since this temple was situated near the harbor, worshippers could stop and pray for safe passage before heading out to sea, as could merchants waiting for the safe arrival of their cargo.

However, Han Yu based his approval of the God of the Southern Sea on an assumed connection of this god to Yellow River cosmology and deities.⁵⁰ According to Han Yu, the god was really the ancient god of fire Zhu Rong—because cosmologically, fire was the element of the south; therefore, a god of the south must be the god of fire. This method of re-branding local gods to fit the imperial pantheon would continue to be used in later dynasties as well.⁵¹ The fact that the local deity needed to be repackaged as an ancient Yellow River god points to the still tenuous nature of southern acceptability among imperial elites. While their gods or ways of life could be considered Chinese, they still needed to connect or conform to imperial standards.

CONCLUSION

Tang dynasty elites saw the Lingnan region and its inhabitants as a bizarre "Other" and feared them for many reasons. However, as time and increased cross-cultural contact brought these elites into the south, some qualities of the south were reconfigured to support or reinforce imperial notions of correct society and behavior. These qualities can be seen in some writings from the later Tang period. A new understanding of the south allowed later Tang writers to move past the fears and Othering that were manifest in earlier writings, which then influenced post-Tang Chinese intellectuals to consider Lingnan an integral part of the Chinese cultural landscape. These historical events demonstrate that fears of the Other are not particular to any one culture or group and also suggest ways those fears and biases can be overcome.

The acceptance of the south by the imperial center derived mostly from the shift in attitudes of the Tang elites themselves. The voices of the indigenous inhabitants of Lingnan had been effectively silenced by the conquering Han Chinese elites, and those aspects of southern culture that survived did so only under approved interpretations from Tang elites. Although southerners actively assisted in the creation of these approved interpretations, this Tang dynasty example remains one of knowledge production about the conquered by the conquerors. Said's model of knowledge production applies here, both before and during the Tang period. Regardless of whether Tang elites feared or accepted the southerners, only the elite opinions about the southerners had any importance, and the Tang elites and their successors continued to control the Lingnan region.

What changed within the Tang elite discourse, however, was the notion that the south was an "Other" to be feared. The fearfulness of the south was broken down by three main factors: (1) prolonged periods of contact between many Tang elites and southerners, (2) increased economic prosperity throughout the region, and (3) growing correlations between imperial cultural norms and southern cultural forms. Loss of fear did not mean a loss of difference; during the Tang and in later periods, the Lingnan region would continue to be described as having unique characteristics. However, Han Chinese society no longer saw these characteristics as threatening.

Pre-modern societies differ from modern societies, but those differences help clarify which aspects of human behavior are intrinsic to the species and which are contingent on surrounding circumstances. Information flows much faster in modern societies, but the smaller number of literate decision-makers in pre-modern times gives much greater importance to the elites who were engaged in knowledge production. The historical experiences of Tang elites and the Lingnan region point out that behaviors that may seem intrinsic to modern societies—fear of the "Other" most of all—have happened before, even though they sprang from different cultural expectations in a different historical environment. Those experiences also reveal how Tang elites moved past their fears of the "Other," which may give confidence that modern societies can find their own ways to do so as well.

NOTES

1. *Taiping Guangji*, 143.1043–1785.

2. Johnson and Peterson, *Historical Dictionary*, 6.

3. Marks, *Tigers, Rice, Silk*, 20–24.

4. For relations between settled and nomadic societies, see Barfield, *The Perilous Frontier*; Pan Yihong, *Son of Heaven*; Di Cosmo, *Ancient China*. For examples of early modern (1500–1800 CE) empire building and knowledge construction, see Crossley, *A Translucent Mirror*; Hostetler, *Qing Colonial Enterprise*; Elliott, *The Manchu Way*; Weinstein, *Empire and Identity*.

5. Wiens, *Han Chinese Expansion*, 130–145. This material was originally published in 1954 by the same press under the title *China's March toward the Tropics*. See also Fitzgerald, *The Southern Expansion*, xxi.

6. Von Glahn, *The Country of Streams*, 215–220.

7. See White, *The Middle Ground*.

8. Walker, *The Conquest*, 8.

9. Walker, *The Conquest*, 9.

10. Armstrong, *Nations before Nationalism*, 7–9.

11. Said, *Orientalism*, 4–8.

12. Robin, *Fear*, 16–23.

13. Schafer, *The Vermilion Bird*, 135.

14. *Song Shu*, 97.2019.

15. Taylor, *The Birth of Vietnam*, 149.

16. Abramson, *Ethnic Identity*, 27.

17. Cleary, *The Sutra of Hui-Neng*, 6. See also Schafer, *The Vermilion Bird*, 92.

18. See, for example, Lau, *Mencius*, 3.

19. *Jin Shu*, 90.2341.

20. *Tong Dian*, 184.978.

21. *Nan Qi Shu*, 32.277 1b.

22. *Sui Shu*, 24.368 20b.

23. Liu, "Jiankang and the Commercial Empire," 46–47.

24. Bielenstein, *Diplomacy and Trade*, 36–100.

25. *Zizhi Tongjian*, 203.2062, 219.2260.

26. Holcombe, "Early Imperial China's Deep South," 140–144.

27. Schafer, *The Vermilion Bird*, 61–69.

28. Schafer, *The Vermilion Bird*, 69. The Tang dynasty territory of Jiaozhou corresponds to the modern-day territory of northern Vietnam.

29. *Taiping Guangji*, 286.1045–1195.

30. Schafer, *The Vermilion Bird*, 102.

31. Schafer, *The Vermilion Bird*, 102–103.

32. Johnson, *T'ang Code: Volume I*, 69, *T'ang Code: Volume II*, 262–265.

33. *Xin Tang Shu*, 115.2846.

34. *Xin Tang Shu*, 115.2846.

35. Schafer, *The Vermilion Bird*, 101.

36. *Taiping Guangji*, 298.1045–1216.

37. Sen, *Buddhism, Diplomacy, and Trade*, 152.

38. Holcombe, *Genesis of East Asia*, 89.

39. Somers, "End of the T'ang," 693–694.

40. Schafer, *The Vermilion Bird*, 78.

41. *Taiping Guangji*, 34.1043–1177. There is no Kaiyuan Monastery in Guangzhou in modern times; however, the names of monasteries frequently changed over time, and this is also a fictional story.

42. Schafer, *The Vermilion Bird*, 97.

43. *Taiping Guangji*, 34.1043–1180.

44. See Johnson, "The City-God Cults," 453. This story is the only reference found to the existence of a City God temple in Guangzhou during the Tang.

45. *Yang Cheng Gu Chao*, 3.198.

46. Quoted in the *Yangcheng Fenghua Lu*, 16.

47. Quoted in the *Yangcheng Fenghua Lu*, 18.

48. Quoted in the *Yangcheng Fenghua Lu*, 18. The body of water next to this temple is currently known as the Huangpu.

49. Quoted in the *Yangcheng Fenghua Lu*, 18.

50. Schafer, *The Vermilion Bird*, 104–105.

51. See Szonyi, "The Illusion of Standardizing the Gods."

BIBLIOGRAPHY

Abramson, Marc S. *Ethnic Identity in Tang China*. Philadelphia: University of Pennsylvania Press, 2008.

Armstrong, John A. *Nations before Nationalism*. Chapel Hill: University of North Carolina Press, 1982.

Barfield, Thomas. *The Perilous Frontier: Nomadic Empires and China*. Oxford: Basil Blackwell, 1989.

Bielenstein, Hans. *Diplomacy and Trade in the Chinese World, 587–1276*. Leiden: Brill, 2005.

Cleary, Thomas, trans. *The Sutra of Hui-Neng, Grand Master of Zen*. Boston: Shambhala, 1998.

Crossley, Pamela. *A Translucent Mirror: History and Identity in Qing Imperial Ideology*. Berkeley: University of California Press, 1999.

Di Cosmo, Nicola. *Ancient China and Its Enemies: The Rise of Nomadic Power in East Asian History*. Cambridge: Cambridge University Press, 2002.

Elliott, Mark. *The Manchu Way: The Eight Banners and Ethnic Identity in Late Imperial China*. Stanford: Stanford University Press, 2001.

Fitzgerald, Charles Patrick. *The Southern Expansion of the Chinese People*. New York: Praeger, 1972.

Holcombe, Charles. "Early Imperial China's Deep South: The Viet Regions through Tang Times." *T'ang Studies* 15–16 (1997–1998): 125–156.

Holcombe, Charles. *The Genesis of East Asia, 221 BC–AD 907*. Honolulu: University of Hawaii Press, 2001.

Hostetler, Laura. *Qing Colonial Enterprise: Ethnography and Cartography in Early Modern China*. Chicago: University of Chicago Press, 2001.

Jin Shu. Beijing: Zhonghua Shu Ju, 1974.

Johnson, David. "The City-God Cults of T'ang and Sung China." *Harvard Journal of Asiatic Studies* 45 (1985): 363–457.

Johnson, Graham E., and Glen D. Peterson. *Historical Dictionary of Guangzhou (Canton) and Guangdong*. Lanham, MD: Scarecrow, 1999.

Johnson, Wallace, trans. *The T'ang Code, Volume I: General Principles*. Princeton, NJ: Princeton University Press, 1979.

Johnson, Wallace, trans. *The T'ang Code, Volume II: Specific Articles*. Princeton, NJ: Princeton University Press, 1997.

Lau, Din Cheuk, trans. *Mencius*. London: Penguin Books, 2003.

Liu, Shufen. "Jiankang and the Commercial Empire of the Southern Dynasties: Change and Continuity in Medieval Chinese Economic History." In *Culture and Power in the Reconstitution of the Chinese Realm, 200–600*, ed. Scott Pearce, Audrey Spiro, and Patricia Ebrey, 35–52. Cambridge, MA: Harvard University Asia Center, 2001.

Marks, Robert B. *Tigers, Rice, Silk, and Silt: Environment and Economy in Late Imperial South China*. Cambridge: Cambridge University Press, 1998.

Nan Qi Shu. Taipei: Yi Wen Yin Shu Guan, 1956.

Pan Yihong. *Son of Heaven and Heavenly Qaghan: Sui-Tang China and Its Neighbors*. Bellingham: Western Washington University Press, 1997.

Robin, Corey. *Fear: The History of a Political Idea*. New York: Oxford University Press, 2004.

Said, Edward. *Orientalism*. New York: Vintage Books, 1979.

Schafer, Edward. *The Vermilion Bird: T'ang Images of the South*. Berkeley: University of California Press, 1967.

Sen, Tansen. *Buddhism, Diplomacy, and Trade: The Realignment of Sino-Indian Relations, 600–1400*. Honolulu: University of Hawaii Press, 2003.

Somers, Robert M. "The End of the T'ang." In *The Cambridge History of China*, vol. 3, ed. Denis Twitchett, 682–789. Cambridge: Cambridge University Press, 1979.

Song Shu. Shanghai: Han Yu Da Ci Dian Chu Ban She, 2004.

Sui Shu. Taipei: Yi Wen Yin Shu Guan, 1956.

Szonyi, Michael. "The Illusion of Standardizing the Gods: The Cult of the Five Emperors in Late Imperial China." *Journal of Asian Studies* 56, no. 1 (1997): 113–135.

Taiping Guangji. Shanghai: Shanghai Gu Ji Chu Ban She, 1990.

Taylor, Keith. *The Birth of Vietnam*. Berkeley: University of California Press, 1983.

Tong Dian. Taipei: Xin Xing Shu Ju, 1963.

Von Glahn, Richard. *The Country of Streams and Grottoes: Expansion, Settlement, and the Civilizing of the Sichuan Frontier in Song Times*. Cambridge, MA: Harvard University Press, 1987.

Walker, Brett L. *The Conquest of the Ainu Lands: Ecology and Culture in Japanese Expansion, 1590–1800*. Berkeley: University of California Press, 2001.

Weinstein, Jodi. *Empire and Identity in Guizhou: Local Resistance to Qing Expansion*. Seattle: University of Washington Press, 2014.

White, Richard. *The Middle Ground: Indians, Empires, and Republics in the Great Lakes Region, 1650–1815*. Cambridge: Cambridge University Press, 1991.

Wiens, Herold J. *Han Chinese Expansion in South China*. Hamden, CT: Shoe String Press, 1967.

Xin Tang Shu. Shanghai: Han Yu Da Ci Dian Chu Ban She, 2004.

Yang Cheng Gu Chao. Guangzhou: Guangdong Ren Min Chu Ban She, 1993.

Yangcheng Fenghua Lu. Guangzhou: Huacheng Chu Ban She, 2006.

Zizhi Tongjian. Zhengzhou: Zhong Zhou Gu Ji Chu Ban She, 2004.

3

Microbe Culture

Germ Politics and the Unseen Racial History of Nature

Melanie Armstrong

MICROBES, NATURE, AND THE FEARFUL OTHER

In the late seventeenth century, a Dutch microscope enthusiast scraped white matter from an old man's teeth and slid it under a microscope, focusing on "an unbelievably great company of living animalcules, a-swimming more nimbly than any I had ever seen . . . in such enormous numbers that all the water . . . seemed to be alive."[1] Antony van Leeuwenhoek put ink to paper to capture a likeness of the rod-shaped motile bacterium and oral cocci, reporting what he saw to the Royal Society of London. He wrote dozens more letters, describing bacteria he'd seen lurking in rainwater or dredged from a beer vat. Page by page, van Leeuwenhoek and other microscope users revealed a natural world invisibly entwined with human bodies. The new technology produced a new category of nature: "little animals" living inside the human body. Long before these microbes were connected to infectious disease, they were painted as monsters, foreign creatures moving unbidden through human spaces. A new fear was born with a few bold strokes of ink, creating a motile nature that acted for its own survival, unknown and seemingly unimpaired by human society. Depicting the microbes made social intervention necessary. Humans had to decide how they would react to these new natures, both as individuals and as part of the new social order that was rising alongside revolutions in science, industry, and government.

Microbes are monsters because they resist classification.[2] From their first discovery, they challenged the social ordering of knowledge. They are hybrids, defying

DOI: 10.5876/9781646420025.c003

categories of nature and culture, human and nonhuman.³ Indeed, to be human means to have a body filled with microbes, but microbes also bring conflict to human physiology. Germs emerge when microbes enter into the body and tamper with the body's processes, and then the microbe monster grows teeth and fangs and threatens human life. We know unseen organisms carry the potential to turn our bodies into sites of turmoil, and this fact creates fear. Knowing that pathogens draw on our body's energy to sustain their own life creates anxiety. And knowing that microbes make human life possible, even as they produce death, creates frustration. We want microbes to be the "Other"—eliminated from our homes by Clorox and our hands by Purel—even though we know they are deeply and vitally entwined with our individual and collective existence. The distress that emerges when we cannot separate the human from the monster shapes society, demanding we negotiate our fears about difference.⁴ The twentieth century began with the rise of a domestic sanitation industry that privileged the white upper class and ended with an HIV/AIDS epidemic that stigmatized homosexuals and caused millions of people to avoid contact with toilet seats.⁵ The current millennium has created new hybrids of war and biology, where "the infected other becomes the terrorist par excellence."⁶

Further, microbes produce social practices that define what it means to be human and to live with other humans. Because of microbes, a kiss can convey both love and death. It is useful to remember that disease preexisted the revelation of the microbe and has long shaped society. Disease took form through the manifestation of symptoms on the body, forging associations between health and social categories such as race and class. However, understanding the pathogenic origins of disease led to disease-control practices that were more systematic and technological, creating mechanisms for a new arrangement for governing collective life. As Michel Foucault theorized, disease became another way of measuring deviance within a group of people.⁷ Health became the normal condition of society; in contrast, abnormality became calculable in terms of health, producing a new space for inscribing countless other social fears and aligning disease with difference. These expressions of deviance manifest in the many ways the human encounter with an unseen microbe is depicted for public comprehension.

We have an irresistible desire to animate the microbe. Microbes have been represented in countless ways, from van Leeuwenhoek's first sketches, to the cartoon germs that dance through television ads for household cleaners to bio-horror blockbusters on the big screen.⁸ Such representations persist in locating microbes outside the healthy body in an environment that is equally portrayed as an unclean, racialized "Other." Moreover, the scientific and medical work to study pathogens and inform social practices through the production of knowledge and quantification of disease relies extensively on metaphor and representation to allow us to grasp the concept of disease. These mechanisms also function as a tool for sorting the normal from the abnormal and, according to Catherine Waldby, are an "immanent narrative of social order."[9] Epidemiology and the work to impact disease is at its core the work to manage people, and it relies on metaphor to translate microbiology into human behavior. One such metaphor is the narrative of war. Bio-military metaphors abound in disease discourse, emerging from and reinforcing deep cultural fears of nature and the promise of modernity to fight, control, and conquer unpredictable natures. Donna Haraway argued that even our metaphors of immunology have shifted alongside changing mechanisms of war, showing how deeply rooted the war-like understandings of disease are, that they seamlessly shift with our new war strategies to stay relevant and useful in understanding disease.[10]

The case study that follows, about the smallpox eradication program, considers at length how representations of disease as a fearful other turned the human-microbe relationship into a public site to negotiate citizenship in the nineteenth and twentieth centuries. When the world declared war on smallpox, new interventions into individual life became possible, ratifying the role and responsibility of governments to care for citizens by creating healthy populations. Motivated by the economic benefit to developed nations, humanitarians entered underdeveloped nations waving banners recruiting native people to "join the fight." The humanitarians were bearing injection guns loaded with vaccines. The propaganda revived colonial narratives, enabling racialized political acts that managed citizens through the management of microbes. Even after the elimination of naturally occurring smallpox, the virus persisted as a mark of otherness and continues to influence governments to act on citizens' bodies out of fear that their bodies are still vulnerable to one of the greatest human killers of all time. The fear of smallpox far exceeds the representation of the microbe itself.

BIOLOGICAL COLONIALISM: SMALLPOX ON THE AMERICAN CONTINENT

> The smallpox was always present, filling the churchyards with corpses, tormenting with constant fears all whom it had not yet stricken, leaving on those whose lives it spared the hideous traces of its power, turning the babe into a changeling at which the mother shuddered, and making the eyes and cheeks of the betrothed maiden objects of horror to the lover.[11]

Lord Thomas Babington Macaulay's description of England during a smallpox epidemic captures the grim fear surrounding a disease that killed a third of the people it touched. The virus has power, not only among the infected but also over those who fearfully anticipate infection. It lingers on bodies so scarred that their most loved ones shudder to look at them. If the high mortality of smallpox did not instill social fear, its gruesome manifestation of infection on the body might. Lesions began in the mouth, growing until they ruptured, spewing the virus into the body through one's own saliva. Pockmarks erupted late in the course of the disease, but the marks left lifelong scars on the bodies of those who survived the infection. Indeed, the *Variola major* virus has been responsible for much of the suffering, blindness, scarring, and death in human history.

Powerful cultural ideas about disease coalesced around smallpox. Historians have credited the European conquest of the Americas to the virus that invading armies left behind on their corpses. With little genetic immunity, native populations were gravely impacted by smallpox. Scholars estimate that, along with measles and flu, smallpox killed up to 95 percent of the native population of the Americas.[12] The native vulnerability to European diseases seemed to some an unfortunate consequence of cohabitation; to others, native vulnerability was the physical expression of divine will. As one so-called gentleman in San Francisco said in 1852, "Providence designed the extermination of the Indians and . . . it would be a good thing to introduce the small-pox among them." The soldier with whom he spoke decried this opinion as "savage sentiment" but at the same time acknowledged the idea to be "the opinion of most white people living in the interior of the country."[13] This exchange shows the racial terms by which disease was known, whether in terms of the vulnerability of native people or the savagery of white populations. Historians also write of soldiers who passed blankets infested with smallpox to native residents of the Ohio Valley during the French and Indian War, though historians debate whether this strategy brought military gain because smallpox was already sweeping through native populations.[14] The most cited account is in a 1763 letter from British general Jeffrey Amherst to one of his commanders: "You will do well to inoculate the Indians by means of blankets, as well as every other method that can serve to extirpate this execrable race."[15] While using a truce to pass a disease-ridden blanket to one's enemy is a reprehensible and inhumane act, these early imaginings of bio-warfare exemplify how microbes have been manipulated throughout history to exploit vulnerability and instill fear.

Whether infected blankets were effective Trojan horses or not, the persistence of the story in the popular history of the Americas affirms the power of the narrative that says the continents were conquered not by Europeans but by their germs. Disease became a weapon of war as a result of the weak immunity of native people.[16] Acts of nature absolved human acts of conquest when deficiencies could be located in the bodies of those who succumbed. By describing the colonization of the Americas in terms of disease, these histories ascribe power to genetics and explain conquest in terms of superior health: people of color were vulnerable because their isolation and in-grouping had left them genetically unprepared for the global world, a state of being that can only be overcome through intermingling and by challenging their immune systems to prove survivability.

VACCINATION: CREATING SECURITY BY FIGHTING VULNERABILITY

Other social practices mitigated contagion before microbes were identified as the sources of infectious disease. Quarantine, funeral rites, and religious traditions prevented infection from dead bodies, food, and other human beings. Because the risk of dying of smallpox was already extraordinarily high, it is no surprise that smallpox motivated the development of some of the earliest medical preventions of disease. Variolation became a common practice. This method produced some level of smallpox immunity by rubbing the liquid from a smallpox pustule over a scratch made on the arm with a needle. The procedure was fatal for 1 percent to 2 percent of those treated.[17] Only in a society so dramatically shaped by disease could an apprentice physician named Edward Jenner inject the neighborhood children with liquid from a cowpox blister on a milkmaid's hand and then variolate them with smallpox to see if they developed the disease. Jenner experimented on folklore claiming that milkmaids wouldn't get smallpox after they'd had cowpox, a bovine cousin to the human strain of poxvirus. He self-published the results of his ethically and scientifically questionable study in 1798, and although his peers looked on his work with skepticism, within a decade his "vaccination" technique had spread throughout Europe, Asia, and the Americas.

With its lower fatality rate, vaccination quickly replaced variolation as the preferred immunization technique for smallpox. By 1801, 100,000 people had been vaccinated in Britain.[18] However, they had to extract the smallpox vaccine from an active rash, and this strategy limited viability in storage, creating problems of distribution. For the first half of the nineteenth century the vaccine was passed through human bodies, drawing live virus from the blister created by the vaccination and injecting it into the next individual. Around 1800, an expedition to take the smallpox vaccine to Spanish America set sail with twenty-two orphans onboard, two of whom were vaccinated every ten days to keep the virus alive during the Atlantic voyage.[19] Around 1840, a technique for producing large amounts of vaccine in cows became popular, and doctors brought infected calves into their offices and scraped the live vaccine right off the animals' flanks. The natural source of immunity was never so apparent as when disease was transferred from cow to human in a doctor's office. Notably, the smallpox vaccine was administered for generations before the *Variola* virus was first seen through an electron microscope. Knowing how to contain the spread of smallpox did not depend on detailed scientific knowledge of the virus itself but on the cultural acceptance of medical practices that seemed to increase human survival. The years following Jenner's discovery saw proposals for mandatory vaccination programs put forth in chambers of government around the globe. The smallpox question became a public platform to negotiate the terms of citizenship in the nineteenth century, raising questions about what governments can and should do to regulate disease in the name of public health and security.

In his lectures on security in the late 1970s, Foucault used the case of smallpox to explain how disease control functions as a mechanism of security. He proposed that despite the radical-ness of the idea, one could infect oneself with disease in hopes of creating immunity. He said vaccination was accepted as common practice because it was reliably safe and statistically successful, evidence that could only be created because of emerging ways of thinking about collective life in terms of a population. Quantitative analysis transformed generalities about the disease prevailing in a town or region into calculations of success and failure within a bounded group of people. The inclination to categorize disease as a problem emerging from "that other" township persisted, now rationalized by statistical evidence. "Cases" of disease could be understood in terms of distribution among the population, making the disease both more and less personal. It also became possible to calculate the risk that any one individual might contract the disease, making smallpox a probability, not a certainty. Moreover, the risks are not the same for all people, aligning disease risk with categories of difference. The outcome of the population, Foucault argued, is the production of mechanisms to keep all forms of deviance, including disease, within the acceptable "normal" conditions of the population. What work will the state do to maintain normal health within a population? As disease control became the responsibility of governments, new interactions between citizens and the state emerged, rationalizing governing acts at the most intimate sites of human life in the name of public health and security for the population as a whole.[20]

Over time, problems of smallpox vaccine distribution were overcome by new technologies that produced air-dried and freeze-dried vaccines, bringing to the surface a quiet hope that the scourge of smallpox could be eliminated from the planet. Indeed, the use of vaccine rapidly reduced the abundance of smallpox across the globe, and mandatory vaccination programs eliminated the disease in most countries by the mid-twentieth century. However, millions of people still suffered from the scourge, and in 1967, the World Health Organization (WHO) began an Intensified Smallpox Eradication Program to eliminate the disease. The WHO campaign is often lauded as an example of innovative thinking, cooperation, and goodwill coming together to alleviate worldwide suffering without regard to borders or politics. Disparagers claim smallpox was already on its way out and that the campaign capitalized on the dwindling incidence of the disease to expand the reach of public health. For whatever ends, the WHO campaign mobilized people to act against disease, using technology to create masses of immunized bodies and destroy the viable habitat of the smallpox virus. The campaign created the microbe as an enemy to be fought, controlled, and eliminated. The effort established the rites of a modern war against a germ, producing the weapons, strategies, tools, and attitudes that continue to characterize health practice as a battle against invasive pathogens.

The push for global eradication followed successes in creating "herd immunity" that inhibited the spread of smallpox by dramatically reducing its incidence in the population. Vaccinating masses of people in endemic countries held much appeal from the perspective of governance: increasing the number of vaccinations would provide an economic boost and a clear show of government engagement in a public health situation. Mass vaccination, however, proved to be expensive and time-consuming, and for decades these programs waned, with little popular support. The 1967 resolution gained momentum, not on moral grounds but by laying out an equation where smallpox-free countries could save billions of dollars on policing their borders against the disease by wiping the virus from the earth. It also allocated 5 percent of the WHO budget, roughly $2.4 million annually, to the work and established a headquarters for the campaign. That was the extent of what the United Nations could do to intervene. As program director Donald A. Henderson explained, "WHO had no authority, other than that of moral suasion, to compel any country."[21] To eliminate the virus, the campaign would have to touch the bodies of millions of people living in more than forty countries. In addition to that hurdle, many of these regions were also tormented by poverty, civil war, and a range of other health concerns.

THE WAR ON SMALLPOX

The decision to declare worldwide war on smallpox might be framed as an act of "humanitarian biomedicine," but it was also a decision to destroy another species.[22] While species extinction is not an uncommon outcome of human-nonhuman interactions, the purposeful work of the smallpox campaign presumed that nature could be managed to achieve a culturally desired outcome. However, managing the nonhuman smallpox organism required managing human bodies, blurring boundaries between that which was human and that which was not human. The fight against smallpox was not a war against a disease or even the management of nonhuman nature; it was a deliberate system of governance that relied on tactics of fear and persuasion to create behaviors among the population. The microbe itself was monster-ized in propaganda to establish it as the nonhuman enemy. Echoing the patriotic refrains of the earlier world wars, the campaign described the duty of all world citizens to submit their bodies to the war against smallpox.

Though Henderson denied that the campaign employed military tactics (or at least that it had similar financial backing, authority, and popular support as a war campaign), the language of war pervaded all aspects of the work. For example, when it became clear that the mass vaccination strategy was not producing lasting results, a new "war plan" was proposed to target and break the chain of transmission. One WHO official recalled, "It was on a hot, blistering June afternoon in 1973 that the 'war plan' that eventually spelt victory over smallpox in India was set in motion. Till then, the relentless war against an enemy that knew no mercy had not been going on too well. If anything, it had become a general's nightmare. Though there was no dearth of 'troops' or 'ammunition,' the problem was to get them to the right place at the right time. Naturally, the casualties were heavy—over 16,000 reported dead and more than five times this number maimed and disabled."[23]

This account overflows with language of war, as the official describes how the new "ring approach" would use quarantine and vaccination to encircle infected areas and block the spread. India's Smallpox Eradication Programme officer chose the following military metaphor: "We decided then that instead of expending our resources against the entire enemy forces simultaneously, we would concentrate on their strongholds."[24] The restructured program recruited "officers" and "advance teams" who were put through "highly intensified training courses" to become "experts" in detecting smallpox. These teams conducted "reconnaissance trips" to identify "enemy" areas. When an outbreak was reported, the team would "blitz" the area with "vaccination devices and vaccine—the guns and bullets of the campaign."[25] These reports from the field suggest that both WHO officials and local workers felt like they were at war with an enemy, though they themselves were immune and need not fear infection. In reality, the fight with the virus took place *inside* human bodies because the vaccine stimulated immune systems to produce antibodies. The primary tactic of the WHO campaign was largely an appropriation of militant ideals to access bodies and control populations. As a vital security mechanism, disease eradication affirmed human relationships with microbes as antipathetic and hostile.

For more than a decade, the WHO and national governments watched populations with an eye focused on disease and deviance. Swift containment of breakouts required that citizens report the disease to authorities. People had to be persuaded to act on a moral imperative, often violating relationships of trust and privacy associated with the sick and dying on behalf of some greater good. Jitendra Tuli reported going into classrooms to ask children to disclose any diseases at home to their teachers.[26] In later years, officials offered a monetary reward to individuals who reported cases of smallpox. No wonder this method turned up hundreds of false leads in poverty-stricken countries, but the strategy successfully cultivated a climate in which people would expose their neighbors' disease. Self-reporting was encouraged in posters and

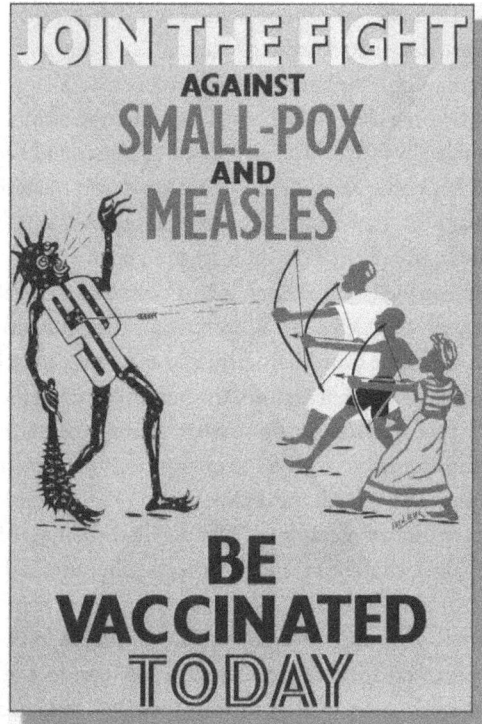

FIGURE 3.1. Public health poster from the worldwide smallpox eradication campaign in Africa. *Courtesy*, CDC/Stafford Smith, taken from the Public Health Image Library, Centers for Disease Control and Prevention (#2587), Atlanta, GA.

pamphlets and even in hand-scrawled messages painted on the backs of buses or slung over elephants. The message was consistently a call to war.

One poster called on citizens to "Join the fight," as if recruiting troops for battle (figure 3.1). The poster shows three Africans in various modes of traditional attire facing off against a personified smallpox giant. Marked with an identifying "SP" on its chest, the monster has distinct human features: arms, legs, fingers, toes, eyes, and hair. Its skin is black with white pockmarks, imitating the way smallpox marks the skin, and it holds a spiked club. Visually, the virus is rendered human or at least human-like but even larger than the people it fights. The individuals facing the monster wield bows and arrows, one of which has been driven into the "heart" of the disease, squarely between the S and P. The scene is of a battle with a monster, in which people armed with primitive weapons hurl projectile points at a foreign body. At the public health clinic, however, the projectile is turned on one's own body, for the fighting behavior promoted by the poster is to "be vaccinated today."

Many posters published between 1968 and 1977 show the vaccination act itself (examples shown in figures 3.2 and 3.3). The injection gun is clearly displayed, poised

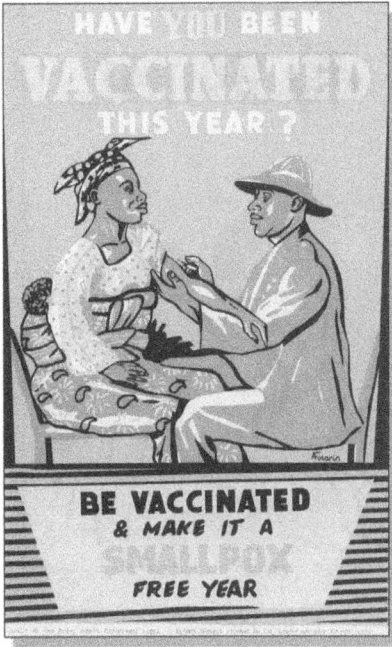

FIGURE 3.2. Poster from Lagos, Nigeria, promoting smallpox vaccination. *Courtesy,* CDC/Stafford Smith, taken from the Public Health Image Library, Centers for Disease Control and Prevention (#2578), Atlanta, GA.

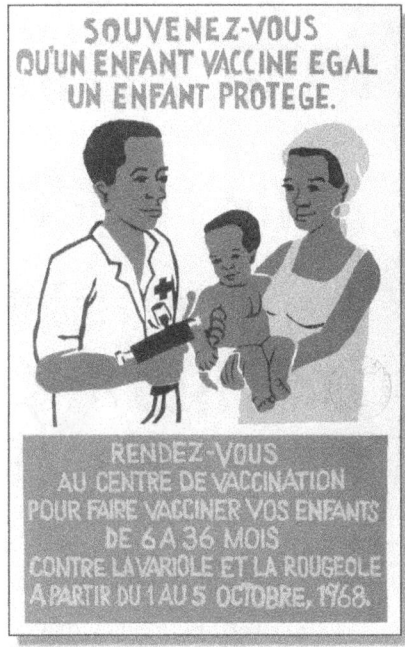

FIGURE 3.3. 1968 poster from the smallpox eradication campaign. *Courtesy,* CDC/Stafford Smith, taken from the Public Health Image Library, Centers for Disease Control and Prevention (#2594), Atlanta, GA.

to shoot a vaccine into the victim's arm. Sometimes a stethoscope or a red cross labels the person holding the gun as a medical professional; sometimes a uniformed officer wearing a hat or badge holds the gun. Typically, the vaccine giver is a man and the recipient is a woman, often carrying a small child. These images depict a critical moment in smallpox eradication, when vaccine is forced into the human body. Such one-on-one meetings between healthy citizens and officials bearing vaccine were the daily work of smallpox eradication. These illustrations of that moment show a power structure in which the unvaccinated individual is under the control of the person administering the vaccine, underlining the vulnerable state of the unvaccinated body. The recipients are women and children wearing some form of "native" attire; the vaccinators are men wearing uniforms. The official holds a gun to the exposed flesh of the recipient, exercising the authority of the state and the medical profession

FIGURE 3.4. Public health poster from the worldwide smallpox eradication campaign. *Courtesy*, CDC/Stafford Smith, taken from the Public Health Image Library, Centers for Disease Control and Prevention (#2591), Atlanta, GA.

(illustrated in figure 3.4). Though written as an invitation to be vaccinated, the poster in figure 3.4 affirms the larger system of social control created through the vaccination program. Race and gender are on display in these clinical encounters, where the body of a woman of color is a target of governance (generally) and a target of a gun (in particular). Repeated depictions of vaccine recipients dressed in robes, headscarves, and other traditional attire associate vulnerability with poor people of color. Such representations suggest that these populations are more susceptible to disease or at a minimum are more in need of being educated and persuaded to be vaccinated. Though vaccines are only effective in people who have not been infected and healthy individuals were the target of the ring approach, the propaganda of the campaign established women and poor, traditional cultures as the greatest obstacle to smallpox eradication. It appeared that these people were the greatest risk to the health of the world's population and therefore most in need of being controlled.

In addition to the voluntary submission to vaccination, smallpox containment required citizens to relinquish cultural practices and social norms to sustain public health. Human social behaviors are not readily relinquished, particularly during times of collective suffering, despite evidence that those practices may be risky.

WHO officers arrived at outbreak sites to find scores of people traveling between towns as they paid their respects to the dead and dying, carrying the virus from a relation's deathbed to their own homes.[27] In India, the spring outbreak of smallpox was welcomed as the annual tribunal of the goddess Shitala Mata, by which she would decide who was strong enough to live. Positive outcomes from collective vaccination, including the end of an epidemic, could be easily attributed to many unrelated factors, including divine intervention. Religious beliefs regarding animals, including the cow, drew skepticism toward the medicine rumored to have bovine origins.[28] The vaccine does have risks and complications, including death, and produces an open wound that must be properly cared for to be effective. In communities with little exposure to modern medicine, a needle with a promise was a hard sell. Field officers employed creative strategies to persuade citizens to participate, including jabbing themselves with the needle to demonstrate that it did no harm, an act that mimicked the scenes depicted on many program posters.[29]

Containment also depended upon identifying and marking both the source of infection and the immune population. WHO officials "read" human bodies to distinguish the "at-risk" population. There are no invisible carriers of smallpox; people who are infected wear the symptoms on their bodies. People who are immune can prove their immunity by showing scars on their arms (from the vaccine) or the scars left on their bodies from the disease itself.[30] Officials traveling from house to house would mark houses where smallpox was present with a number and then vaccinate everyone who lived within a quarter mile, moving outward in concentric rings until they got ahead of the disease. (House marking is shown in figure 3.5.) At the bull's-eye of the ring was a house marked with disease and a number telling anyone who passed by just that. The home became a place to be feared, stigmatized by the presence of an unseen organism.

Like a marker on a home or a scar on a body, the cultural production of disease marks bodies of color as bearers of disease risk. Such associations at the level of the individual and the population allow white people to contain their fear because the threat is located in geographically distant countries and biologically different bodies. By pinpointing "other" bodies as the source of risk, public health practice expresses racial politics and naturalizes the control of bodies as the management of microbial natures.

As the blight of smallpox began to fade, WHO officials combed the planet for signs of any outbreak. Tentatively at first, then more emphatically, they began to suggest the disease had been contained. In 1977, a man in Somalia became the last person to catch contagious smallpox from the body of another human being. His antibodies fought off the virus, and without another vulnerable body to infect, the disease succumbed. The chain of contagion had been ruptured, and the 10,000-year-old virus

FIGURE 3.5. Paint marking a home where a person with smallpox lives. *Courtesy,* CDC/ WHO, Stanley O. Foster, MD, MPH, taken from the Public Health Image Library, Centers for Disease Control and Prevention (#7524), Atlanta, GA.

no longer passed freely from host to host. WHO president Dr. Abdul Rahman Al-Awadi signed the death certificate for smallpox on May 8, 1980, declaring solemnly that "the world and its peoples have won freedom from smallpox, which was the most devastating disease sweeping in epidemic form through many countries since earliest time."[31] Not only were people's bodies freed from the disease, but the global economy was freed from the cost of smallpox. WHO declared that the total expense of the campaign was $112 million, and they predicted a worldwide savings of $1 billion annually through the eradication of smallpox.[32] Fieldworkers were recognized as the "heroes who conquered smallpox." At a celebratory parade in Sierra Leone, "The vaccination team members wore their field uniforms and displayed their jet injector guns for the public to see."[33] Such military-like parades helped people commemorate a victory that was largely invisible: the elimination of a threat to which much of the population was already individually immune.

In the end, perhaps the most significant outcome of the WHO campaign was not the elimination of a disease that was on decline but the worldwide expression of how humans could impact infectious disease. The war-like campaign established disease as an oppressive enemy that could and should be battled with all the weapons of modern medicine and government. Even WHO's final victory shout, "Smallpox

Is Dead," echoed in headlines around the globe, reaffirmed that the war had been against a living enemy. Clearly, success was to be marked not in healthy bodies but in the obliteration of the smallpox virus. Such approbation further ratified the body checks, quarantines, and bounties for exposing your neighbor as necessary displays of force to kill the virus. Moreover, the smallpox campaign has enduring outcomes in global understandings of disease and the production of biological citizens. The global campaign expressed colonial power in the terms of the modern era, in this case the global spread of public health and the advancement of medical technology. Abiding fears of disease, largely in the developed nations where vaccination was an economic burden and long life a cultural expectation, rationalized the extension of state power over foreign nations, particularly nations where people of color lived according to their own cultural understandings of disease. The depiction of the war on smallpox as a battle against microbes naturalized the colonial work as a necessary practice. It had been necessary to manage fearful natures, creating racialized subjects. These subjects, then, must depend on foreign governments to create health and security. As in the colonization of the Americas, native people's vulnerability to disease is at the crux of the conquest, though four centuries later the colonial encounter is not explained as an expression of divine will but is produced as an opportunity to use modern technology to overcome nature to achieve a perceived advancement of society.

CONCLUSION: THE POLITICS OF SMALLPOX IN THE TWENTY-FIRST CENTURY

Though the world commemorated the death of smallpox more than two decades ago, *Variola major* is still alive, held hostage in freezers in the United States and Russia. WHO's post-eradication program called for all countries to send their laboratory stocks of the smallpox virus to two repositories, where after a ten-year window for scientific study, all remaining live virus would be destroyed. A series of UN resolutions has since delayed the destruction of the stockpiles. The reluctance to destroy a microbe—even the most deadly germ to present itself in human history—expresses a strong cultural belief that scientific study will ultimately extract social benefits from the germ, even as citizens concurrently acknowledge mistrust of the nation-state. Some people speculate that countries may be harboring live virus in secret violation of international diplomacy.[34] The existence of the virus stocks creates an arena for debates about the calculation of risk, trust in government, and the value of every organism, even a deadly virus.

Moreover, modern biotechnologies and the public imagination have made smallpox into a twenty-first-century monster, preying upon the fears of a population no longer vaccinated and therefore vulnerable to the smallpox virus. In 2002, scientists successfully created a polio virus from 70-letter bits of its DNA sequence. While the smallpox virus is more complex (185,000 letters in smallpox virus to polio's 7,000), the possibility of artificially manufactured viruses has been realized, and smallpox may live forever through its DNA.[35] Much of the smallpox DNA sequence has become publicly available, as pieces have been doled out for research on vaccines and antidotes. In fact, in 2006, a *Guardian* reporter ordered a smallpox sequence over the internet using a fake company, a cell phone, and a residential address.[36] Others fear that the virus might be captured in glaciers or cemeteries, set to reemerge in nature as global temperatures climb. In 2003, a librarian in New Mexico discovered smallpox scabs in an envelope inside a library book. Though the material contained no live virus, the genetic technologies of the twenty-first century might allow the production of smallpox from such matter.[37] Today, it may be impossible to "kill" smallpox.

Because smallpox still exists in all these forms, it continues to produce vulnerable bodies. Perhaps, even if the stockpiles were destroyed, the possibility that the virus could be revived would continue to sustain the cultural fear of smallpox. Medical professionals are now discouraged (and at times prohibited) from vaccinating individuals against smallpox, on the grounds that the risks associated with the vaccine pose a greater threat than the disease. An entire generation—in some countries, two or three generations—has not been vaccinated against smallpox. Unvaccinated bodies can be perceived as vulnerable. As so frequently in the history of the disease, smallpox is still used to manage vulnerable bodies and create categories of difference.

In the last moments of a 2005 hearing in the US Congress, Representative John Linder provoked a panel of bio-terror experts with this question: "What would you say if I told you a scientist from Sweden said that Iranian children emigrating with their parents from Iran to Sweden have all been vaccinated for smallpox; what would that mean to you?"[38] The question asked scientists to assess a political threat by reading marks on human bodies. Children's bodies would be too young to carry a scar left by vaccines administered pre-eradication. Their bodies exist in a social context that also labels them as Middle Eastern, Iranian, emigrant, and foreign—categories that might be read as risky. The scar links them to larger political meanings of disease and the possibility that Iran is immunizing its citizens against a terrorizing release of smallpox. Cultural fears of Iran and the Middle East converged with fears of disease on the body of a child with a scar. One scientist on the panel presented an alternative reading, saying that people in Iran are not convinced that smallpox has been eradicated, insinuating that Iranians are either uneducated and ignorant or brainwashed by the state. Here, rumors of vaccination can be read as both an act of personal control and an act of state dominance and international warfare.

The exterminated smallpox virus continues to produce meanings about nationhood, terrorism, and fear—not only of disease but of the wide range of politics and practices that align with the care of human bodies in a world of microbial monsters. Narratives of race and difference continue to be naturalized through the production of microbes as a nonhuman "other" that threatens a normal society. Military rule and other extremes of social control emerged for smallpox eradication, and these forms of control are refined in public health practice today. Though smallpox scars are fading on the bodies of the population, the possibility that the virus could emerge again sustains fear in society; along with this fear come all the markers of difference in race, class, and gender that can be used to explain risk and manage human bodies. Thus the politics of the modern microbe are politics of difference, rationalized for the survival of the human species.

NOTES

1. Dobell, *Anthony van Leeuwenhoek.*
2. Wald, "Bio Terror," 101.
3. Latour, *We Have Never Been Modern.*
4. Magnusson and Zalloua, *Contagion,* 12.
5. See, for example, Tomes, *The Gospel of Germs*; Treichler, *How to Have Theory in an Epidemic*; Brier, *Infectious Ideas.*
6. Magnusson and Zalloua, *Contagion,* 12.
7. Foucault, *Security, Territory, Population.*
8. Wald, *Contagious,* 42.
9. Waldby, *AIDS and the Body Politic,* 51.
10. Haraway, "The Biopolitics of Postmodern Bodies."
11. Macaulay, *The History of England from the Accession of James II,* 423.
12. For a cultural history of smallpox and detailed biological information, see Hopkins, *Princes and Peasants.*
13. Croffut, *Fifty Years in Camp and Field,* 395.
14. Peckham, *Pontiac and the Indian Uprising,* 226; Anderson, *Crucible of War,* 809b; Ranlet, "The British, the Indians, and Smallpox."
15. Grenier, *The First Way of War,* 144; Nester, "Haughty Conquerors," 114–115.
16. Most famously, Diamond, *Guns, Germs, and Steel.*
17. Behbehani, "The Smallpox Story."
18. Behbehani, "The Smallpox Story," 19.
19. Hopkins, *Princes and Peasants*; Smith, "The 'Real Expedicion Maritima de la Vacuna' in New Spain and Guatemala"; Bowers, "The Odyssey of Smallpox Vaccination."
20. Foucault, *Security, Territory, Population.*

21. Henderson, *Smallpox*, 421.

22. Lakoff, "Epidemic Intelligence."

23. Tuli, "India's 'War Plan.'"

24. Tuli, "India's 'War Plan.'"

25. Davies, "A Job Well Done," 7–9 (quotation); Henderson, "A Victory for All Mankind," 4; Tuli, "India's 'War Plan,'" 13.

26. Tuli, "India's 'War Plan.'"

27. Henderson, "A Victory for all Mankind."

28. Tuli, "India's 'War Plan.'"

29. Chacko, "A Goddess Defied," 15.

30. Notably, the vaccine is only effective for a decade, though the scar will last much longer. Only about 80 percent of smallpox cases leave facial scars, so this surveillance could not be considered to be foolproof.

31. World Health Assembly Resolution 33.3, 1980.

32. Henderson, "A Victory for All Mankind."

33. Davies, "A Job Well Done," 8.

34. A Federation of American Scientists fact sheet on smallpox, for example, sustains the rumor of countries harboring smallpox reserves: http://www.fas.org/programs/bio/fact sheets/smallpox.html. See also Tucker, *Scourge*.

35. Cello et al., "Chemical Synthesis of Poliovirus CDNA."

36. Randerson, "Did Anyone Order Smallpox?" *The Guardian*, 6/23/2006.

37. "Century-Old Smallpox Scabs in N.M. Envelope," *USA Today*.

38. US Congress, "Reducing Nuclear and Biological Threats at the Source."

BIBLIOGRAPHY

Anderson, Fred. *Crucible of War: The Seven Years' War and the Fate of Empire in British North America, 1754–1766*. New York: Alfred A. Knopf, 2000.

Behbehani, Abbas M. "The Smallpox Story: Life and Death of an Old Disease." *Microbiology Review* 47 (1983): 455–509.

Bowers, John Z. "The Odyssey of Smallpox Vaccination." *Bulletin of the History of Medicine* 55 (1981): 17–33.

Brier, Jennifer. *Infectious Ideas: US Political Responses to the AIDS Crisis*. Chapel Hill: University of North Carolina Press, 2009.

Cello, Jeronimo, Aniko V. Paul, and Eckard Wimmer. "Chemical Synthesis of Poliovirus CDNA: Generation of Infectious Virus in the Absence of Natural Template." *Science* 297, no. 5583 (2002): 1016–1018.

"Century-Old Smallpox Scabs in N.M. Envelope." *USA Today*, December 26, 2003.

Chacko, Arun M. "A Goddess Defied." *World Health: The Magazine of the World Health Organization* (May 1980): 14–16.

Croffut, William Augustus, ed. *Fifty Years in Camp and Field: The Diary of Major General Ethan Allen Hitchcock*. New York: G. P. Putnam's Sons, 1909.

Davies, Marcella. "A Job Well Done." *World Health: The Magazine of the World Health Organization* (May 1980): 6–9.

Diamond, Jared. *Guns, Germs, and Steel: The Fates of Human Societies*. New York: W. W. Norton, 1999.

Dobell, Clifford. *Anthony van Leeuwenhoek and His "Little Animals."* London: John Bale, Sons, and Danielsson, 1932.

Federation of American Scientists fact sheet on smallpox. http://www.fas.org/programs /bio/factsheets/smallpox.html.

Foucault, Michel. *Security, Territory, Population: Lectures at the Collège De France, 1977–78*, trans. Graham Burchell, ed. Michel Senellart, François Ewald, and Alessandro Fontana. New York: Palgrave Macmillan, 2007.

Grenier, John. *The First Way of War: American War Making on the Frontier, 1607–1814*. Cambridge: Cambridge University Press, 2005.

Haraway, Donna J. "The Biopolitics of Postmodern Bodies: Determinations of Self in Immune System Discourse." *Differences: A Journal of Feminist Cultural Studies* 1 (1989): 3–43.

Henderson, Donald A. *Smallpox, the Death of a Disease: The Inside Story of Eradicating a Worldwide Killer*. Amherst, NY: Prometheus Books, 2009.

Henderson, Donald A. "A Victory for All Mankind." *World Health: The Magazine of the World Health Organization* (May 1980): 3–5.

Hopkins, Donald R. *Princes and Peasants: Smallpox in History*. Chicago: University of Chicago Press, 1983.

Koplow, David A. *Smallpox: The Fight to Eradicate a Global Scourge*. Berkeley: University of California Press, 2003.

Lakoff, Andrew. "Epidemic Intelligence: Rethinking the War on Terror." In *Contagion: Health, Fear, Sovereignty*, ed. Bruce Magnusson and Zahi Zalloua, 44–70. Seattle: University of Washington Press, 2012.

Latour, Bruno. *We Have Never Been Modern*. Cambridge, MA: Harvard University Press, 1993.

Macaulay, Thomas Babington. *The History of England from the Accession of James II*, vol. 4. New York: Harper and Brothers, 1898.

Magnusson, Bruce, and Zahi Zalloua. "Introduction." In *Contagion: Health, Fear, Sovereignty*, ed. Bruce Magnusson and Zahi Zalloua, 3–24. Seattle: University of Washington Press, 2012.

Nester, William R. *"Haughty Conquerors": Amherst and the Great Indian Uprising of 1763.* Westport, CT: Praeger, 2000.

Peckham, Howard H. *Pontiac and the Indian Uprising.* Princeton, NJ: Princeton University Press, 1947.

Peters, Stephanie True. *Smallpox in the New World.* New York: Benchmark Books, 2005.

Randerson, James. "Did Anyone Order Smallpox?" *The Guardian*, June 23, 2006.

Ranlet, Philip. "The British, the Indians, and Smallpox: What Actually Happened at Fort Pitt in 1763?" *Pennsylvania History* 67, no. 3 (2000): 427–441.

Smith, Michael M. "The 'Real Expedicion Maritima de la Vacuna' in New Spain and Guatemala." *Transactions of the American Philosophical Society* 64, part 1 (1974): 1–74.

Tomes, Nancy. *The Gospel of Germs: Men, Women, and the Microbe in American Life.* Cambridge, MA: Harvard University Press, 1998.

Treichler, Paula A. *How to Have Theory in an Epidemic: Cultural Chronicles of AIDS.* Durham, NC: Duke University Press, 1999.

Tucker, Jonathan B. *Scourge: The Once and Future Threat of Smallpox.* New York: Grove, 2002.

Tuli, Jitendra. "India's 'War Plan.'" *World Health: The Magazine of the World Health Organization* (May 1980): 12–13.

US Congress. "Reducing Nuclear and Biological Threats at the Source." Serial no. 109–87, June 22, 2006. http://www.gpo.gov/fdsys/pkg/CHRG-109hhrg33959/pdf/CHRG -109hhrg33959.pdf.

Wald, Priscilla. "Bio Terror: Hybridity in the Biohorror Narrative, or What We Can Learn from Monsters." In *Contagion: Health, Fear, Sovereignty*, ed. Bruce Magnusson and Zahi Zalloua, 99–122. Seattle: University of Washington Press, 2012.

Wald, Priscilla. *Contagious: Cultures, Carriers, and the Outbreak Narrative.* Durham, NC: Duke University Press, 2007.

Waldby, Catherine. *AIDS and the Body Politic: Biomedicine and Sexual Difference.* London: Routledge, 1996.

World Health Assembly Resolution 33.3, 1980.

Reinforcing or Spreading Fear of the "Other"

4

"They'll Take Away Our Birthrights"

How White-Power Musicians Instill Fear of White Extinction

Kirsten Dyck

Fantasies of racist violence often appear in the lyrics of white-power and neo-Nazi music.[1] For instance, Jocke Karlsson, frontman of the Swedish band Pluton Svea, in a 2001 song called "Hail the Swastika," sings lyrics professing to fight daily for "the existence of the white race" and telling "Niggers and Jews, gooks and communists" that they "have to pay."[2]

Listeners who are unaccustomed to hearing songs full of blatant racism might be shocked by this celebration of the Holocaust, not to mention Pluton Svea's violent threat that non-whites "have to pay!" The racist violence inherent in "Hail the Swastika" is certainly one of the most obvious features of the song. Yet upon further examination, this lyric excerpt displays not only an ethos of violent racism and aggression but also a sense of fear that the white race is under threat. The idea that whites must fight for "existence" on a day-to-day basis suggests that their racial and political enemies are putting the white race's future in jeopardy. In fact, many musicians who participate in the international web of contemporary white-power music—including not only Pluton Svea but also groups from European-descended populations around the world—have used song lyrics to proclaim that without intervention from white-power activists, the white race is in danger of disappearing in the near future.

This chapter will illustrate how and why white-power bands have adopted a form of rhetoric that centers on a fear of white extinction. To explain why this rhetoric matters to white-power musicians and their fans, as well as why it should matter

DOI: 10.5876/9781646420025.c004

to people who do not usually interact with white-power music, this chapter will show how white-power musicians link the fear of white extinction to a purported Jewish world conspiracy. What follows is an analysis of the goal of this conspiracy rhetoric, arguing that white-power musicians use fear in their songs both to justify violence against racial "Others" and to subvert others' claims to racial victimhood. This chapter will also explore how white-power musicians' rhetoric of white racial extinction relates to wider issues of racism and inequality in the Western world. It will examine the premise that the fear inherent in white-power songs is a manifestation of racism that is present in the mainstream as well as on the radical racist fringes of Western society.

WHITE EXTINCTION AND JEWISH WORLD CONSPIRACY THEORY

To many scholars of colonialism and European history, the idea that peoples of European descent are in danger may seem strange. Centuries of European colonial violence and exploitation have devastated many non-European groups, giving Europeans and their progeny control of the majority of the world's physical and financial resources.[3] However, when white-power musicians discuss the idea of white extinction, they are typically referring to something other than the processes of naked violence and cultural obliteration European powers have used for centuries against indigenous populations under colonial control. Rather, white-power musicians and their fans tend to perceive the threat of white extinction lurking in the mundane world around them, seeing risks for whites not only in violent attacks from racial Others but also in social structures and interpersonal interactions that might seem for people outside white-power circles to have nothing to do with racial conflict.

While not all white-power believers share the same racist ideologies, one central anti-Semitic conspiracy theory does appear consistently in the lyrics of white-power music. This theory of Jewish world conspiracy links issues such as immigration, pornography, drug abuse, non-white criminality, white race mixing, white prostitution, and white anti-racism. Their belief in this conspiracy stems directly from the century-old *Protocols of the Elders of Zion*, a forged, anti-Semitic redaction of a non-racist nineteenth-century French text that first appeared in the wake of the 1905 Russian Revolution.[4] The *Protocols* claimed to be the minutes of a secret meeting at which Jewish leaders discussed a plan to take over the world by seizing covert control of international media and financial institutions. Despite reputable studies as early as the 1920s which determined that the *Protocols'* provenance was illegitimate, anti-Semitic movements, including both Hitler's original Nazi party and subsequent neo-Nazi groups, have cited the text as proof of an evil Jewish world conspiracy.[5]

The *Protocols*-descended conspiracy theory that appears most often in white-power music developed among neo-Nazi ideologists in the United States during the 1970s and 1980s. Racist activists of that time, such as Eric Thomson, were frustrated with the fact that since the end of World War II, mainstream public opinion in many Western countries had shifted away from overt racism. Thomson and others took the turn-of-the-century racist conspiracy theory they found in the *Protocols* and updated it. They suggested that whites were beginning to accept non-whites as equals not because non-whites and whites could ever be real equals but rather because Jews had succeeded sometime after World War II in implementing the *Protocols'* clandestine control strategies.[6] These writers argued that the increasing multicultural tolerance among European-descended populations derived simply from the fact that Jews were controlling institutions such as the international media and banking conglomerates, national governments, the United Nations, and the World Bank and then using this power to convince unsuspecting whites to act against their racial self-interests.[7] Thomson's term for the Jewish conspiracy was the *Zionist Occupation Government*, or ZOG, although other white-power ideologists have used phrases such as New World Order to refer to similar constructs.[8]

The period in the late 1970s and early 1980s when ZOG theory first appeared as a popular element of international white-power ideology was also the window of time when contemporary white-power music first arose as a coherent and transnational phenomenon. The music originated in England under the leadership of seminal racist oi! punk bands such as Skrewdriver, Brutal Attack, and No Remorse. By the mid-1980s, white-power bands had begun to appear across western Europe, North America, Australia, and South America, in some cases even taking hold in eastern Europe before the fall of the Iron Curtain. Many of these bands quickly abandoned the old-style, ultra-nationalist rhetoric of their parents' generation in favor of a more transnational form of neo-Nazi philosophy. The updated version included ZOG theory as one of its core tenets. The bands played together at international white-power music festivals that sometimes drew four-digit crowds. They produced their music on white-power music labels that could gross hundreds of thousands of dollars per year, although exact sales figures are often impossible for researchers to find because musicians, distributors, and fans are often leery of providing such information to outsiders, given that many white-power songs express political sentiments that are illegal or semi-legal in many countries.[9] This growing cadre of premier 1990s white-power bands, like Germany's Landser, the US's Bound for Glory, and Russia's Kolovrat, began to argue that all individuals of European descent really belonged to *one* nation and that the future of that white nation would be uncertain until whites could purge racial Others from the earth.[10]

Key aspects of ZOG theory began to enter white-power song lyrics during this period. Songs during the 1990s began to say that all whites needed to come together as one nation to fight their common Jewish arch-enemy. For example, the lyrics to the 1999 song "Forked-Tongue Lies" by the Canadian white-power heavy metal band Battlefront draw on both medieval ideas of Jewish greed and Third Reich tropes of Jews as vermin and predators. The song, which appears on the same Battlefront album as a cover of the Skrewdriver song "One Fine Day," dwells on fear that the ZOG conspiracy is trying to exterminate the white race. One verse, for example, suggests that Jews are inherently greedy: "Greed flickers in their eyes." The next lines attribute a "master plan of white genocide" and planned destruction "of our kind" to Jews, who, according to Battlefront, "call themselves the New World Order."[11]

Here, Battlefront suggests that Jews want to commit genocide against whites to claim the resources white populations currently control. By characterizing Jews as snakelike, "[w]ith a serpent's smile and forked-tongue lies," the band references Third Reich propaganda materials and draws on the common image of the snake as both untrustworthy and predatory. This metaphor supports the band's allegation that because of Jewish avarice, dishonesty, and aggression, Jewish community leaders want to concentrate resources in their community by destroying Jews' racial competitors. Partly as a result of this lyrical content, "Forked-Tongue Lies" and other songs on the Battlefront album *Into the Storm* have received favorable reviews from white-power music fans who post on internet message boards like the Stormfront community. A prolific Stormfront CD reviewer who identified himself by the username JU-87, the serial number of the World War II–era German Stuka fighter plane, wrote a 2006 review of *Into the Storm* that stated, "This is a very tasty release [...] Too bad this band was yet another 'one day fly', like we use to say in the Netherlands [...] (8.5/10)" [*sic*].[12]

Despite positive fan response, however, this song makes several problematic assumptions. Most glaring, it assumes that a Jewish world conspiracy exists, a supposition that does not appear to match the reality of world power structures. Jewish world conspiracy theories are, however, non-falsifiable; in other words, no one person or organization can observe all Jews all the time to give absolute proof that Jews cannot be conspiring to take over the world, so no amount of counterevidence will be enough for some diehard believers. Also, the song's lyrics talk about biological racial categories as immutable, suggesting that all members of these immutable racial groups share fixed social and moral characteristics; natural scientists have long demonstrated that the concept of race, unlike the concept of biological descent, actually rests almost entirely on ever-changing social constructs, not immutable biology.[13] Moreover, the idea that Jews view whites as their enemies is problematic, too. It presupposes that whites are the strongest and noblest race of humans. If so, whites would be the key obstacle to Jewish world domination and therefore the natural primary targets for Jewish aggression. Neo-Nazis, however, suggest that whites are naturally superior to all other groups of people. How could Jews pose such a serious threat to whites if whites are naturally superior to Jews? The song addresses this paradox by positing that successful Jewish control and white genocide could only be achieved by methods that are underhanded, deceitful, and covert. Overall, then, the ZOG rhetoric in Battlefront's "Forked-Tongue Lies" and many other white-power songs about Jews rests on flawed conceptions of the world, some of which the band addresses directly and some of which it leaves unexamined.

Neither Battlefront's "Forked-Tongue Lies" nor Pluton Svea's "Hail the Swastika" establishes in any detail, however, how white-power musicians fit non-white races *other* than Jews into their conception of a Jewish world conspiracy. Whereas supporters of ZOG theory tend to view Jews as intelligent adversaries, albeit evil ones, most of the musicians refer to other non-white groups like Africans, Asians, Latinos, and Roma/Sinti as stupid, genetically inferior, and improperly evolved. These traits are not characteristics one would normally associate with groups of people who might pose any significant risk to the white race if one assumed that the white race really were superior. Yet ZOG theory has a place for these groups, too.

Take, for instance, songs by the prominent 1990s white-power band Nordic Thunder, which morphed into an even more influential Delaware-based band called Blue Eyed Devils after the murder of Nordic Thunder's lead singer, Joe Rowan. Members of Blue Eyed Devils actually claimed in a *Resistance* magazine interview to have once played a concert to an audience of 2,600 fans in Germany, and their 1999 album *Retribution* was hailed by *Resistance* as a CD whose "thirteen tracks of uncompromising hatecore [racist hardcore punk music] will get you ready for the racial revolution."[14] On a 1994 Nordic Thunder album, the band discusses the relationship between Jews and non-Jewish "Others" in the song "The Truth Will Set You Free." One verse describes "Niggers running wild, backed by Jewish greed," as well as what the narrator perceives as the "corrupting" theory of the melting pot, "devised by the Zionist pigs to destroy the white man."[15]

In this verse, Nordic Thunder insinuates that non-Jewish racial "Others" constitute a threat to the white race because greedy Jews are "backing" them. The idea is that Jews are using these non-Jewish, non-white groups as pawns in their efforts to "corrupt" areas that would normally belong to whites. This stanza says Jews are advocating that whites assimilate and interbreed with genetically inferior non-Jewish racial Others in a racial "melting pot" that will dilute the supposed purity, power, and dominance of the white race. As in the lyrics to Battlefront's "Forked-Tongue Lies," Nordic Thunder's lyrics use the metaphor of Jews as disgusting animals to remind listeners that even if Jews are intelligent and cunning, one should still view whites as the superior race. The idea that Jewish masterminds are controlling the behavior of other non-white groups allows supporters of ZOG theory to maintain a crucial idea: that non-Jewish racial Others still pose a threat to whites in the fight against ZOG, even if Jews remain the white race's arch-enemies. Under ZOG theory, non-white non-Jews become the unwitting minions of Jewish greed, unable to achieve cultural sophistication or political power on their own and dependent on the Jewish world conspiracy for advancement at the expense of whites.

In another example, the 1999 song "Loss of Identity" by the Australian band Fortress uses imagery of Jews as snakes ("[t]he New World Order tightens the coils"). The lyrics argue that genocide against whites is occurring because of both Jewish-controlled non-white immigration and Jewish-derived taboos against overt racism: "equality dogma" and "massive immigration."[16]

In this song, Fortress implies that white genocide is being accomplished through "government-sanctioned," lenient immigration legislation. As a result, say the lyrics, whites are losing the resources that should be their "birthright." This premise ignores the fact that Australia had been ruled by an indigenous Aboriginal population for thousands of years. Settlers from Europe and elsewhere immigrated to Australia for increased economic opportunity, displacing the Aborigines.

Many white-power musicians, like those quoted above, argue that ZOG is destroying the white race by means of a wide range of government policies from different Western nations. Members of the Ukrainian white-power band Sokyra Peruna, for example, responded to an interview question about the 2004 Ukrainian election crisis by saying, "Both of the candidates have many different features, but one they have in common—like twin brothers—is that Yanoukovich and Youshchenko are puppets in the hands of Zionist puppeteers. The only reason this pair was allowed in the elections is that both of them have faithfully served their Jewish masters for years [...] We should not let the Jews turn our homeland, which was granted to us by our glorious ancestors, into a battlefield for the war of different Jewish clans."[17]

In the same issue of *Resistance* magazine, a member of the German band Anger Within likewise told interviewers, "The 'German' government is no topic of my interest; it's part of a system that was installed in 'Western countries' to destroy them in culture and race."[18] When a government passes legislation that seems to conflict with white-power goals, then, individuals who agree with the sentiments of musicians like these can say that this legislation is proof of ZOG's evil power. ZOG theory becomes an explanation for almost anything these musicians fear about contemporary Western society, from overbearing law enforcement to non-white enfranchisement to anti-racist education in public schools. To them, this is why centuries-old racist structures should remain in place. The fear of white extinction thereby helps to justify the use of violence to safeguard the white race from imminent destruction.

FEAR OF WHITE EXTINCTION AS MOTIVATION AND
JUSTIFICATION FOR RACIAL VIOLENCE

Several of the songs discussed so far imply that whites should respond to the threat of the ZOG conspiracy with violence. The Pluton Svea lyrics quoted at the beginning of the chapter say that the struggle against racial Others is a daily battle. Battlefront's song gives whites two choices in the face of ZOG: "fight or die." References to struggle and fighting are often found in white-power music. Lyrics often use the fear of ZOG and white extinction to justify violence against racial and ideological "Others," as if such violence is self-defense. In this line of thinking, whites are the *victims* of racism and genocide, and violence against racial Others is therefore a reasonable response to the threat.

The purpose of such music, at the most basic level, is often to attract new followers for white-power groups and ideologies. This is evident from the writings of the late William Pierce, founder of the once-prominent US neo-Nazi group the National Alliance and former owner of Resistance Records, which was the biggest white-power record label in the world under Pierce's leadership in the late 1990s and early 2000s. In the Winter 2000 issue of the label's glossy *Resistance* magazine, Pierce stated: "We want resistance music to be much more available, not just from Resistance Records, but in record stores and everywhere else that people buy music. We want to bring it out from under the counter and put it on display. We want millions of young, White Americans and Europeans to make resistance music their music of choice, instead of the Negroid filth churned out by MTV and the other Jewish promoters of anti-White music intended to demoralize, corrupt, and deracinate young Whites."[19]

During his lifetime, Pierce's label distributed thousands of white-power songs and albums that urged new listeners to take up racist activism in an effort to preserve what Pierce saw as a dying way of life. Although Pierce died in 2002 and Resistance Records then underwent several management upheavals that included one long-term closure, new owners recently reopened the business, selling albums through an internet store. One of the groups whose music is still for sale on the Resistance Records website is the British neo-Nazi oi! punk band Skrewdriver, which, according to most scholars, was the first and most important band to have played white-power rock music.[20] Lyrics in "Eyes Full of Rage" include calls to "[stand] up for our nations" and "stand against the traitors."[21]

The song never explicitly names the white race's enemies. However, the singer openly advocated neo-Nazism during his lifetime, working to forge links between white-power bands and neo-Nazi political organizations. In the 1980s and early 1990s, Ian Stuart Donaldson, who died in a 1993 car accident, used his connections in the music scene to make friends with veterans of Hitler's SS.[22] In a 1988 interview, Donaldson even stated, "Eventually there will be a race war and we have to be strong enough in numbers to win it. I'll die to keep this country pure and if it means bloodshed at the end of the day, then let it be."[23] Like the songs discussed previously, the lyrics of "Eyes Full of Rage" say that someone is stealing the land that should be a white "birthright" and that the "white rights" undergirding "life as once we knew it" are in imminent danger. The song urges whites to "stand up" and "sacrifice" for "our nations" and "our rights." It urges the listener to fight anyone who jeopardizes the white-dominated social structure.

Although Skrewdriver's music is several decades old, white-power music distributors such as Micetrap Records still list Skrewdriver albums among their bestsellers.[24] Skrewdriver songs have served as the inspiration for decades of new songwriters who support violent retribution against racial Others. For instance, the US band Youngland uses the fear of white extinction as a reason for advocating sweeping violence against non-whites in the 2003 song "I Wanna See the Day," which was originally written by the Welsh white-power musician Billy Bartlett.[25]

The lyrics to this song, written for Youngland by Bartlett, argue that the presence of "mud" in "our land"—referring to the racial slur "mud people," a common derogatory phrase for non-white non-Jews among white-power activists—justifies waging holy war on the "evil plague" of non-whites who are supposedly usurping land and resources from deserving whites. Bartlett here draws on a racist variant of Scandinavian revival paganism in suggesting that "the hammer of mighty Thor" will help whites in their race war against Jews and other non-whites. By deploying neo-pagan symbolism such as the hammer of the god Thor, Bartlett and Youngland allege that whites deserve by reason of both innate racial superiority and divine provenance to inherit land that has historically belonged to people of European descent—again ignoring the fact that European settlers in recent centuries stole the land that has become Youngland's home country, the United States, from indigenous groups who had previously controlled it for millennia. In this conception, whatever method white-power activists must use to "rid these lands from the evil plague" of Jewish-controlled non-whites becomes acceptable because a divine figure wills violence. Suggesting that white-power groups are fighting absolute evil with the absolute good of a pure-white, European-derived deity like Thor thereby lends their white-power cause a sense of significance beyond mere bigotry. Because most listeners condone self-defense more readily than they do wanton ideologically motivated attacks on innocent victims, construing racist violence as a divine mission to eliminate a serious threat is an important rhetorical device that helps white-power musicians like Bartlett and Youngland argue the virtue of their cause.

Bartlett's imagery in "I Wanna See the Day" is meant to be compelling. It is meant to incite listeners to action. Of course, one might dismiss the violence in such songs as simply the toothless blustering of a few lunatics who have no impact on the rest of society. Regrettably, however, over the past several decades, individuals with links to the white-power music scene have carried out numerous violent attacks. For example, during the 1980s, Skrewdriver frontman Ian Stuart Donaldson assaulted an elderly Nigerian man, a crime for which he spent a year in prison.[26] In the early 1990s in Norway, members of a small, neo-Nazi black metal circle murdered two people. They also committed numerous arsons, going so far as to burn down the twelfth-century Fantoft wooden-stave church in Bergen to protest the presence of the purportedly foreign, Jewish-derived Christian religion in Scandinavia.[27] Between 2000 and 2006 in Germany, a neo-Nazi terrorist cell assassinated nine immigrants working at fast-food restaurants around the country, a series of events that featured in a 2010 song by the German neo-Nazi band Gigi & die braune Stadtmusikanten. A macabre twist was that the song was released a full year before the German police or mainstream public discovered that any of the murders had connections to neo-Nazi groups, leading German courts to sentence frontman Daniel "Gigi" Giese to a seven-month suspended prison term and several fines for the crime of inciting racial hatred.[28] In another incident, in the summer of 2011, just months before the German killing spree made headlines in Europe, seventy-seven people died in a two-pronged terrorist attack on left-wing political organizations in and around Oslo. The man responsible was a Norwegian, Anders Behring Breivik, who professed in a personal manifesto to be a fan of a female Swedish neo-Nazi singer who performs under the stage name Saga.[29] Then, in 2012, Wade Michael Page killed six people and wounded four others in an attack on a Sikh temple in Milwaukee, Wisconsin.[30] Page had been frontman for the white-power band 13 Knots and had played bass for both Youngland and Billy Bartlett's band Celtic Warrior. In fact, Page had been the bassist on Youngland's 2003 album *Winter Wind*, which included the aforementioned "I Wanna See the Day."

Clearly, individuals with ties to white-power music have committed numerous acts of ideologically motivated violence. It is important to note that this link does not mean that white-power music *caused* any of these attacks. Clinical researchers have only begun to study the complex connections between music and human violent behavior, meaning that while the *correlation* between white-power music and violence may appear to be strong, it remains impossible to prove that racist music was actually the main factor that triggered white-power musicians and fans to harm themselves and others. Nonetheless, white-power songs remain important ideological statements, providing a crucial lens into the multifaceted world of recent white-power thought. The fact that white-power musicians place so much emphasis on the fear of white extinction, as well as the fact that some of them later go on to commit extreme acts of violence against the racial and ideological Others they have threatened in the lyrics to their songs, suggests that for contemporary white-power and neo-Nazi musicians and fans, the fear expressed in their music represents a powerful motivator to violent action.

CONCLUSION: WHY THEIR FEAR MATTERS

The fear-driven rhetoric of white extinction, one of the most prominent justifications white-power musicians use to excuse violence in their song lyrics, is a key factor in explaining why some individuals are willing to harm seemingly innocent victims. This link between violent rhetoric and real-world violent actions alone should be enough reason to argue that white-power musicians' rhetoric of fear ought to matter to the mainstream public. However, this is not the only reason why white-power musicians' fears should matter to people who might otherwise have nothing to do with white-power music. In fact, white-power musicians' racial and racist anxieties overlap strongly with attitudes that many individuals who consider themselves non-racist also hold. To understand why white-power musicians continue to attract new fans with their rhetoric of fear, as well as why members of the white-power counterculture keep committing spectacular acts of violence, one must examine how mainstream racism in many Western countries interacts with the more visible racism of white-power groups.

Most European-derived societies tolerate overt acts of interpersonal racism, such as violent racist attacks and the use of racial slurs in anger, to a far lesser degree than they did in the pre–World War II era. As a result of civil rights movements in Europe and many of its former settler colonies, mainstream populations in countries like the United States, Canada, Britain, Germany, and Australia typically consider overt white-power racism taboo. However, this newfound focus on multicultural tolerance belies continuing issues with subtler forms of racial prejudice and discrimination among European-descended populations. In some cases, public commentators use the rhetoric of multiculturalism to argue that non-whites no longer have any cause to complain about interpersonal or structural racism, using this rhetoric to dismiss reports of continuing racism as it actually exists. In other cases, mainstream publics are willing to tolerate racist humor and stereotyping from entertainment and news media like US professional wrestling television shows, which often give wrestlers racially stereotyped personae—such as the African American wrestling team Cryme Time, which reinforces the misconception that African American males are fundamentally predisposed to criminal activity. Mainstream demographics in some countries may even support supposedly non-racist policies that are actually designed to target specific minority groups, like France's 2011 "burqa ban" law that claimed to outlaw all religious garb in public places but was in reality constructed primarily to target Muslim women who wore traditional head and face coverings.[31] Many of the individuals who espouse such practices would consider themselves to be non-racist or even anti-racist to the degree that they oppose the kinds of overt racism that emanate from organized white-power and neo-Nazi groups. However, the pervasive racist rhetoric mainstream Western societies are willing to tolerate in public discourse falls on a spectrum with and does not stand in opposition to more extreme forms of racist discourse such as those that appear in white-power music.

At a basic level, white-power musicians' fear of white extinction is really a fear that European-derived populations will lose the privileges they have amassed through centuries of unjust enrichment. White-power musicians might complain that whites are swiftly losing their birthright to non-whites, but this allegation does not match the reality of wealth or power distribution in the contemporary world. In the United States, for instance, a 2009–2010 study found that at the rate the racialized income gap was then closing, the difference in income between US citizens of European and African descent would only disappear in 634 years, a longer span of time than has passed since Christopher Columbus arrived in the Americas.[32] Despite the progress civil rights movements have made toward eliminating racial disparities such as the black/white wealth gap in the United States, whites both in the United States and elsewhere truly do bear privilege both statistically and anecdotally. Nonetheless, even people who bear phenomenal privilege in an *absolute* sense may view small *relative* changes in social status, such as the shift in Western popular opinion away from overt racism and toward surface-level multicultural tolerance since World War II, as sincere threats to individual and group well-being.[33] Slight shifts in racial dynamics have been enough provocation to convince a small percentage of whites in many Western countries to participate in white-power music and other forms of racist activism even though they know they are violating mainstream standards of multicultural decency. Far more than this, however, white-power musicians' relatively extreme fears of white extinction and white genocide reflect fears that circulate widely in many mainstream European-descended populations—fears that the West in general and that whites in particular might continue to lose social status and political power to new immigrants, national minorities, and populations in developing countries.

White-power musicians' fears of white extinction really matter, despite the fact that white-power music is a small niche genre, because they represent a particularly visible and pronounced manifestation of mainstream fears. Simply put, white-power music scenes would no longer continue to attract new fans or performers if safeguarding the future of white privilege no longer mattered to anyone. Although mainstream Western societies may now marginalize white-power musicians and other racist activists, the racist rhetoric one finds in white-power music developed out of ideas that helped establish Europe and a few of its settler colonies as leaders in world politics, finance, and mass culture. Examining the rhetoric of fear in white-power music as part of a wider problem with racism in the West, then, provides a window not only into the violent rhetoric of today's semi-legal web of organized white-power hate but also into the fears and anxieties of many people who profess to be non-racists. Thankfully, however, this view also suggests that if Western societies address structural racial inequality and mainstream racism as the root causes of white-power and other so-called extremist forms of racism, it may be possible, albeit profoundly difficult, to create a truly tolerant future in which the ideas of race mixing and white extinction no longer frighten anyone.

NOTES

1. define the term *white-power music* as *music created and distributed by individuals who are actively trying to advance an overtly pro-white racist agenda.* Following Christian Dornbusch and Jan Raabe, I refer to international white-power music structures as a "web" rather than a "movement" to illustrate that white-power musicians play in many de-centered and yet intersecting scenes and sub-genres rather than in one coordinated movement with central leadership (Dornbusch and Raabe, "'White-Power'-Music in Germany").

2. The band name "Pluton Svea" is Swedish for "Swedish Platoon." Pluton Svea, "Hail the Swastika," *Utgivna Latar.*

3. Powell, *Barbaric Civilization*, 5–9.

4. *The Jewish Peril.*

5. Goodrick-Clarke, *Black Sun*, 1; Gardell, *Gods of the Blood*, 102–103.

6. Goodrick-Clarke, *Black Sun*, 25; Thomson,. "Welcome to ZOG-World."

7. Simi and Futrell, *American Swastika*, 2.

8. Thomson, "Welcome to ZOG-World."

9. Southwell, "White Pride World Wide," 78.

10. The band name "Landser" is an old-fashioned German word for "foot soldier," a term that was used to refer to German soldiers during World War II. The band name Kolovrat is Russian (Коловрат) for "spinning wheel," but it is also the Russian word for "swastika."

11. Battlefront, "Forked-Tongue Lies," *Into the Storm.*

12. JU-87, "Re: CD Reviews."

13. Anderson, *Vancouver's Chinatown*, 11.

14. "Blue Eyed Devils," 58; "CD Reviews," 61.

15. Nordic Thunder, "The Truth Will Set You Free," *Final Stand.*

16. Fortress, "Loss of Identity," *The Fires of Our Rage.*

17. "Pagan of Ukraine," 26.

18. "What Fuels the Fires of Activism," 37.
19. Pierce, "Message from the Publisher," 3.
20. Jackson, "The Hooked-Cross, the Symbol of Re-Awakening Life," 85–86.
21. Skrewdriver, "Eyes Full of Rage," *After the Fire*.
22. Silver, "Blood and Honour 1987–1992," 13.
23. Donaldson quoted in Silver, "Blood and Honour 1987–1992," 13.
24. Micetrap Records, www.micetrap.net/shop/catalog.
25. Youngland, "I Wanna See the Day," *Winter Wind*.
26. Lowles and Silver, "From Skinhead to Bonehead," 5.
27. Gardell, *Gods of the Blood*, 306–307.
28. Barlen, "Nach 'Döner-Killer Song,'"; Jüttner and Ternieden, "Rechtsrocker bekommt Bewährungsstrafe"; "Richter bestätigen Urteil gegen Rechtsrocker." The band name "Gigi & die braune Stadtmusikanten" is German for "Gigi & the Brown City Musicians." In Germany, the color brown is associated with far-right politics because of its association with Hitler's Sturmabteilung, who wore brown uniforms and were known colloquially as "brownshirts." The color brown also has a connection with the contemporary far-right political party the Nationaldemokratische Partei Deutschlands (National Democratic Party of Germany, or NPD), which uses brown as its official party color.
29. Lewis and Lyall, "Norway Killer Gets the Maximum"; Breivik, *2083: A European Declaration of Independence*, 847.
30. Yaccino et al., "Gunman Kills 6 at a Sikh Temple Near Milwaukee." The band name "13 Knots" derives from the fact that there are thirteen knots in a noose.
31. Erlanger, "Has the 'Burqa Ban' Worked in France."
32. Feagin, *The White Racial Frame*, 219.
33. Ferber and Kimmel, "White Men Are This Nation," 151–152.

BIBLIOGRAPHY

Anderson, Kay. *Vancouver's Chinatown: Racial Discourse in Canada, 1875–1980*. Montreal: McGill-Queen's University Press, 1991.

Barlen, Julian. "Nach 'Döner-Killer Song'–Anklage gegen 'Gigi & die braunen Stadtmusikanten.'" *Endstation Rechts*, February 20, 2012. http://www.endstation-rechts .de/news/kategorie/straftaten/artikel/ nach-doener-killer-song-anklage-gegen-gigi-die -braunen-stadtmusikanten.html.

Battlefront. "Forked-Tongue Lies." *Into the Storm*. Panzerfaust Records, 1999. Sound recording.

Blee, Kathleen M. *Inside Organized Racism: Women in the Hate Movement*. Berkeley: University of California Press, 2002.

"Blue Eyed Devils." *Resistance* (Winter 2000): 58–59.

Breivik, Anders Behring [as Andrew Berwick]. *2083: A European Declaration of Independence*. Self-published, 2011.

"CD Reviews." *Resistance* (Winter 2000): 60–61.

Dornbusch, Christian, and Jan Raabe. "'White-Power'-Music in Germany: Development, Dimensions, Trends." Presentation at the workshop White-Power Music: Germany in the World, Göttingen, Germany, June 4, 2012.

Erlanger, Steven. "Has the 'Burqa Ban' Worked in France?" *International Herald Tribune*, September 2, 2012. http://rendezvous.blogs.nytimes.com/2012/09/02/has-the-burqa -ban-worked-in-france/?r=0.

Feagin, Joe R. *The White Racial Frame: Centuries of Racial Framing and Counter-Framing*. 2nd ed. New York: Routledge, 2013.

Ferber, Abby L., and Michael S. Kimmel. "'White Men Are This Nation': Right-Wing Militias and the Restoration of Rural American Masculinity." In *Home-Grown Hate: Gender and Organized Racism*, ed. Abby L. Ferber, 143–160. New York: Routledge, 2004.

Fortress. "Loss of Identity." *The Fires of Our Rage*. Great White Productions, 1999. Sound recording.

Gardell, Mattias. *Gods of the Blood: The Pagan Revival and White Separatism*. Durham, NC: Duke University Press, 2003.

Goodrick-Clarke, Nicholas. *Black Sun: Aryan Cults, Esoteric Nazism, and the Politics of Identity*. New York: New York University Press, 2002.

Jackson, Paul. "'The Hooked-Cross, the Symbol of Re-Awakening Life': The Memory of Ian Stuart Donaldson." In *White Power Music: Scenes of Extreme-Right Cultural Resistance*, ed. Anton Shekhovtsov and Paul Jackson, 85–100. Ilford, UK: Searchlight, 2012.

The Jewish Peril: Protocols of the Learned Elders of Zion. London: The Britons, 1920. Reprinted by Elibron Classics, 2005.

JU-87. "Re: CD Reviews." *Stormfront*, April 3, 2006, 6:59 a.m. https://www.stormfront .org/forum/t198817-9/?s=5b2f0a48322e998df4b83718f8fdce36.

Jüttner, Julia, and Henrik Ternieden. "Rechtsrocker bekommt Bewährungsstrafe." *Spiegel Online*, October 15, 2012. http://www.spiegel.de/panorama/justiz/volksverhetzung -daniel-giese-zu-bewaehrungsstrafe-verurteilt-a-861296.html.

Lewis, Mark, and Sarah Lyall. "Norway Killer Gets the Maximum: 21 Years." *New York Times*, August 24, 2012. http://www.nytimes.com/2012/08/ 25/world/europe/anders -behring-breivik-murder-trial.html?pagewanted=all.

Lowles, Nick, and Steve Silver. "From Skinhead to Bonehead: The Roots of Skinhead Culture." In *White Noise: Inside the International Nazi Skinhead Scene*, ed. Nick Lowles and Steve Silver, 1–8. London: Searchlight, 1998.

Micetrap Records. www.micetrap.net/shop/catalog.

Nordic Thunder. "The Truth Will Set You Free." *Final Stand*. Tri-State Terror Records, 1994. Sound recording.

"Pagan of Ukraine: Interview with Sokyra Peruna." *Resistance* (Winter 2005): 25–27.

Pierce, William L. "Message from the Publisher." *Resistance* (Winter 2000): 3.

Pluton Svea. "Hail the Swastika." *Utgivna Latar*. Bootleg album, 2001. Sound recording.

Powell, Christopher. *Barbaric Civilization: A Critical Sociology of Genocide*. Montreal: McGill-Queen's University Press, 2011.

"Richter bestätigen Urteil gegen Rechtsrocker." *Spiegel Online*, March 27, 2014. http:// www.spiegel.de/panorama/justiz/daniel-giese-olg-oldenburg-bestaetigt-urteil-wegen -volksverhetzung-a-961112.html.

Silver, Steve. "Blood and Honour 1987–1992." In *White Noise: Inside the International Nazi Skinhead Scene*, ed. Nick Lowles and Steve Silver, 9–27. London: Searchlight, 1998.

Simi, Pete, and Robert Futrell. *American Swastika: Inside the White Power Movement's Hidden Spaces of Hate*. New York: Rowman and Littlefield, 2010.

Skrewdriver. "Eyes Full of Rage." *After the Fire*. Rock-O-Rama Records, 1988. Sound recording.

Southwell, Cliff. "'White Pride World Wide'? The Internet and the Global Marketing of White Power Rock." In *White Noise: Inside the International Nazi Skinhead Scene*, ed. Nick Lowles and Steve Silver, 77–83. London: Searchlight, 1998.

Thomson, Eric. "Welcome to ZOG-World." 1999 [1976]. http://www.faem.com/eric/2000 /et047.htm.

"What Fuels the Fires of Activism? Interview with Anger Within." *Resistance* (Winter 2005): 36–38.

Yaccino, Steven, Michael Schwirtz, and Marc Santora. "Gunman Kills 6 at a Sikh Temple Near Milwaukee." *New York Times*, August 5, 2012. http://www. nytimes.com/2012/08 /06/us/shooting-reported-at-temple-in-wisconsin.html.

Youngland. "I Wanna See the Day." *Winter Wind*. Panzerfaust Records, 2003. Sound recording.

"... or Suffer the Consequences of Staying"

Terror and Racial Cleansing in Arkansas

Guy Lancaster

This was the notice posted by vigilantes in Black Rock, Arkansas, on the night of Friday, January 12, 1894: "All negroes must leave this town inside of ten days or take what follows, and all who have houses rented to them must fire them or we will fire the houses inside of ten days. Negroes, don't let this slip your mind." After this initial notice, the vigilantes issued more verbal and written warnings to major area employers, namely local mills and factories, threatening owners with the burning of their property should they fail to dismiss their African American employees. African Americans had reportedly been run off from other towns near Black Rock, and the *Arkansas Gazette* observed that "if driven from Black Rock [they] will be without friends and money in an inhospitable country." Governor William Meade Fishback took a personal interest in the situation and stated that he was willing to take action "necessary to the protection of life and property," as did several local employers. Despite this backing, the largest firm in the town dismissed its entire African American workforce. One-third of the African American population of the town, estimated then at 300, reportedly fled, even though no actual acts of violence had been committed.[1]

Vigilantes such as those in Black Rock were commonly known as "whitecappers" or "nightriders." They were "bands of armed white men ... engaged in what they viewed as community 'regulation' and retaliation, moving against those who violated norms, transgressed boundaries, or threatened livelihoods." In many areas, as the economy in the late nineteenth century soured, whitecappers targeted and

DOI: 10.5876/9781646420025.c005

attacked African Americans, specifically those who "rented farms, owned land, or otherwise worked for merchants or large planters," as well as those who had found "alternative employment in newly opened railroads, lumber camps, and sawmills," with the aim of opening those jobs up to unemployed whites.[2] However, economic competition was not the only motivation behind white attempts to expel local African American populations. Whites also linked expulsive violence against African American communities either to a desire to restore political domination—especially in the post-Reconstruction years, when white Democrats tried to curb the success of the Republican Party, which depended on African American voters—or as collective punishment for a crime allegedly committed by one or more African Americans.

Sometimes, such violence occurred without a stated cause. On December 28, 1906, the *Sharp County Record* of Evening Shade reported that "unknown parties" had posted notices warning African Americans to leave the area and had also attacked one African American resident, Joe Brooks. These actions resulted in the near evacuation of the area by African Americans, most of whom lived in a small colony just outside town. The newspaper identified no misdeed committed by any local African American resident that might have supplied motivation for such an attack.[3] The following week, the newspaper reported that another notice had been posted. By the time of this report, there were "very few negroes remaining here, a majority of them having left last week and [in] the early part of this week."[4]

One might well ask why African Americans fled so often in response to anonymously posted notices. But such notices were not the only tools available to those who desired to expel African Americans from a particular locality. This chapter examines three common tactics used by whites to generate the level of fear and terror among African Americans in Arkansas that made their expulsion feasible. These tactics included personal visitations during which a threat was delivered face to face, the anonymous posting of notices, and the presentation of threats through semi-official means, such as the publication of anti-black editorials in a newspaper or the communication of hostility through the US mail. In some of the cases covered in this chapter, actual violence was combined with these tactics to effect a population transfer—of African Americans, away from whites—while in other cases, a simple notice or visitation proved to be just as effective.

What these various tactics have in common is their shared production of fear and terror among African American populations. As anthropologists Andrew Strathern and Pamela J. Stewart note: "Terror is based on an interlocking feedback between memory and anticipation, the same nexus that makes possible continuity in human action generally. Here, however, the feedback is based on a sense of rupture. Terror consists precisely in intrusions into expectations about security, making moot the mundane processes on which social life otherwise depends. Repeated ruptures shift people's perceptions and render them progressively more anxious and vulnerable to disturbance."[5] To employ an analogy illustrating the idea, an abused child or animal may flinch when the abuser's hand is raised, regardless of whether a slap or punch is forthcoming, precisely because that feedback between memory and anticipation holds that a strike is possible, even if not likely. Or as the philosopher Claudia Card writes, terrorism "creates an *atmosphere of grave uncertainty and insecurity* in the face of what could be imminent danger. Uncertainty and insecurity can make fears *reasonable*."[6] In many cases, the threat of violence became the reality of violence as white mobs attacked African Americans, thus creating a new feedback loop between memory and anticipation that made it progressively easier to intimidate African American communities and thus carry out projects of racial cleansing, for a range of motives and occasionally in the face of white elite disapprobation.

Communities that experienced racial-cleansing violence often became "sundown towns," defined by sociologist James W. Loewen as "any organized jurisdiction that for decades kept African Americans or other groups from living in it and was thus 'all-white' on purpose."[7] This created, through the decades, another level of fear for African Americans, who often avoided moving into or even passing through such communities based merely on their reputations.[8] Although this chapter does not examine the long-term maintenance of the all-white status of sundown towns, it does focus on the immediacy of racial-cleansing violence within the time frame in which it was perpetrated. The conclusion examines how these acts of intimidation and violence served a communicative function, inculcating a specific form of terror within African American communities targeted for racial cleansing.

PERSONAL VISITATIONS

Despite the menace presented by a personal visitation from a group of white vigilantes—especially if they arrived armed—warning away African Americans, it appears that this tactic was not a preferred method for most would-be whitecappers. As historian Story Matkin-Rawn has observed, whitecappers—unlike participants in lynch mobs—occasionally faced arrest, had their identities revealed, and were convicted, given that their actions could threaten the profits of white mill or planta-tion owners.[9] This possible result is why many vigilantes worked at night, in disguise, and through the medium of anonymous notices rather than exposing themselves to possible recognition and punishment. However, a few cases of personal visitation do stand out.

In 1880, according to the US Census, only forty-three African Americans were listed as residents of Clay County, which is in the northeastern corner of the state. Certain locals were so determined to keep this population at a minimum that they even targeted outside workers who were laying railroad tracks through Clay County. Two different versions of the central story exist. According to one account, once the African American railroad workers had crossed the St. Francis River from Missouri into Arkansas, "a group of white men, with lighted lanterns, marched single file past these tents, opened the tent flaps, passed their lanterns inside, just looked around and passed on."[10] As a result, the laborers moved back to the Missouri side of the river and refused to work in Arkansas. Another account holds that Bill Waddle, then overseeing an African American labor crew on the Missouri side of the river, recruited a group of white locals (possibly members of the Ku Klux Klan, as he reportedly was) and "led a shot gun parade" to the Missouri line, where he "told the bosses and Negroes, who were doing the work, that was where the Negroes stopped and the whites would take over."[11]

Just south of Clay County, in late October 1892, "twenty-five or thirty men went to the houses and residences of most of the colored population" of the Greene County community of Paragould "and notified them to leave within three days and nights." According to the *Arkansas Gazette*, many African Americans had apparently left or were making plans to do so, despite the fact that "leading citizens are opposing this and doing all in their power to quiet the negroes, as there is [*sic*] a lot of them here who are perfectly harmless, also industrious and attend to their own affairs and are owners of property in their own right."[12] In August 1899, Paragould was also the site of racial violence when vigilantes (described as "the lowest element of the white population") attacked local African Americans. This attack led to an exodus that the *Arkansas Gazette* reported under the headline "Negroes Are Leaving Paragould by Hundreds." According to the news story, a "self-appointed vigilance committee visited the negro citizens of Paragould" on the night of Thursday, August 3, warning them "to leave the city of Paragould, bag and baggage, on or before next Saturday night, and never return again, for any purpose whatsoever, or suffer the consequences of staying." By the following day, "the trains leaving Paragould were crowded with darkies who were fleeing to other parts of the state. None of them had been killed and none were shot at, but they were alarmed for their safety." During the weekend following the visitations by the vigilance committee, homes and businesses owned by African Americans were stoned. At the time of the *Gazette*'s reporting, fewer than twenty-five African Americans remained in town.[13]

POSTING OF NOTICES

A more popular tactic of intimidating African Americans was the posting of anonymous notices. This practice began in the immediate post-Reconstruction years, when African Americans still had a measure of political power as a result of Reconstruction reforms, and the tactic continued well through the early twentieth century. As a means of intimidation, notices not only allowed perpetrators to remain unknown and thus free from potential prosecution but also prevented recipients from knowing the actual power behind the warnings—whether it was a large, armed group or a single individual. African American populations thus targeted were faced with unknowns rather than a quantifiable force and so perhaps lived in a greater state of anxiety, wondering whether their decisions to stay or to flee were wise or foolish.

On August 30, 1882, a notice was posted against Burrell Lindsay, an African American who had settled on land in Van Buren County in north-central Arkansas. The warning read: "Notice is her by giving That I sertify you, Mr. Niggro, just as shore as you locate your Self her death is your potion. the Cadron [Creek] is a ded line. your cind cant live on this side a tall and this is all you air going to git And I dont know what cind the next warning will Bee." Lindsay was unmoved, and on December 13, 1882, he made a homestead entry for his tract of land. However, on the night of January 10, 1883, a group of disguised men (later said to number ten) visited his house "with the intention of making him leave the country." Lindsay, having anticipated trouble, had gathered a group of neighbors in his house on account of "demonstrations" the previous evening and barricaded the door against attack. Once the masked party began firing at the house, the Lindsay group fled out a back door, whereupon they were pursued by the vigilantes. The group fired on the vigilantes, felling one man, and then "traveled all night through the mud, and landed at Conway worn out and nearly frightened to death."[14]

The posting of notices usually preceded acts of violence, as in the case just described. Sometimes notices were posted to tap into the local collective memory of earlier outbreaks of mob activity. For instance, on the night of Friday, July 16, 1897, unknown persons posted notices "in a few places about town . . . warning negros [sic] to leave Mena," which is in Polk County in southwestern Arkansas. The local newspaper reported that "after diligent inquiry no one can be found to father, or even favor, this move." The paper added, "There are not many colored people here, and those who are here are industrious and law-abiding and have just as good a right to live in Mena as any other 'citizens,' and as citizens of Arkansas they must be protected in this right."[15] However, the following year, notices were once again posted in town, and these were accompanied by "outward demonstrations made by a certain organized gang against the negro population in this city."[16] These notices and demonstrations must surely have called to mind a widely reported "race war" that had occurred in 1896 during the building of the railroad through the county, which had its genesis in local attempts to keep African Americans from entering the county. According to the *Arkansas Gazette*, approximately thirty African American railroad workers who entered Polk County on August 5, 1896, were driven off. Though contractors managed to have the next group of African American workers met by armed guards and escorted by the sheriff of neighboring Sevier County, this maneuver could not prevent the outbreak of violence. According to the *New York Times*, "Italian, Swedish, and Hungarian laborers, together with a number of natives," teamed up to raid a camp occupied by African American railroad workers, killing three and wounding many more. Numerous other African American workers fled the county in fear.[17]

Sometimes, it was not simply a small group of vigilantes posting threats against African American populations but a significant portion of the white community doing so in a crypto-official capacity. This scenario is what happened in the coal mining town of Bonanza, in Sebastian County just south of Fort Smith, near the Oklahoma border. There, on the night of Wednesday, April 27, 1904, approximately 200 white citizens met and passed a resolution "demanding that about forty negroes employed by Central Coal and Coke Company leave town." In addition, plans were made to effect the removal by force if the company should resist.[18] The faction posted the following notice in public:

> At a mass meeting of several hundred citizens of Bonanza and surrounding country, held at Bonanza on the night of April 27, 1904, the following resolutions were unanimously passed:
>
> Whereas, There has recently been a large influx of negroes into this coal camp, with a prospect of many more to come, it was
>
> Resolved, That the white citizens of this community are bitterly opposed to the negro living in our midst, and that those now here are requested to leave at their EARLIEST CONVENIENCE.

Local No. 1199 of the United Mine Workers of America, attempting to combat rumors that it was behind the notice, adopted its own resolution reaffirming "the principles as set forth in our preamble not to discriminate against a fellow union miner on account of creed, color, or nationality."[19] The community was in a state of high tension for a few days after the posting of the notice. A fight between white and black patrons at a local saloon on the night of Saturday, April 30, escalated into a town-wide exchange of bullets, most of which were fired into the homes of African American workers. More shots were fired the next day, but by Monday morning "it was found that the negroes were quietly leaving town, a few at a time," and was predicted that the town would be emptied of African Americans by the end of the week.[20]

A recurring motif of these racial-cleansing events was the limited ability of local elites to prevent the violence and bring its perpetrators to justice. This lack of support was the case in the Lawrence County town of Walnut Ridge, in northeast-ern Arkansas, in April 1912. A group calling itself "Kit Karson and Band" posted notices demanding that local African Americans leave the area. As in Bonanza, a local committee opposed this threat, even posting its own notices warning vigilan-tes that they faced prosecution and that whites in town were likely to "arm their servants with instructions to shoot the first intruders who disturb them." However, on the night of April 19, a crowd of white men succeeded in dynamiting the home of one African American and terrorized "the entire [African American] section of the city for several hours," finally quitting only "when practically all of the negroes had fled from the district." Governor George Washington Donaghey called out the local militia to restore order, but by the time the militia arrived, half of an estimated African American population of 400 was reported to have already fled the city.[21]

ELITE POWER

Although the posting of notices may have had some semi-official backing, as per the example of Bonanza, this tactic was usually the strategy employed by rela-tively powerless whites. Their posted notices were occasionally ignored or resisted by African Americans who understood—and could occasionally exploit—the class difference between political and business elites and poor white vigilantes. However, when statements regarding the undesirability of African American resi-dents received prominent placement in a local newspaper or when threats against African Americans were delivered through the US mail (which had a respected aura of authority in this era), African Americans tended to see themselves in a much more precarious position. This use of the newspaper and mail, more than anything, had to make fear *reasonable*, to use the words of Claudia Card, for it drove home the fact that African Americans had no local protectors.

A well-known example of semi-official intimidation of African Americans is the case of the railroad town of Cotter, located in Baxter County in northern Arkansas. Its newspaper, the *Cotter Courier*, openly expressed antipathy toward the local African American population, a group that had migrated to the area to work on the railroad. According to an August 25, 1905, article: "Nine out of ten inquirers ask as to negroes. Until within the last month there was but one colored family in the county, and a few extra colored men who came here to work on the railroad. There is a strong feeling against the negro in Cotter and the county, and the feeling is growing. It is quite likely there will not be a colored person in Baxter county within a year. They are not wanted."[22] The following year, an April 6, 1906, editorial titled "Too Many Negroes" opined:

Cotter bids fair to be over run with the colored race if the present rate of increase continues. It is far from a pleasant thought and is causing not a little uneasiness. A few months ago there were but three colored people in town, the Mason family, and excellent colored people they have proven themselves to be, but of late the dark-eys are coming in by gangs and are most unwelcome. Cotter is a white town and proposes to remain white and the feeling is daily growing that the negroes should move on. Cotter and North Arkansas can get along without them. There are rumors of resorting to drastic measures to keep the colored men out of town, but it is hoped such steps will not be resorted to.

The editorial ended with this warning: "It would be unfortunate indeed should any colored person at this time commit any offense in Cotter, for it would be taken as an excuse to put the race on the run."[23] Which was exactly what happened when, on August 24, 1906, a fight between two local African Americans gave the white townspeople the excuse they wanted. Notice was served that all African American residents were to leave town immediately.[24]

The Cotter example serves as a contrast to the riots and other cases of violence discussed in this chapter. What happened in those areas of Arkansas—and of the nation—that "went sundown" was often much more low-key. Intimidation usually consisted of the implied threat behind a quiet "shot gun parade" or the posting of anonymous notices in town or newspaper editorials that purported to repre-sent broad public opinion on the desirability of removing African Americans from town. And because these threats might possibly be backed up with violence (because such violence had happened elsewhere), the threats created precisely that state of anxiety that is the goal of terrorists everywhere. Such fears on the part of the African American community were quite reasonable, for whites had proven them-selves capable again and again of immense violence. What happened in the town of Catcher in 1923–1924 stands as a prime example of this capability.

Catcher is in Crawford County in western Arkansas, sited in the rich bottomland of the Arkansas River. Thirty-five to forty families, mostly African American, lived there. On Friday, December 28, 1923, Effie Latimer, a twenty-five-year-old white woman, was found near death at her home by a visiting neighbor. Despite having been shot in the back of the head with a shotgun and clubbed, before she died she was reportedly able to identify her attackers as three African American men, naming one as William "Son" Bettis. Bettis was arrested, as were alleged accom-plices Charles Spurgeon Rucks and John Henry Clay, the latter only fourteen years old. These three suspects were taken first to Fort Smith and then spirited away to Little Rock to keep them safe from a growing white mob, which, when denied its charge for revenge, went on a rampage in Catcher, threatening local residents and

desecrating graves in the African American cemetery. This mob's rampage continued for days, with local law enforcement apparently joining in. A deputy sheriff
shot and killed Rucks's sixty-five-year-old father. Governor Thomas Chipman
McRae, instead of using his power to protect the local African American population as previous governors had, ordered the transportation of a machine gun to the
Catcher area to be used against a group of eleven African American men locked
up inside a cabin. Seeing what they faced, these men promptly surrendered and
were, in an example of supreme irony, charged with violating the state's law against
nightriding. Bettis and Rucks stood trial on January 4–5, 1924, and were convicted
and sentenced to death, while Clay received a sentence of hard labor after providing a signed confession.[25] (Local residents who have delved into the spotty history
of the riot have recorded oral histories and uncovered other evidence that suggests
Latimer's husband was having an affair with the neighbor who found his wife on
that fateful day, lending credence to stories that perhaps they arranged his wife's
murder. Nothing has yet been proven, though research is ongoing.)[26]

In Catcher, the demands that African Americans leave the area did not precede the
violence but rather came afterward and consisted of a combination of posted notices
and warnings communicated in a more official capacity. On the evening of Saturday,
January 13, 1924, unsigned notices were posted throughout Catcher "warning the
negroes to get out of the county within five days."[27] Similar warnings were reportedly
sent through the US mail to those African American defendants accused of nightriding. According to the motion for a change of venue filed by the accused nightriders
in March 1924, one of the defendants, Gus Richardson, received a letter that read: "It
becomes necessary for the safety of the community to ask you to leave it. You will be
given a few days to straighten out your affairs. If you are out of Crawford County in
five days you will not be bothered; otherwise, you will have to suffer the consequences."
According to this same document, anonymous notices were also posted in the nearby
town of Shibley "advising that no negroes would be tolerated in that community, and
that all negroes there should not be found around that place, or to that effect."[28] As
a result, by the morning of January 15, there were only three African American families left in the Catcher settlement, and all were reportedly making plans to depart.
The January 18, 1924, issue of the *Van Buren Press-Argus* reported that the black out-
migration "continued until that settlement was strictly a white settlement."[29]

CONCLUSION

German literary scholar Jan Philip Reemtsma argues that violence assumes social
significance when it carries out a communicative function in which the perpetra-
tor's act upon a victim conveys a special message to a third party. "In all forms of

war," writes Reemtsma, "the bullet is meant for two soldiers: the one it strikes and the one it does not. With the first soldier, the intention is to kill. With the second, the intention is to communicate that he's next."[30]

If we can assume a similar communicative significance in the violence of racial cleansing, then what might it be? The answer is this—nothing less than the placement of its victims outside what Helen Fein has called "the universe of obligation." This phrase refers to "the range of people to whom the common conscience extends: the people toward whom rules and obligations are binding, who must be taken into account, and by whom we can be held responsible for our actions."[31] Of course, one may assume that the praxis of white supremacy at this time placed all African Americans outside the universe of obligation, but this assumption was not the case, for the rhetoric of the "white man's burden" contained a measured obligation toward supposedly inferior non-whites. Even the practice of lynching could imply some level of obligation by providing examples of punishment and thus a helpful warning to African Americans not to transgress certain boundaries. As Amy Louise Wood points out, large-scale "spectacle" lynchings often entailed the victim-to-be giving "an execution speech, which often read as a lengthy religious confessional, in which he testified to his own sin and accepted the suffering he must endure as a means to his salvation." Thus even the victim of a lynching is arguably included in the universe of obligation, at least insofar as his execution is done for the good of his soul.[32]

Unlike lynching, however, the violence of racial cleansing did not have an immediately perceptible horizon beyond which normality, such as it was, might return. Being an African American in Arkansas—in America—during these times often meant surviving through the regular practice of deference toward one's "racial betters," especially in the immediate aftermath of massive white-on-black violence such as lynchings. Those were the rules, but racial cleansing threw out the rules, depriving African Americans of their regular strategies for surviving in a white supremacist society—for these communities made it clear that there was no place at all for African Americans, not even at the bottom of the social scale. As the notice delivered to Burrell Lindsay testifies: "Notice is her by giving That I sertify you, Mr. Niggro, just as shore as you locate your Self her death is your potion. the Cadron is a ded line. your cind cant live on this side a tall and this is all you air going to git." African Americans were accustomed to the many behavioral lines they could not cross, but these new "dead lines" were physical and geographical. Beyond these many "dead lines" that ran across this country, African Americans could not live with the assurance that a properly subservient attitude would protect them. Their behavior was not the issue; rather, their very existence was the issue. By understanding that fear, we can begin to comprehend the level of existential terror this sort of violence produced, to comprehend why so many people fled their homes and their jobs at the first hint of danger, even if it was simply a sign posted anonymously during the night. Such acts signified their removal from the universe of obligation, and outside that universe anything could happen—and often did.

NOTES

1. "Whitecaps," *Arkansas Gazette*, January 17, 1894, 2; "Negroes Ordered out of the County," *New York Times*, January 17, 1894, 8. According to the *New York Times*, two days later Black Rock had settled into an armed quiet, and "no overt acts have been committed by the persons who have attempted to drive the negroes from town," though whitecappers had by then published three notices. "Armed Quiet in Black Rock," *New York Times*, January 19, 1894, 6. See also "Indignant Citizens," *Arkansas Gazette*, January 20, 1894, 2; "The Facts in the Case," *Arkansas Gazette*, January 21, 1894, 4; Perkins, "Race Relations." Whitecappers are mentioned as having been operating in the same county four years later. See "Negro's Bloody Deed," *Arkansas Gazette*, November 23, 1898, 1; "White Caps Shot in Arkansas," *New York Times*, November 24, 1898, 1.

2. Hahn, *A Nation*, 427. Historical anthropologist Alf Lüdke observes that expulsions and removals carried out by subaltern populations "suspend the top-down relationship that seems so characteristic of power and domination" and that "self-mobilization imbues a sense of domination to those who actively participate in subjugating others." See Lüdke, "Explaining Forced Migration," 28–29.

3. The newspaper—which editorialized that "We have little use for the negro as a citizen and on general principles"—insisted that local black residents deserved to live in peace "unless the negro commits some crime, or interferes in some way with white people or with white people's business." "Negroes Leaving," *Sharp County Record*, December 28, 1906, 1.

4. "Negro Trouble," *Sharp County Record*, January 4, 1907, 1; Jaspin, *Buried in the Bitter Waters*, 219–223. The local newspaper followed up on the case in 1907, reporting that J. D. May was arrested on a charge of slander for having accused local resident Caleb Evans of having masterminded the expulsion of black residents. See "Slander Is Charged," *Sharp County Record*, April 12, 1907, 2; "Local News," *Sharp County Record*, June 7, 1907, 2.

5. Strathern and Stewart, "Introduction," 7.

6. Card, *Confronting Evils*, 166; original emphasis.

7. Loewen, *Sundown Towns*, 2. In Arkansas, these sundown towns were found mostly in the upland regions of the state, the Ozark and Ouachita Mountains, and communities in northeastern Arkansas that emerged with post–Civil War railroad and industrial development.

8. Loewen, *Sundown Towns*, 345–349.

9. Matkin-Rawn, "We Fight for the Rights of Our Race," 97–98.

10. O. L. Dalton, "More about St. Francis . . . ," *Piggott Banner*, August 30, 1963, 2.

11. Letter from C. E. (Nub) Jewell, published in column titled "Some More about Greenway," *Piggott Banner*, September 27, 1963, 13; Laymon, *Pfeiffer Country*, 73–75.

12. "Ordered to Leave the County," *Arkansas Gazette*, November 1, 1892, 3. This attempt at racial cleansing reportedly occurred as a response to the murder of one Monroe Pulley. The *Gazette*, however, gave no details about this murder, and no record of it has been found.

13. "Negroes Are Leaving Paragould by Hundreds," *Arkansas Gazette*, August 8, 1899, 1.

14. "Trouble at Faulkner," *Arkansas Gazette*, January 14, 1883, 4; "Conway Condensations," *Arkansas Gazette*, January 18, 1883, 1; "Land Troubles," *Arkansas Gazette*, January 16, 1883, 5; "Brought to Justice," *Arkansas Gazette*, January 25, 1883, 4. The title of the first report betrays an early misrepresentation of events as occurring in Faulkner County near Pinnacle Springs rather than farther north in Van Buren County. Lindsay's name is variously represented throughout the newspaper reports as C. G. Lindsey, Burrill Lindsey, Burnet Lindsey, and Burrill Lindsay. This instance of nightriding eventually led to the US Supreme Court case *United States v. Waddell et al.*; see "*United States v. Waddell and Others*," 221.

15. "Those Warning Notices," *Mena Weekly Star*, July 21, 1897, 2.

16. On August 16, 1898, a dozen "men and boys" were arrested in connection with this campaign but were let off after receiving a friendly warning from the mayor. "The Mayor Gives Good Advice," *Mena Weekly Star*, August 17, 1898, 4.

17. "Not Wanted in Polk," *Arkansas Gazette*, August 6, 1896, 1; "Race War in Arkansas," *New York Times*, August 10, 1896, 1.

18. "Negroes Warned to Leave Town," *Arkansas Gazette*, April 30, 1904, 1; "Bonanza Budget," *Fort Smith Times*, May 1, 1904, 7; "Object to Negro Miners," *Van Buren Press*, May 7, 1904, 4.

19. "The Bonanza Miners," *Fort Smith Elevator*, May 6, 1904, 2; "Quiet at Bonanza," *Arkansas Gazette*, May 3, 1904, 2.

20. "War at Bonanza," *Fort Smith Times*, May 2, 1904, 1; "Negroes Leave Town of Bonanza," *Arkansas Gazette*, May 7, 1904, 1; "Bonanza Budget," *Fort Smith Times*, May 3, 1904, 4; "Bonanza Budget," *Fort Smith Times*, May 4, 1904, 4.

21. "Citizens Join to Protect Negroes," *Jonesboro Evening Sun*, April 18, 1912, 1; "Citizens Join to Protect Negroes," *Arkansas Gazette*, April 19, 1912, 2; "Whites Dynamite Home of Negro," *Arkansas Gazette*, April 21, 1912, 1, 3; "Walnut Ridge Negroes Ordered to Leave by Whites, Militia Called," *Jonesboro Evening Sun*, April 22, 1912, 1; "Militia in Camp at Walnut Ridge," *Arkansas Gazette*, April 22, 1912, 2.

22. "Just How It Is," *Cotter Courier*, August 25, 1905, 1.

23. "Too Many Negroes," *Cotter Courier*, April 6, 1906, 2.

24. "Negroes Ordered to Leave," *Cotter Courier*, August 24, 1906, 4; "Negroes Warned to Leave Cotter," *Arkansas Gazette*, August 25, 1906, 1.

25. "Woman Slain by Negro Assailant," *Arkansas Gazette*, December 29, 1923, 1; "Negro Held for Slaying White Woman," *Southwest American* (Fort Smith, Arkansas), December 29, 1923, 1; "Mob Is Pursuing Negro Prisoners," *Arkansas Gazette*, December 30, 1923, 1; "Negro Is Killed Resisting Arrest," *Arkansas Gazette*, December 31, 1923, 1; "Negro Is Dead Following Near Riot at Catcher," *Southwest American*, January 1, 1924, 1; "Negroes Are Indicted by Jury Tuesday," *Southwest American*, January 2, 1924, 1; "Negro Trial Is Scheduled Next Friday," *Southwest American*, January 3, 1924, 1; "Brutal Black Murderers on Trial for Most Inhuman Act," *Van Buren Press-Argus*, January 4, 1924, 1; "Death Sentence Given Slayer of Woman," *Southwest American*, January 5, 1924, 1; "Guilty Given as Verdict at Bettis Trial," *Southwest American*, January 6, 1924, 1; Nathan Hopkins, "Mob Is Pacified When Death Verdict Is Given," *Chicago Defender*, January 12, 1924, 3.

26. Lancaster, "Remembering Catcher," 12, 19.

27. "Negroes Are Fleeing from Murder Scene," *Southwest American*, January 15, 1924, 1.

28. "Motion for Change of Venue," March 19, 1924.

29. "'Colony' Negroes Flee from Wrath of Whites," *Van Buren Press-Argus*, January 18, 1924, 1. For more on the Catcher riot, see Gray, "Catcher Race Riot."

30. Reemtsma, *Trust and Violence*, 270.

31. Fein, "Scenarios of Genocide," 4.

32. Wood, *Lynching and Spectacle*, 39.

BIBLIOGRAPHY

Card, Claudia. *Confronting Evils: Terrorism, Torture, Genocide.* New York: Cambridge University Press, 2010.

Fein, Helen. "Scenarios of Genocide: Models of Genocide and Critical Responses." In *Toward the Understanding and Prevention of Genocide: Proceedings of the International Conference on the Holocaust and Genocide*, ed. I. W. Charny, 3–31. Boulder: Westview, 1984.

Gray, Wanda M. "Catcher Race Riot." *Encyclopedia of Arkansas History and Culture.* http://www.encyclopediaofarkansas.net/encyclopedia/entry-detail.aspx?entryID=5885.

Hahn, Steven. *A Nation under Our Feet: Black Political Struggles in the Rural South from Slavery to the Great Migration.* Cambridge, MA: Harvard University Press, 2003.

Jaspin, Elliot. *Buried in the Bitter Waters: The Hidden History of Racial Cleansing in America.* New York: Basic Books, 2007.

Lancaster, Guy. *Racial Cleansing in Arkansas: Politics, Land, Labor, and Criminality.* Lanham, MD: Lexington Books, 2014.

Lancaster, Guy. "Remembering Catcher, Ark.: 90 Years after the Race Riot." *Arkansas Times*, November 20, 2013, 12, 19. https://arktimes.com/news/arkansas-reporter/2013/11/21/remembering-catcher-ark-90-years-after-the-race-riot.

Laymon, Sherry. *Pfeiffer Country: The Tenant Farms and Business Activities of Paul Pfeiffer in Clay County, Arkansas, 1902–1954*. Little Rock: Butler Center Books, 2009.

Loewen, James W. *Sundown Towns: A Hidden Dimension of American Racism*. New York: New Press, 2005.

Lüdke, Alf. "Explaining Forced Migration." In *Removing Peoples: Forced Removal in the Modern World*, ed. Richard Bessel and Claudia B. Haake, 13–34. New York: Oxford University Press, 2009.

Matkin-Rawn, Story L. "'We Fight for the Rights of Our Race': Black Arkansans in the Era of Jim Crow." PhD dissertation, University of Wisconsin–Madison, 2009.

"Motion for Change of Venue." *State of Arkansas v. Gus Richardson, et al*. Circuit Court of Crawford County, Arkansas, March 19, 1924.

Perkins, Blake. "Race Relations in Western Lawrence County, Arkansas." *Big Muddy: A Journal of the Mississippi River Valley* 9, no. 1 (2009): 7–21.

Reemtsma, Jan Philip. *Trust and Violence: An Essay on a Modern Relationship*, trans. Dominic Bonfiglio. Princeton, NJ: Princeton University Press, 2012.

Strathern, Andrew, and Pamela J. Stewart. "Introduction: Terror, the Imagination, and Cosmology." In *Terror and Violence: Imagination and the Unimaginable*, ed. Andrew Strathern, Pamela J. Stewart, and Neil L. Whitehead, 1–39. Ann Arbor, MI: Pluto, 2006.

"*United States v. Waddell and Others*." In *The Federal Reporter*, vol. 16: *Cases Argued and Determined in the Circuit and District Courts of the United States, June–July 1883*. St. Paul, MN: West, 1883. http://openjurist.org/16/f1d/221.

Wood, Amy Louise. *Lynching and Spectacle: Witnessing Racial Violence in America, 1890–1940*. Chapel Hill: University of North Carolina Press, 2009.

6

Making "The Case against the 'Reds'"

Racializing Communism, 1919–1920

Julie M. Powell

On November 15, 1919, readers opened the latest weekly edition of the *Literary Digest* and settled in for an evening of entertainment and edification. On the front page, they read of the impending failure of a coal strike that had been characterized by President Woodrow Wilson as "wrong both morally and legally," a stand—the article heralded—endorsed by the US Congress. Four pages into the magazine, then-governor of Massachusetts Calvin Coolidge proclaimed a "Victory for Law and Order" against the "threats and intimidation of the Reds." On page seventeen, preceding an article titled "To Stop Race Suicide in France" and the weekly feature "Education in Americanism: Lessons in Patriotism," readers were treated to a political cartoon (figure 6.1), borrowed from the pages of the *Brooklyn Eagle*. The caption, "The Red: 'Let's Go to the Bottom First,'" accompanied an image of a man struggling near a shoreline, who represented "civilization" and was reaching for "solid ground" but was being pulled into the murky depths of "chaos" by the bearded, menacing figure of "Bolshevism."[1] The cartoon (which visually, allegorically, and discursively marked "Bolshevism" as non-white) was standard fare during America's first Red Scare and served a very specific purpose for those people who kept such images in circulation.

The communist Red Scare of 1919–1920 came in the midst of the redefinition of whiteness in the United States. As D. H. Lawrence once observed, Americans have always defined themselves by what they are *not*. As so-called new immigrants poured into the country from southern and eastern Europe, the established stock

DOI: 10.5876/9781646420025.c006

THE RED: "LET'S GO TO THE BOTTOM FIRST."

----Harding in the Brooklyn Eagle.

FIGURE 6.1. "Bolshevism" drags "Civilization" into "Chaos." Originally published in the *Brooklyn Eagle*; republished in the *Literary Digest*, November 15, 1919. *Courtesy*, Red Scare (1918–1921), an Image Database (#79).

of Anglo-Saxons sought to consolidate their power by creating distance between themselves and the new arrivals.[2] Their solution was a eugenic restructuring of the racial state. This change scrapped the black/white binary. They created instead a racial caste system. This system relegated immigrants from southern and eastern Europe to an inferior racial status that was viewed as not-quite-white by the Anglo-Saxons who laid claim to the state and its levers of power. This relabeling of ostensibly "white" immigrants had significant implications for the reception of foreign ideologies, namely communism, which would become so entwined and associated with the eastern and southern European "type" as to become inextricable. This association formed the explosive nucleus of domestic anticommunism and was by no means accidental. The manner by which it was constructed is the focus of this chapter.

Dispensing once and for all with threadbare notions of a grassroots *hysteria*, it can be posited, rather, that Red Scare anticommunism (an expression of racist nativism) was deliberately deployed by white business interests to cripple unionized labor. Souring American citizens on working-class solidarity required an appeal to fear—not of the dangers of an intangible ideology but of the threat of the not-quite-white outsider. In 1919, elites and business interests inaugurated a campaign of racializing communism, drawing on the rampant nativism of early twentieth-century Americans and a new racial hierarchy to ensure that the ideology and its attendant union collectivism gained no ground stateside. Ultimately, what elites needed to maintain the social order—and what emerged during the Red Scare—was a closed chain of signification that equated unionized labor with the not-quite-white "Other" and the vague specter of communism. This closed chain forced immigrant Americans to abjure all forms of collectivism—marked as "non-white"—and to adopt anticommunism, its binary opposite. Political cartoons from the Red Scare era serve as extant links in this chain (evidence of the racialization of communism) and are examined at length for their role in the early twentieth-century anticommunism campaign. This racial campaign inaugurated a shift in the nature of American anticommunism in which conservative opposition gained ground through fear and hatred of a racialized Other.

RED SCARE ANTICOMMUNISM

Anticommunist historiography characterizes postwar anticommunism as either a continuity of American political and social traditions or a discrete event, a hysteria, which defies historicization in the American narrative. Analyses of the latter approach are few and dated—typically shaded by the fury of the McCarthy era. These analyses view domestic anticommunism as a reaction to the Russian Revolution. From this vantage, anticommunism begins and ends with the rise and fall of Soviet communism, its reason for being.[3] Such analyses, for all their empirical value, suffer from a myopia that isolates the postwar manifestation of anticommunism from the framework of nativism, xenophobia, and racism in which *longue durée* analyses have situated it. (*Longue durée* means to look at the "forest" of broad historical structures over the "trees" of events.) In my view, when properly historicized, the contours of the first Red Scare become all too clear. Instead of a popular genesis of domestic anticommunism, historicized accounts of the Red Scare have unanimously identified a reverse transmission, orchestrated from above.[4] Regin Schmidt writes that Red Scare anticommunism was "at bottom, an attack on . . . movements for social and political change and reform, particularly organized labor, blacks and radicals, by forces of the status quo."[5] William M. Wiecek argues similarly that "government, civic, business, labor and religious groups leagued themselves in a crusade to stamp out radicalism as they variously defined it . . . Seeing their opportunity, all those hoping to shore up the status quo made the most of it, using patriotism as a cover for their differing agendas of control and suppression."[6] M. J. Heale contends that as early as the 1870s, "anticommunism was being developed as a weapon to isolate labor organizations and control the untamed urban masses. Invoking republican values . . . it mobilized public support behind the business community."[7]

A mechanism for this mobilization was racism, sometimes coded as "nativism"— though such a term inserts notions of ethnicity into an analytical space where they do not belong (an anachronism to which I will soon return). While "nativism" serves as the portmanteau of "racism" for John Higham and Heale, others are more direct. For example, Joel Kovel argues that white America originally united around hating Native Americans and exerted a similarly vehement organizing power with the enslavement of Africans, a tradition of Othering that supplied anticommunism with its racist dimension.[8] "Drawing upon their profound hatred and using the voices of the press and politicians," he writes, "the elites transmitted fear to the populace by arousing a dread of the dark outsider, whose symbol was assigned to Communism."[9] Wiecek likewise writes plainly of the "obvious racial and ethnic slants" of the countersubversive movement and of the "racial, ethnic and religious hostility [that] . . . drove anticommunism and its antecedents."[10]

Establishing racism as a mechanism by which elites mobilized anticommunist sentiment opens an intellectual space in which to explore the question of how such sentiments were accessed and exploited. Schmidt asserts, "The Red Scare was not *caused* by popular nativism or political intolerance, but it might be argued that they *made it possible* for the elite to pursue such a repressive line for a time during 1919 and 1920."[11] An analysis of Red Scare editorial cartoons can serve to expose the manner by which communism was racialized, thereby preventing working-class cohesion and repressing labor collectivism.

RACE IN THE EARLY TWENTIETH CENTURY

To understand how communism was racialized, one must first appreciate the nature of race in early twentieth-century America and the relative position of Slavic peoples in the racial hierarchy. The articulation of racial identities is understood here as a product of "the process by which social, economic and political forces determine the content and importance of racial categories."[12] Understanding racial ideology as a historicized construction allows one to avoid the dangerous pitfall articulated by Matthew Frye Jacobson in which "American scholarship . . . has generally conflated race and color, and so has transported a late-twentieth-century understanding of 'difference' into a period whose inhabitants recognized biologically based 'races' rather than culturally based 'ethnicities.'"[13] Race in the late nineteenth and early twentieth centuries was, at bottom, an expression of national origin, which—according to pseudo-scientific theories of eugenics, then in their ascendancy—ascribed to the foreign national a corresponding set of fixed, biological traits. Mae M. Ngai reminds scholars that early twentieth-century nativism "articulated a new kind of thinking, in which the cultural nationalism of the late-nineteenth century had transformed into a nationalism based on race . . . *Race, people*, and *nation* often referred to the same idea."[14]

The nation-based, eugenic view of humanity created a racial hierarchy in which not-quite-white peoples from southern and eastern Europe were seen as innately inferior to their northern and western European peers. According to Thomas Borstelmann, this hierarchy—delineating varying degrees of whiteness—consisted of "Anglo-Saxons, Teutons, Latins, Celts, and so on, down to Slavs, who were seen as partly Asian."[15] The Asianness of eastern Europeans was an enduring concept—Truman foreign policy adviser George Kennan claimed that Soviet despotism was a by-product of its peoples' "century-long contact with Asiatic hordes . . . [and] its attitude of Oriental secretiveness and conspiracy."[16] The allusion is significant in assessing the perceived relative whiteness of eastern Europeans; the Chinese constituted the only group explicitly barred from US citizenship, having been singled out as racially unassimilable outsiders.[17] The Dillingham Commission on immigration—which met from 1907 to 1911—had begun the pseudo-scientific work of redefining whiteness in a legal sense. Attributing the perceived intellectual and social deficiencies of southern and eastern Europeans to biologically degenerate racial stock, the committee assessed them as unfit for citizenship in white America and recommended a literacy test that was aimed at keeping them out. The targeted immigration provision passed Congress in 1917.

While the commission laid the legal groundwork for the racialization of formerly "white" Europeans, it was the continued, racially charged clamor for immigration restrictions—borne out in the Johnson-Reed Act of 1924—that is perhaps most revealing about Anglo-Saxon opinions of their Mediterranean and Slavic contemporaries. Madison Grant's book, *The Passing of the Great Race*, achieved significant popularity in the early 1920s. It cautioned Americans against the dangers of diluting their Anglo-Saxon stock with that of the racially inferior immigrants who made up the second wave of European immigration. According to Grant, the "new immigration" consisted of "the weak, the broken, and the mentally crippled of all races drawn from the lowest stratum of the Mediterranean basin and the Balkans, together with hordes of the wretched, submerged populations of the Polish Ghettos."[18] His racial characterization of southern and eastern Europeans was not unique. In a June 1896 article in the *Atlantic Monthly*, census superintendent Francis Walker espoused his belief that the recent wave of immigration represented "vast masses of peasantry, degraded below our utmost conceptions . . . beaten men from beaten races, representing the worst failures in the struggle for existence."[19]

For all the efforts by elites to articulate a more exclusionary meaning of whiteness, it is important to remember that the relationship between racial meaning and the socio-political environment is a reciprocal one and that the racial Othering of so-called new immigrants reverberated through all ranks of society. Jacobson writes that "although it may be tempting in retrospect to identify the likes of Madison Grant . . . as extreme in [his] views, it is critical to recognize that . . . it was not just a handful at the margins who saw certain immigrants as racially distinct; nor did the eugenic view of white races emerge in a vacuum. The consensus on this point was impressive."[20] Particularly at the working-class level, the racial ranking of immigrant nationalities and the indisputable social premium placed on whiteness proved to be predictably divisive. For those people situated in the vague middle ground of the racial hierarchy, creating distance between themselves and those people who were marked as not-quite-white was not just a way to maintain their position in the racial order but, conceivably, an opportunity to improve it. To gain acceptance in a country where citizenship was awarded to "free white persons" and the meaning of "white" was becoming ever more circumscribed, creating a wide berth between oneself and the racialized Other had become increasingly critical. Jacobson writes that for "the various probationary white races . . . whiteness *could* emerge by its contrast to nonwhiteness . . . [but perhaps more important,] immigrants who were white enough to enter as 'free white persons' could also lose that status by their association with nonwhite groups."[21] It was a risk many were unwilling to take.

RACIALIZING COMMUNISM

As the historiography of Red Scare anticommunism suggests, the ability of elite conservatives and business interests to undermine unionized labor and working-class solidarity was contingent on their capacity to capitalize on the racist notions of workers, largely immigrants themselves, who were keenly aware of the dynamics of the American racial order. Schmidt writes of powerful employer organizations in which "in order to win support for what was at bottom a union-breaking campaign, an extensive propaganda drive was organized . . . to discredit unions as subversive, Bolshevistic and alien to basic American values."[22] Imbedded in these campaigns was a set of pedagogical oppositions that functioned in this way:

| American (insider) | White | Conservatism | Free market labor |
| Foreign (outsider) | Non-white | Radicalism | Unionized labor |

The conflation of unionism and Bolshevism signaled a concomitant merging of the communist identity with that of (according to Harry H. Laughlin) the degenerate and unassimilable "mongrel" races of southern and eastern Europe.[23] In his charge to stamp out domestic communism, Attorney General A. Mitchell Palmer spoke of "Bolsheviks" and labor leaders interchangeably, writing of the former that "out of the sly and crafty eyes of many of them leap cupidity, cruelty, insanity and crime. From their lopsided faces, sloping brows and misshapen features may be recognized the unmistakable criminal type."[24] The unapologetically racial overtones were unmistakable. Yet importantly, the racialization of communism was not confined to political rhetoric. It penetrated far into the realm of popular culture, in which working-class citizens picked up on unambiguously racial cues and adopted anticommunism to secure their own purchase on whiteness.

During the Red Scare, newspapers and journals provided fertile ground for cultivating the racial image of communism. Jacobson writes that "notions of variegated whiteness" were "reflected in literature, visual arts, caricature, political oratory, penny journalism and myriad other venues of popular culture."[25] Past accounts of domestic anticommunism, such as that of Robert K. Murray, have been sabotaged by the tendency to interpret newspaper content as an expression of popular sentiment rather than the manifestation of elite agendas to influence it. Schmidt argues for the latter explanation: "Most of the larger influential dailies . . . reflected the conservative ideological preferences of their owners and followed a clear pro-business and anti-radical line."[26] The campaign of racializing communism is perhaps most evident in editorial cartoons of the period, which can best be understood by bifurcating them into descriptive and prescriptive expressions of domestic communism, presented in more or less equal measure during the years 1919 and 1920. Descriptive expressions provoked fear of the communist Other, who was racialized as a menacing, savage outsider—un-American in origin, appearance, and comportment. Prescriptive cartoons supplemented such notions, calling on Americans to repel the radical invasion through deportation and violent reprisal. Taken together, anticommunist Red Scare editorial cartoons (of both descriptive and prescriptive hues) provide a window into the comprehensive manner in which communism was racialized in the postwar press.

DESCRIPTIVE EDITORIAL CARTOONS

Descriptive anticommunism cartoons drew on allusions to savagery and European origin to racialize communism. Michael H. Hunt writes that cartoons of the period "equate[d] social revolution with indiscriminate death and destruction . . . the threat the 'Reds' posed to civilization . . . [was] embodied by a brutal, stereotypically Slavic type."[27] The savage European, who exhibited all the exaggerated biological features of the "lower races," was then labeled a "Bolshevik" or a "Red," thus imbuing communism with a distinctly racial identity. What Borstelmann calls the "traditional color-coding of savagery in the American National narrative" is indeed a persistent theme.[28] Following the 1867 New York City draft riots, Anglo-Saxons employed references to savagery to assert their whiteness by questioning the comparative racial integrity of the Irish. Jacobson writes that "many non-Irish onlookers and commentators . . . registered their own republican claims by questioning the rioters' full status as 'white persons' . . . The *Times* . . . decr[ied] the 'barbarism' of the riots and . . . characterize[d] the rioters themselves as 'brute,' 'brutish,' and 'animal' . . . The *Tribune* routinely characterized the Irish as a 'savage mob,' a 'pack of savages,' 'savage foes,' 'demons,' and 'incarnate devils.'"[29]

A December 1920 *Literary Digest* sketch embodies the savage type, featuring an imposing uniformed figure with Asian features, baring his teeth amid a nest of facial hair. "Bolshevism" is visible on his sash as he crosses the threshold of "Civilization," shoving the door open with his bloodied palm. Behind him there is darkness and a dead body—presumably slaughtered with the figure's long bloody knife. Themes of knives, blood, and death are used in several descriptive cartoons to signify savagery. Of twenty descriptive cartoons examined, four contain images of knives, three feature deaths, two display blood, and seven augur a physical threat to the viewer. Three of twenty feature the signifying figure of communism positioned outside a space defined as "civilization."

Kovel writes that "fantasies of bearded, filthy alien-radicals plotting against democracy and Western civilization [were] promulgated by the press," and indeed these racialized images of savage outsiders abound.[30] A January 1919 cartoon from the *Atlanta Constitution* includes an anthropomorphized "Bolshevik/Anarchist" storm cloud hovering menacingly over the United States, its dark trail reaching back into the recesses of Europe. Wild hair and a Russian Cossack hat cap the swarthy, snarling face amid the dark billows. Hands grip a bloody dagger and a bomb—the fuse is lit. The lightning bolts that pierce the sky above the United States feature the words "Murder," "Arson," and "Plunder." All of the allegorical elements of savagery are present, as is a clear visual representation of the extra-American origin of communism. At least 55 percent of the descriptive cartoons examined include such an allusion.

Another rhetorical device employed by illustrators of the period to mark the savage as un-American was the use of an oppositional figure. A cartoon from the *Memphis Commercial Appeal* (figure 6.2) republished in a July 1919 issue of *Literary Digest* shows a greasy, hook-nosed figure with droopy eyes crouched threateningly behind the Statue of Liberty. Wrapped in the cloak of "European Anarchist," the figure, clutching a dagger in one hand and a bomb in the other, prepares to attack Lady Liberty from the rear. Oppositional figures such as Uncle Sam and open-shop laborers provide the "American" or white counterpoint in at least four other descriptive images. Yet what is perhaps most interesting about this image is the placement

FIGURE 6.2. The "uncivilized" attack of the "European Anarchist." Originally published in the *Memphis Commercial Appeal*; republished in the *Literary Digest*, July 5, 1919. *Courtesy*, Red Scare (1918–1921), an Image Database (#16).

"COME UNTO ME, YE OPPREST!"
—Alley in the Memphis *Commercial Appeal*.

of the two figures vis-à-vis one another. Paul A. Kramer reminds us that "within the Euro-American world, patterns of warfare were important markers of racial status: civilized people could be recognized in their civilized wars, savages in their guerrilla ones."[31] The irredeemable savagery of the anarchist is clear in his unwillingness to engage Lady Liberty head-on.

Perhaps the most frequently employed racializing device in descriptive cartoons of the Red Scare era—embodying the savagery and extra-American origin of the communist—was the rhetorical use of the "Red" designation. What Kovel calls a "transposition of color" works here on two levels. First, "Red" was a direct reference to the revolutionary Russian Red Army, which—beyond representing the racial wasteland of Slavic territories—had become legend in the American popular imagination for its savagery. Congressman Henry L. Myers of Montana "elaborated on the precise meaning of this Soviet-style revolution, saying it augured a government founded on murder, assassination, robbery, rapine, rape, force, violence, and, presumably, other—more unspeakable—crimes against mankind."[32] Meanwhile, the *Baltimore American* characterized the Soviet government as "an outlaw of civilization and a stench in the nostrils of humanity," and a June 1919 *New York*

Times headline announced: "Thug with a Rifle: Russia's New Czar; Refugee Tells of Murder and Robbery under Bolsheviki—Rule of Criminals: Bourgeoisie Burned Alive; Men Whose Only Crime Was Decency Herded Together and Drowned to Make a Holiday."[33]

A *Literary Digest* cartoon from October 1919—originally printed in the *Philadelphia Inquirer*—features a beady-eyed, bearded figure creeping out from under the American flag. He brandishes a torch that reads "Anarchy" and a dagger that reads "Bolshevism"; his cap marks him as a "Red." "Put them out and keep them out" was the caption. Stereotypical facial features, outsider status, and savagery all come together under the "Red" moniker. A similarly racist sketch, published initially in the *New York Evening World* and subsequently in the *Literary Digest* in January 1920, highlights the efficacy of the "Red" device. The unkempt, shifty communist spreads his arms wide, proudly displaying a desecrated American flag. The panel of stars has been removed from the tattered banner, along with all of the white stripes. The remaining streamers are labeled "Red" and the caption reads "All they want in our flag." Without relying on knives, death, or allusions to extra-American origin, the savage un-Americanism of communism resonates. Forty-five percent of the Red Scare descriptive cartoons examined used explicit "Red" language to racialize communism.[34]

"Red" allusions worked on another level by referencing the original "savage outsider" of the American narrative: the American Indian. Kovel argues that such references "were adaptable to social conflicts between groups that had no collective memory of the encounter between Puritan and Indian . . . [and] the national wave of strikes in 1877 signified the transfer of the darkest images of the Indian onto the labor agitator. After Custer's Last Stand, Indian rebellions never again were a real threat to white society. The workers, though, were another story . . . thus was anticommunism officially born, as the prime signifier of the Devil passed from one kind of 'Red' to another."[35]

Cartoon depictions that included devils, monsters, wild animals, and nature themes—at least five of the descriptive cartoons—in conjunction with "Red" language were particularly adept at soliciting such connections. A July 1919 cartoon from the *Portland Telegram* captioned "Hell's Masterpieces" provides a striking example. The nude, red Devil—bearing a resemblance to Trotsky with an exaggerated hooknose—sits at an easel putting the finishing touches, with his "Red" brush, on a canvas titled *Bolshevik*. Behind him is a grotesque portrait of the recently humiliated Kaiser Wilhelm II, and at his feet are three completed portraits titled *Nero, Judas,* and *Caligula.* Nero's features are somewhat Asian, with the addition of a pig nose; Judas has a wild beard and hooknose; Caligula, for his part, bears a striking resemblance to the modern DreamWorks Studios–animated ogre, Shrek.

The "Bolshevik" snarls at the reader, his hair wild, his teeth rotted, and his eyes glaring past his bulbous nose. The meaning is unmistakable: the "Red," a savage Bolshevik, represents the racial heritage of the "Red," a savage Devil, and is cut from the same cloth as the criminals and ne'er-do-wells of the degraded Mediterranean and Slavic races.

The transposition of color from the American Indian to the radical, while highly effective in racializing the target, was, like many of the devices used in descriptive Red Scare cartoons, not new. David R. Roediger described the case of radical Finns in a Minnesota mining community who, racially marked as "red Finns," fell victim to violent attack. He writes that "after 1905, special (anti) Indian agents began a concerted campaign to close saloons and arrest bootleggers on and near the Iron Range. With the Mesabi iron strike of 1915, these 'Indian bulls' went after saloons used by 'red Finns'—the term connoted socialism . . . but also resonated with comparisons to Indians . . . the repression that eventuated on the Iron Range was nothing short of savage."[36] If savage repression was the remedy for those marked as successors to the "savage" American Indian, cartoons such as the one in a July 1919 issue of *Outlook*—reprinted from the *Brooklyn Eagle*—were setting radicals up as the new targets of the American extermination campaign. The sketch (figure 6.3) features a large tree, "America," from whose trunk spring the snarling, beady-eyed heads of "Red Aliens." Their protruding brows recall images of wild, uncivilized Neanderthals. The caption, "Fungus," leaves little doubt as to what must be done. Once again, white Americans would take the cue to excise the red outsider from the American landscape.

PRESCRIPTIVE EDITORIAL CARTOONS

Thus descriptive editorial cartoons of the Red Scare marked the communist as a savage. Recall that contact with a racial outsider could cause Americans to forfeit claims to whiteness. So prescriptive cartoons about racial outsiders reminded viewers of the proper way to deal with the Other—with rejection through violent suppression and removal. With racist contempt, inevitably, comes violence. The appetite for violence against the racialized communist during the Red Scare was remarkable in its voraciousness. Kovel argues that "fear had opened the collective mind not only to tolerate state repression, but to demand it; and the sense of horror surrounding radicalism both legitimized and impelled violence on the part of the government."[37] On January 2, 1920, in a series of raids in more than thirty cities in twenty-three states, Attorney General Palmer and the government complied. Thousands were arrested in a campaign whose hallmark was unmitigated violence. Murray reported that in the New York arrests,

FIGURE 6.3. "Red Aliens" bring about the decay of "America."
Originally published in the *Brooklyn Eagle*; republished in *Outlook*,
July 2, 1919. *Courtesy*, Red Scare (1918–1921), an Image Database (#12).

brutality was practiced to an excessive degree. Prisoners in sworn affidavits later testified to the violent treatment they had received. One claimed he had been beaten by a Justice Department operative without any explanation; another maintained he was struck repeatedly on the head with a blackjack . . . Still another testified: "I was struck on my head, and . . . was attacked by one detective, who knocked me down again, sat on my back, pressing me down to the floor with his knee and bending my body back until blood flowed out of my mouth and nose."[38]

Civil liberties were dismissed out of hand as the Red Scare program expanded into warrant-less arrests, illegal searches and seizures of persons and property, and cruel and unusual punishments. The treatment of radicals by federal officers bore all the markings of racial repression. Yet racial violence was not only within the purview of the federal government.

Locally, businessmen, patriot groups, and American Legionnaires were viciously lashing out against unionized labor, which had been conflated in the popular imagination with the radical, not-quite-white outsider. This was the type of racially charged response that obtained in prescriptive cartoons of the Red Scare years. Depictions of violence represent 45 percent of the prescriptive cartoons examined. In one such image from a September 1919 issue of the *San Francisco Examiner*, a grinning Legionnaire looms large in the foreground, poised with a baseball bat of "100 per cent Americanism" at the ready. From "US" soil, he looks across the ocean, where a "Revolution Maker" prepares to pitch a worker—who is clutching a lunch pail and a sheaf of "Propaganda for US"—onto American shores. There is a mix of satisfaction and pleasure on the batter's face as he readies to meet the foreign worker with a violent blow. What is noteworthy in this depiction and in at least fourteen other prescriptive cartoons is the novel approach to characterization of the communist. In a departure from the menacing depictions used in descriptive illustrations, these radicals, with their big noses, tattered clothes, wild facial hair, slack jaws, and stupefied expressions, appear inept and imbecilic. As in the illustration of the Legionnaire, the oppositional figure in such images is always above and large, while the radical is below and small. In print as in reality, violence follows diminution and dehumanization.

Oppositional figures play a significant role in prescriptive sketches, modeling the proper response to the racialized communist, who retains many of the trappings of the savage outsider present in descriptive cartoons. Thus the Other deserves the violent reprisal of the civilized, white opponent. Oppositional figures appear in nine of the twenty prescriptive cartoons, often in the form of Uncle Sam or the "American"/white, open-shop laborer. Two such cartoons—both from the summer of 1919—feature the foreign extremist laid low by US labor. The first (figure 6.4), from the *Chicago Tribune*, titled "The Patriotic American," depicts the figure of "American Labor," with rolled-up sleeves and a clenched right fist, standing over a dazed "Foreign Extremist" he has just knocked to the ground. The bearded, beady-eyed vagabond is sitting up and feeling for his face. His hat and a "Red" flag are on the ground beside him. "I'm kind of particular about who calls me 'brother,'" quips the laborer. In point of fact, this was perhaps just as prescriptive as it was reflective, given how rampant racial prejudice against eastern and southern Europeans was within craft unions. According to Roediger, "New immigrants . . . had less access to craft jobs in unionized sectors than did whites of northwestern European origin . . . [partially because of] a hard core of union opinion seeing [them] as mirroring the biological unsuitability of Asians."[39] Such images reinforced and encouraged workplace segregation. A similar cartoon from the *New York Tribune* features a burly woman labeled "Labor" standing on her doorstep; a radical (so identified by his facial hair and "Red" flag) is crumpled at the foot of the steps. "Capital" stands behind her as she proclaims, "Who told *you* I needed any help to manage my husband!" Both cartoons prod laborers to legitimize their Americanness, their

FIGURE 6.4. "American Labor" takes down the Reds. Originally published in the *Chicago Tribune*; republished in the *Literary Digest*, June 28, 1919. *Courtesy*, Red Scare (1918–1921), an Image Database (#9).

whiteness, by rejecting the "Red" outsider, often through violent means that are justified by the communists' racial inferiority.

Depictions of deportation were other prescriptive means used to remind Americans that the communist was a racial outsider, unfit for citizenship in a country in which "free and white" were the only requirements to legitimization. A cartoon from the *New York Evening World*, republished in January 1920 in the *Literary Digest*, features the American bald eagle engaged in "Cleaning the Nest!" Five comically flailing radicals, their papers, and "Red" flags are shown suspended in an endless sky—tossed out like garbage, unfit for the American aerie—presumably to descend on baser lands. At least half of the prescriptive cartoons examined reference deportation explicitly or implicitly. A December 1919 sketch from the *New York Tribune*, titled "Deporting the Reds," features Uncle Sam plucking miniature, bearded communists from his feet and sending them down a chute that terminates at an ocean liner marked "Deportation." In an allusion to the unstemmed tide of racially "new" immigration, the "Bolsheviki," "Reds," and "Revolutionaries"—as their banners identify them—just keep coming, frustrating the efforts of the bigger, stronger, whiter Uncle Sam. Another appearance by the oppositional figure in a March 1919 image from the *Columbus Dispatch* has Uncle Sam skimming the indigestible "Scum" from "The World's Melting Pot." The foul froth he ladles from the American stew is composed of the "Red Flag," the "I.W.W.," "Bolshevism," "The Mad Notions of Europe," "Anarchy," and "Unamerican [*sic*] Ideals." The cartoon uses the melting pot—which represented the assimilation of immigrants into white America—to mark out Wobblies, Bolsheviks, anarchists, and Reds as decidedly unassimilable, not-quite-white outsiders of the rankest sort.

The dehumanization that impelled and underwrote the racial violence of the Red Scare period also made its way into prescriptive cartoons as a validation of the deportation of alien agitators. November 1919 raids by the US Department of Justice had culminated in the deportation of 249 alleged communists and radicals, who were sent to sea aboard the USS *Buford*. The vessel became known as the "Soviet Ark" or "Red Ark," and its cargo was allegorically reduced to mere animals. Prescriptive cartoons of the period reflect the theme. An April 1919 sketch from the *New York Tribune* features a crate of howling, wild radicals awaiting deportation on the dock. Arms, legs, and wildly maned heads push their way through the gaps between the planks of the crate. The side of the shipping crate reads "Disloyal Aliens. Violence Advocates and I.W.W. Leaders." A shipping label declaring "Not Called For: Return to Sender" is affixed with a nail. When the radicals were racialized as caged beasts, who could protest their removal? Another such cartoon, originally published in the *Cleveland Plain Dealer* (figure 6.5) and later featured in a February 1920 issue of *Literary Digest*, depicts a wild-eyed animal in a suit and tie. He carries "Poison Literature" in his pocket and a gun in his hands, tagged with the label "Free Speech." The suited animal, it is suggested, has "No Brains," and in the second of three panels we see that the shots from his gun create bursts of "Sedition" and "Treason." The final panel shows the mad radical confined inside a cage on the dock. The tag "To Russia" leaves little doubt as to the creature's lowly, Slavic racial identity.

CONCLUSION

Descriptive and prescriptive cartoons—just a part of the Red Scare arsenal used to racialize communism—proved spectacularly effective for the white business elites of America in whose papers they were featured. Kovel argues that "ordinary citizens, the working people whom the radicals wanted to emancipate, had learned that they

FIGURE 6.5.
Dehumanizing the
foreign radical.
Originally published
in the *Cleveland Plain-
Dealer*; republished
in the *Literary Digest*,
February 7, 1920.
Courtesy, Red Scare
(1918–1921), an Image
Database (#126).

could avoid estrangement through anticommunism. For to hate and fear communism was the sure way of proving one's American identity."[40] With the rise of eugenics and the racial ranking of immigrant nationalities, working-class Americans sought to assert their own claims to whiteness by distancing themselves from the racialized outsider. If, as suggested by the historiography of domestic anticommunism, the racial Othering of organized labor was meant to marginalize and destroy the threat to the social order, its efficacy is indisputable. Even as the *Wall Street Journal* reported that "never before . . . has a government been so completely fused with business," working-class solidarity remained an elusive chimera.[41] So successful was the fusing of the "degraded" Slavic and southeastern European racial identity with that of the communist ideologue that business elites were forced to confront an unintended consequence of the campaign: the persistent stigmatization of alien workers and radicals augured immigration reform and an end to cheap labor.[42] The damage was done.

The racialization of communism would exhibit a peculiar staying power, even as the Red Scare subsided and the Johnson-Reed Immigration Act of 1924 passed, granting immigrants from southern and eastern Europe institutional access to the path toward whiteness. The act, while ranking all nationalities on a eugenically based scale of desirability and assigning immigration quotas accordingly, *did* serve to define all Europeans as racially white. While immigration from Russia and Italy was reduced by the national origins quota system to 7 percent and 9 percent of their previous allowances, respectively, the generational assimilation—the whitening—of southern and eastern Europeans meant that the racializing power of Red Scare rhetoric, extant in political cartoons of the period, would progressively diminish. Yet as anyone familiar with the modern American political landscape can discern, cries of "communist" are still an effective means of Othering one's opponent, marking him or her at once as un-American, opposite, and unequal.

NOTES

1. *Literary Digest*, 11–96.

2. Deloria, *Playing Indian*, 3.

3. This historiographic view is best represented by Robert K. Murray. See Murray, *Red Scare*, 15; Powers, *Not without Honor*, 426.

4. Heale, *American Anticommunism*; Higham, *Strangers in the Land*; Kovel, *Red Hunting*; Schmidt, *Red Scare;* Wiecek, "Legal Foundations."

5. Schmidt, *Red Scare*, 26.

6. Wiecek, "Legal Foundations," 385.

7. Heale, *American Anticommunism,* 27.

8. Kovel, *Red Hunting*, 220–221.

9. Kovel, Red Hunting, 16.

10. Wiecek, "Legal Foundations," 390, 384.

11. Schmidt, *Red Scare*, 40; emphasis added.

12. Omi and Winant, *Racial Formation*, 61.

13. Jacobson, *Whiteness of a Different Color*, 6.

14. Ngai, *Impossible Subjects*, 23; original emphasis.

15. Borstelmann, *Cold War*, 13.

16. Cited in Borstelmann, *Cold War*, 50.

17. This was done in the 1882 Chinese Exclusion Act.

18. Grant, *The Passing of the Great Race*, 87.

19. Cited in Ngai, *Impossible Subjects*, 30.

20. Jacobson, *Whiteness of a Different Color*, 88–89.

21. Jacobson, Whiteness of a Different Color, 57, original emphasis.

22. Schmidt, *Red Scare*, 33.
23. Ngai, *Impossible Subjects*, 24.
24. Palmer, "Address of A. Mitchell Palmer," 619.
25. Jacobson, *Whiteness of a Different Color*, 41–42.
26. Schmidt, *Red Scare*, 37.
27. Hunt, *Ideology and US Foreign Policy*, 120.
28. Borstelmann, *Cold War*, 185.
29. Jacobson, *Whiteness of a Different Color*, 54–55.
30. Kovel, *Red Hunting*, 21.
31. Kramer, *Blood of Government*, 90.
32. Cited in McNiece, "Un-Americans," 59.
33. Kovel, *Red Hunting*, 14.
34. Based on my examination of forty editorial cartoons.
35. Kovel, Red Hunting, 226–227.
36. Roediger, *Working toward Whiteness*, 64.
37. Kovel, *Red Hunting*, 19–20.
38. Murray, *Red Scare*, 214.
39. Roediger, *Working toward Whiteness*, 82.
40. Kovel, *Red Hunting*, 22.
41. Cited in Miller, *New World Coming*, 88.
42. Schmidt, *Red Scare*, 39.

BIBLIOGRAPHY

Borstelmann, Thomas. *The Cold War and the Color Line: American Race Relations in the Global Arena*. Cambridge, MA: Harvard University Press, 2001.

Deloria, Philip J. *Playing Indian*. New Haven, CT: Yale University Press, 1998.

Feuerlicht, Roberta Strauss. *America's Reign of Terror: World War I, the Red Scare, and the Palmer Raids*. New York: Random House, 1971.

Fields, Barbara J. "Ideology and Race in American History." In *Region, Race, and Reconstruction: Essays in Honor of C. Vann Woodward*, ed. J. Morgan Kousser and James M. McPherson, 143–177. New York: Oxford University Press, 1982.

Grant, Madison. *The Passing of the Great Race: Or the Racial Basis of European History*. New York: Charles Scribner's Sons, 1918.

Heale, Michael J. *American Anticommunism: Combating the Enemy Within, 1830–1970*. Baltimore: Johns Hopkins University Press, 1990.

Higham, John. *Strangers in the Land: Patterns of American Nativism, 1860–1925*. 2nd ed. New York: Atheneum, 1971.

Hoyt, Edwin P. *The Palmer Raids, 1919–1920: An Attempt to Suppress Dissent*. New York: Seabury, 1969.

Hunt, Michael H. *Ideology and US Foreign Policy*. New Haven, CT: Yale University Press, 1987.

Jacobson, Matthew Frye. *Whiteness of a Different Color: European Immigrants and the Alchemy of Race*. Cambridge, MA: Harvard University Press, 1998.

Klein, Leo Robert. Red Scare (1918–1921), an Image Database. http://leoklein.com/red scare/index.htm.

Kovel, Joel. *Red Hunting in the Promised Land: Anticommunism and the Making of America*. 2nd ed. London: Cassel, 1997.

Kramer, Paul A. *The Blood of Government: Race, Empire, the United States, and the Philippines*. Chapel Hill: University of North Carolina Press, 2006.

Literary Digest. November 15, 1919. http://books.google.com/books?id= Nqk5AQAAMAAJ&printsec=frontcover&dq=The+Literary+Digest+Volume+63 &hl=en&sa=X&ei=nOwCU9iVItChogT_ooKYDQ&ved=0CCsQ6AEwAA#v= onepage&q=The%20Literary%20Digest%20Volume%2063&f=false.

McNiece, Matthew A. "'Un-Americans' and 'Anti-Communists': The Rhetorical Battle to Define Twentieth-Century America." PhD dissertation, Texas Christian University, Fort Worth, 2008. http://search.proquest.com/docview/250789688?accountid =13802 (250789688).

Miller, Nathan. *New World Coming: The 1920s and the Making of Modern America*. New York: Scribner, 2003.

Murray, Robert K. *Red Scare: A Study in National Hysteria, 1919–1920*. Minneapolis: University of Minnesota Press, 1955.

Ngai, Mae M. *Impossible Subjects: Illegal Aliens and the Making of Modern America*. Princeton, NJ: Princeton University Press, 2004.

Omi, Michael, and Howard Winant. *Racial Formation in the United States: From the 1960s to the 1980s*. New York: Routledge, 1987.

The Opper Project at the Ohio State University: The Red Scare. 2019. http://hti.osu.edu /opper/lesson-plans/the-red-scare.

Palmer, A. Mitchell. "The Case against the 'Reds.'" *Forum* 63 (1920): 173–185.

Palmer, A. Mitchell. "Address of A. Mitchell Palmer at the Dinner of the New York County Lawyer's Association, Hotel Astor, New York City, Friday Evening, February 27, 1920." In *Charges of Illegal Practices of Department of Justice, January 1, 1921, to March 3, 1921*, 617–628. Washington, DC: Government Printing Office, 1921.

Powers, Richard Gid. *Not without Honor: The History of American Anticommunism*. New Haven, CT: Yale University Press, 1995.

Roediger, David R. *Working toward Whiteness: How America's Immigrants Became White.* New York: Basic Books, 2005.

Schmidt, Regin. *Red Scare: FBI and the Origins of Anticommunism in the United States, 1919–1943.* Copenhagen: Museum Tusculanum Press, 2000.

Wiecek, William M. "The Legal Foundations of Domestic Anticommunism: The Background of Dennis v. United States." *Supreme Court Review* (2001): 375–434.

7

Toward a Post-Racial Society, or a "Rebirth" of a Nation?

White Anxiety and Fear of Black Equality in the United States

Travis D. Boyce and Winsome M. Chunnu

The more things change, the more things stay the same.

FRENCH NOVELIST JEAN-BAPTISTE ALPHONSE KARR
(1808–1890), *LES GUÊPES*, JANUARY 1849

February 8, 2015, marked the 100th anniversary of the release of D. W. Griffith's controversial film *The Birth of a Nation*. Although the opening credits note "this is an historical presentation of the Civil War and Reconstruction Period, and is not meant to reflect on any race or people of today,"[1] the reality was that the film heightened preexisting racial, social, and political tensions in a country that was already structured around the dominant ideology that blacks are inferior. Since its debut, this film has served as a glaring illustration of the country's white anxiety rooted in the fear of black equality. The film was well received by the US mainstream (including US president Woodrow Wilson) as a cinematic masterpiece; sadly, Ku Klux Klan (KKK) membership skyrocketed under its anti-immigrant, anti-Semitic, anti-black, and anti-Catholic agenda, which appealed to the white, Protestant mainstream.[2] In 2007, film historian Melvyn Stokes noted that *The Birth of a Nation* "functioned as a propaganda and recruitment film."[3] For example, in Atlanta, Georgia, in 1915, the Klan printed advertisements of *Birth* in local newspapers and held public meetings with cross burnings in the days leading up to the opening of the movie in their members' cities.[4] The use of *Birth* as a recruitment tool for the Klan continued into the late twentieth century. Most notably, white

DOI: 10.5876/9781646420025.c007

supremacist David Duke (b. 1950), a Louisiana state legislator and candidate for US Senate who also ran for the presidency of the United States,[5] used this film and even narrated it to prospective supporters during the 1970s.

The Birth of a Nation, based on Thomas F. Dixon Jr.'s 1905 novel *The Clansman*,[6] is a fictional account of the US Civil War. It features a prominent family in South Carolina before, during, and after the Civil War. While the family is prosperous and optimistic before the war (and even partially during the war), its members (along with the entire white South) experience social, political, and economic hardship during Reconstruction under black American rule. The film's protagonist, Ben Cameron, is credited with organizing the Ku Klux Klan after witnessing two white children dressed in white sheets (while at play), scaring a group of their African American peers.[7] Thus Cameron makes it his duty to save the South from Radical Reconstruction. His goal was to defend white womanhood and facilitate white masculinity (such as carrying firearms and voting). His agenda includes a paternalistic/racial supremacist sense of entitlement to govern oneself and the "Other."

Thomas Dixon (1864–1946) and David Llewelyn Wark "D.W." Griffith (1875–1948), both southerners, had influential patriarchal figures (Dixon's uncle and Griffith's father, respectively) who fought for the Confederacy. Thus Dixon and Griffith sought to construct a skewed narrative of Reconstruction drawn from the perspective of the "Redeemers" (ex-Confederates who aligned with the Democrats and sought to overthrow the Racial Republican agenda).[8] The Redeemers asserted that African Americans were inferior and thus not capable of self-rule. As a result, they sought to regain what they perceived as their political birthright. In the wake of the fall of Reconstruction, J. R. Ralls states:

> The brief political history of the Negro at the South has brought out two important facts that may be useful in the future in solve [*sic*] the political problem that presents itself in connection with this race. One of these facts is that he has no affinity for the white race in politics, as well as in social life and religion, and as soon as all extraneous force is removed, he will become isolated, and independent, as far he can, of the control and contact of the white man. The other important fact disclosed by his brief political career is, that he, though possessed of a clannish spirit in a high degree, is incapable of organization, and if left to himself, without the leadership and drilling tact of the white man, must, irrespective of numerical power, yield political control to the superior race.[9]

The Redeemers' perspective on Reconstruction is firmly grounded in the ideology of anti-black thought as espoused by the likes of J. R. Ralls. Redeemers' politics used similar rhetoric during and after Reconstruction to both suppress black American political enfranchisement and enhance their own political careers. They instigated a sense of anxiety and fear of black political empowerment. Benjamin "Pitchfork" Tillman (1847–1918) exemplifies the use of these fear tactics in his political campaigns. Tillman rose to political relevancy in the 1880s on the political rhetoric of populism. He was South Carolina's governor from 1890 to 1894, as well as a US senator from 1895 until his death in 1918. He posited that Radical Reconstruction was a complete failure under black rule in South Carolina politics. Tillman forcefully advocated white patriarchal rule and welcomed violence against African Americans who sought political enfranchisement as well as social and economic equality.[10] In July 1876, he was involved in a particularly tragic event in Hamburg, South Carolina (the town is now defunct). An all-black militia, after a drill, refused to yield to two white farmers passing by. The white farmers subsequently complained to a local judge. The farmers' attorney demanded that the militia disband and relinquish their arms, which they refused to do. Over 100 white men with weapons and a cannon brought from neighboring Augusta, Georgia, convened on the town.[11] They captured 20 African Americans and brutally executed 5 others. This disastrous event, known as the Hamburg Massacre, was one of many racially violent outrages that occurred during the Reconstruction period.[12] Tillman, who said he had been one of the rioters, used his participation in these shocking murders to enhance his political career.[13]

In *Birth*, African Americans in the South were depicted as powerful enough to gain control of the political economy, but they were simultaneously portrayed as buffoons—uppity and incapable of self-rule. Even more dangerous, the film portrayed blacks as violent and as rapists. Much of this rhetoric came from Harvard-educated historian William Garrott Brown (1868–1913), who defended whites' reaction to the evils of Reconstruction in a 1901 article. Brown also noted that this reaction should have been expected in light of interference from the North. In addition, he stressed that the Klan was fighting with a moral goal in mind. Similarly, in 1914, Walter Henry Cook addressed the Faculty of Friends at Western Reserve University, Ohio, where he gave an overwhelming defense of racism and the Klan. What is the point of negative rhetoric? Speech professor Cal M. Logue (b. 1935), in a 1977 article, dissects how newspapers and speeches in the South employed negative language in their discussion of blacks. Their goal was to frame blacks as lazy and a threat to whiteness. Logue notes that these frames are still used today. For example, history professor emeritus Jack Maddex Jr., in a 1974 publication, defends slavery and the Confederacy on the notion that blacks are inferior. Claude H. Nolen's 1967 book addresses the vigorous defense of white supremacy by southern whites during Reconstruction. This rhetoric was used to disenfranchise blacks.[14]

The movie *Birth of a Nation* showed the Ku Klux Klan as the gallant heroes who ultimately saved the South from black rule, protecting white womanhood and reaffirming white masculinity. Thus the movie reinforced anti-black scholarship and political rhetoric that had emerged after Reconstruction and particularly during the early twentieth century.[15] Consequently, anti-black rhetoric as well as the film served as a parading of dominant ideas as truth rather than as an opinion. As the first major motion picture of its kind, *Birth* used a race-based narrative that hinged on black violence to reorganize racial politics. *Birth* focused the gaze of white anxiety on blacks as violent and reminded its white viewers that black equality was to be feared.

Birth left an immediate and lasting legacy pertaining to both film studies and race relations in the United States. From a cinematic perspective, Griffith believed motion pictures could reach out to a larger, more mainstream audience than the small audience gained by professional historians.[16] Today, the "movie version" of period pieces can overpower or replace actual historical fact. For example, the Civil War film *Glory* features recruits who had been former southern slaves. In fact, the regiment had been mostly freemen from the North. Although *Birth* is deemed one of the most controversial films in US cinematic history, it continues to be cited by film schools and historians as a good example for its "aesthetic and technical qualities."[17] Griffith and his team recruited individuals who were surveyors and engineers with military experience to create exact replicas of battlefield scenes—particularly the critical Battle of Petersburg. Moreover, the media praised Griffith for the historical accuracy of the scene in which Lee surrenders at the Appomattox Courthouse, a scene in which General Ulysses S. Grant was correctly represented wearing a muddy uniform and boots.[18]

Despite the film's cinematic achievements, the immediate and lasting legacies of its construction of black bodies as a violent force that must be opposed by a state-supported mechanism of social control such as laws and public policy continue to mar the film. Upon its release in 1915, progressive organizations such as the National Association for the Advancement of Colored People (NAACP) staged protests across the country. The people who opposed *Birth* achieved small victories. Parts of the film were censored or banned in some cities. But it was overwhelmingly well received by the US mainstream and served as a catalyst for the revival of the Ku Klux Klan.[19] More important, it was screened at a private showing at the White House as well as before members of the US Supreme Court and Congress, who lauded the film.[20]

Of course, the movie *Birth* is not the only cause of the long-term perpetuation of institutional racism in the United States. Rather, it is merely a reflection of the country's racial divide, which is fundamentally grounded in white anxiety and fear of black equality. Both implicitly and explicitly, millions of white viewers in 1915 were reminded by *Birth* to fear black equality (because of the supposed vulnerability of white women, the possibility of black-on-white violence, and the peril of black elected officials). Subsequent generations also received that message: black men are rapists, former slaves are fundamentally violent, and blacks need to stay in their place, particularly *out* of politics. Therefore, it was considered the duty of mainstream institutions to suppress black equality.

This suppression of black equality was evident in the fearful rhetoric that was espoused during the 2008 election and 2012 reelection of President Barack H. Obama. Obama's election ushered in a new century, one in which many people hoped race would no longer influence social and economic equality. However, race-based assaults against the Obama presidency worsened.[21] In fact, the United States continues to experience a "rebirth" of a nation grounded in the fears of black equality. Specifically, anti-black rhetoric portraying blacks as rapists, violent, and incapable of self-rule continues to be spread by white pundits or politicians who seem motivated to fight for every inch of black equality.

Using select themes and scenes of the film *The Birth of a Nation*, this chapter presents current and historical events to examine the use of fear tactics (fearful framing) against black equality. On its 100th anniversary, we are putting forth a "re-birth" of *Birth*. We are examining *Birth* as a historical piece to help make sense of the present. *Birth* is also a truncated version of a history that we should not forget. *Birth* is a historical and contemporary construction of oppression. It is also important to situate our analysis and resistance in history. However, examining *Birth of a Nation* as a purely historic piece without contemporary political reflection and dialectic tensions would be to take a linear view of the film. How do the fears shown in *Birth of a Nation* apply to today's political culture? This chapter will examine the fearful framing through construction of the fictive Black Beast and the use of public policy/law as a means of controlling the demonized black body. The chapter will conclude with an examination of the construction of fear through black militancy, including when black men are armed. A discussion of black elected officials includes the reaction of the mainstream during both Reconstruction and post-Reconstruction to expound a contemporary interpretation of *Birth* and illustrate how US society continues to be enmeshed in the problems shown in D. W. Griffith's controversial film.

FEAR THE BLACK BEAST

On December 26, 1908, Jack Johnson (1878–1946) was crowned the first black American heavyweight boxing champion of the world. He had successfully defeated Tommy Burns, a Canadian national, in a rough fight. After fourteen rounds in which Burns took a severe beating from Johnson, local police intervened and stopped the match.

The fight took place in Sydney, Australia. Although the match was not in the United States, where Johnson had faced intense discrimination, he was met with an equally hostile Australian crowd that hurled racial epithets at him during the bout. Johnson ignored the crowd and at times smiled and chatted with fans or taunted hecklers near ringside before defeating Burns. Conveniently, a camera crew stopped rolling before Johnson's climatic punch that knocked out Burns.[22]

Johnson's seven-year reign as champion of the world vexed whites everywhere but especially in his home nation, the United States. Although boxing was illegal in the majority of states in the early twentieth century, it still represented the essence of white masculinity. Black athletes, compared to white athletes, were generally viewed as weak cowards who lacked strategic intellectual capacity. The implication of Johnson's reign was much bigger than the sport itself. His athletic prowess revealed the vulnerability of white supremacist ideology. Johnson, in effect, embodied social equality, which was reflected outside the boxing ring.[23] "The Galveston Giant" (as he was called) wore expensive tailored clothes, drove fast cars, and lived in predominately white or all-white neighborhoods.

But this blurring of the lines that separated blacks and whites in the early twentieth century was minor compared to Johnson's ultimate transgression: three marriages to white women. Only one generation prior, the white mainstream/Redeemer contingent had created a narrative to overturn Reconstruction and justify the lynching of black men (to protect white womanhood) through the Black Beast image.[24] In Johnson's case, the press focused particularly on this issue and framed him as the "menacing, lustful black male [whites] had to come to fear."[25] Johnson, in effect, was constructed as a Black Beast. During his championship years, countless images were printed in newspapers depicting him as an extremely dark-skinned man with ape-like traits.

The construction of the Black Beast in *Birth* serves as a framework for understanding the use of the law to control Johnson. In the film, after the South has been controlled politically and militarily by black Republican rule, the viewer is introduced to Gus, a soldier. Like Johnson, Gus embodies the spirit of social equality. He is an officer in the US Army (a captain), and his promotion reflected the unlimited possibilities for blacks who sought equality. In one scene, Gus and his soldiers are seen pushing whites from the sidewalk. They have a brief confrontation with the film's white protagonist, Ben Cameron. Gus later develops an attraction to Ben's sister, Flora. Eventually, Gus encounters Flora alone, and she flees. He chases her to the edge of a cliff, and she jumps to her death rather than give in to his advances. Ben Cameron and the Klan capture Gus, execute him, and leave his body at the door of Lt. Governor Silas Lynch (a corrupt, biracial politician). The narrative surrounding Gus is made clear to the audience: black men are hyper-sexual and will prey on white women. White womanhood has to be protected at all costs.

The white mainstream was determined to curtail the access to white women that Johnson's fame afforded him. They worked under the banner of white supremacy with the aims of protecting the color line and white womanhood. This they achieved through the law and public policy—specifically, the 1910 White Slave Traffic Act, also known as the Mann Act. Named after its author, Rep. James R. Mann (R-IL), the law was originally intended to combat forced prostitution.

In 2013, history professor Theresa Runstedtler provided a compelling documentation of Johnson's case.[26] In 1913, Johnson was convicted of transporting a prostitute from Pittsburgh to Chicago. However, the so-called prostitute was actually Johnson's white girlfriend. No force was involved—the couple simply took a trip together over a state boundary. Nevertheless, the championship boxer was convicted and given the maximum sentence: one year and one day. Sojourner says that the rhetoric of the law was rooted in black migration to the North and its concurrence with the rising number of young, single white women in urban areas.

The case against Johnson became a full-fledged, racist moral panic. One Democratic congressman attempted to add an anti-miscegenation clause to the US Constitution. Bills were later passed to ban black-white marriage in some northern states. In addition, there was a sharp increase in police clampdowns on interracial social gathering areas. Consequently, there was widespread public condemnation of Johnson for openly engaging in sexual relationships with white women. It is against this background that the Mann Act was conceptualized as a legal means to police black bodies.

After Johnson defeated a series of boxers considered "Great White Hopes" (along with surviving a series of controversies in his personal life that were enthusiastically covered by the media), he lost the championship on April 5, 1915, to a white man, Jess Willard. The match happened about three months after the release of *The Birth of a Nation*. The Black Beast had been destroyed. Ironically, the most controversial and lauded part of *Birth* centered on interracial sexual politics and glorified the destroying of the Black Beast.

Groups such as the Ku Klux Klan, the White League in Louisiana, and the Knights of the White Camelia obstructed, assassinated, and intimidated black and white Republican officials. They engaged in violence as a means of voter suppression. Fundamentally, they were determined to restore white supremacy. However, lynching remains the most disturbing form of intimidation from this period. As Jessie Parkhurst Guzman (1898–1996) makes clear in a 1952 black history yearbook with sociologist Lewis Ward Jones (1910–1979), "not only [was] the act itself [horrific], but [it was] the impunity with which it was used as an instrument of terror and subjugation throughout the South. Thousands of black people were tortured, branded, mutilated, dismembered, and finally hanged or burned by mobs who knew their mode of 'justice' would go unpunished."[27] Guzman, a historian with the Tuskegee Institute, explains that although anti-lynching bills were submitted, neither Congress nor US presidents at the time made any effort to engage in serious consideration of these bills.

While blacks were lynched for committing various infractions, both written and unwritten, many of these lynchings were conducted for the alleged rape of white women.[28] The media exaggerated these fears and conversely reinforced the image of the Black Beast. Despite the pleas for anti-lynching laws by the NAACP in the 1920s, the practice continued. There was even an insistence by southern civic leaders to curb lynchings out of economic interest for their respective cities. Yet lynchings continued with a rape narrative as a justification well into the 1930s (when lynchings surged).[29] Perhaps one of the best-known lynchings occurred in August 7, 1930, in Marion, Indiana. Three black teens (Tom Shipp, Abe Smith, and James Cameron) were accused of murdering a white man (Claude Deeter) and raping a white woman (Mary Ball). The *Marion Chronicle* essentially tried and condemned the young men. A mob broke into the teens' jail cells, brutally beating and murdering Shipp and Smith. Cameron, the youngest of the three, was spared. Shipp and Smith were hanged and mutilated in front of thousands, and the scene was captured by a local photographer. That photograph became the iconic image of US lynching.[30] The idea of the Black Beast and the preservation of white womanhood remained fixed in the minds of the white US mainstream. This myth perpetuated itself in many forms outside the realm of the hanging tree.

According to Guzman's 1952 account, of the three major sources of lynching statistics—the *Chicago Tribune*, the Tuskegee Institute, and the NAACP—none captures the complete history of lynching in America. Although the numbers of lynchings listed in each source varies slightly, according to the Tuskegee Institute figures, between the years 1882 and 1951, 4,730 people were lynched in the United States.

THE BLACK BEAST IN THE WORKPLACE

On December 22, 1955, almost forty years after the release of *Birth*, the fear of the Black Beast resulted in the dismissal of a black worker (James Major) at a Detroit Dodge plant. As noted by historian Kevin Boyle (b. 1960), the culture in these car plants at the time was grounded in white supremacy.[31] Boyle, who researches class and race in the workplace, says that white male workers used their racial and gender identity as a tool to control that arena. Skilled positions and foreman spots were reserved for white men. Black men and white women were relegated to menial and gender-specific tasks. Assigning black men to tedious but dangerous jobs was justified by whites, who viewed black men as physically strong but lacking intelligence and skill. As for access to women, there was a double standard. White men openly sexually pursued white women at work. But white men demonized black men who dated white women.

However, after World War II, technological advancement brought new social customs to the workplace. Skilled employers were losing ground. For example, departments at Dodge in Detroit that were historically reserved for white men were now employing black men and white women. Unfortunately, James Major entered the trim department during an extreme volatile time.[32] Major, a black man, and colleague Leona Hunt, a white woman, had shared a celebratory kiss to usher in the Christmas holidays. Immediately, Hunt was confronted by two white male colleagues who berated her for the kiss.[33] Although the Supreme Court had recently ruled that racial segregation was unconstitutional (*Brown v. Board of Education*), black equality was still viewed as a threat at the Dodge plant in Detroit.[34] The kiss that occurred on December 22, 1955, gave Major's white colleagues the justification to do something to get him fired. Perhaps they saw Major as a Black Beast who had assaulted a white woman. At the least, they must have felt his job was historically reserved for white men. Hunt likely began to fear her white male colleagues and the possibility that she could be fired. She told management that Major had "come up behind her, put his arm around her, spun her around, then kissed her."[35] She claimed she was anxious that Major would hurt her if she protested the kiss. Her testimony reinforced the white male automobile workers' prejudicial views of black men. Major was subsequently terminated. The white workers may have felt vindicated in using fear to restore the racial order of white supremacy.

This incident demonstrates that although some progress (with regard to racial equality) had been made in the United States forty years after the release of *Birth*, the "*rebirth* of a nation" mentality still promoted the fear of black equality. In this scenario, it was the duty of whites to tame and destroy the Black Beast. While interracial sexual politics within the context of black equality was pivotal in Griffith's *Birth*, the film also illustrated other aspects that reinforced white fear and anxiety of blacks seeking equality. The next section will explore the construction of fear through black militancy, including when black men are armed, as well as the fear of black elected officials during both Reconstruction and post-Reconstruction to expound a contemporary interpretation of *Birth* and illustrate how US society continues to be enmeshed in the problems shown in D. W. Griffith's controversial film.

FEAR OF BLACK ARMED MILITANCY (OR BLACK CRIMINALITY)

History professor Carole Emberton (b. 1975) astutely observed, "Loaded or not, guns symbolize freedom in profound ways."[36] After the Civil War, many southern whites feared black independence. The idea that blacks could own guns was very unsettling to southern whites. What if there were an insurrection? In 1866, in Walton County, Georgia, the Ku Klux Klan attacked Charles Smith, an African American, and broke his gun into several pieces as a reminder of how they regarded his independence and manhood. During the Reconstruction era, one of the fears surrounding African American masculinity and citizenship was blacks' right to bear arms.[37] Although it was mostly whites who perpetuated crimes against blacks, the white public imagined armed black men committing violence. Just after the war, Nevada senator James Nye (1815–1876) stated, "We have gone on . . . wisely or unwisely, converting the colored population into beings of power through military discipline . . . We have taught one hundred and sixty thousand of them in the art of killing . . . It must be a poor observer of human nature who does not realize that the colored people [of the] South can be goaded into desperation."[38] While African Americans did engage in combat against paramilitary insurgents such as the Ku Klux Klan, blacks were not the aggressors. Nevertheless, Democratic politicians, ex-Confederates, or anyone who opposed black independence claimed there were armed blacks who were aggressive and hostile. This claim translated years later into scenes in D. W. Griffith's *The Birth of a Nation*.

In *Birth*, viewers are presented with multiple scenes of an occupied South both before (briefly) and during Reconstruction under black Republican rule. Armed African Americans are depicted as violent and criminal. One scene in *Birth* depicts a predominately African American federal army invading Piedmont, South Carolina, and attacking the Cameron residence. They injure the elder Dr. Cameron as he defends his home; white women and children take refuge in the basement. Although a local Confederate regiment comes to the Camerons' assistance and drives off the federal troops, Piedmont is devastated from the attack. The Cameron home is set on fire. Further examples occur in subsequent scenes in *Birth*. At the point in the movie where the South is officially under African American Republican rule, viewers see African American soldiers pushing whites off the street when they cross paths, intimidating them at the polls on Election Day, and beating and murdering ex-slaves who remained loyal to their former masters. African Americans dressed in federal blue uniforms and armed with rifles represent the fear not only of black equality but also of black criminality.

Highly telling of this fear is an 1876 editorial cartoon by Thomas Nast (1840–1902) published in *Harper's Weekly*. Titled "He Wants Change Too," the cartoon indicts the white South for its paramilitary violence against blacks—particularly in wake of the recent Hamburg Massacre, in which the federal government did not intervene. However, as Emberton points out, this cartoon from Nast, as well as his critiques of Democratic paramilitary activities, had the opposite effect in the South. There, the image gave white paramilitary groups a degree of respectability and legitimacy. In the cartoon, they saw a black, shirtless, gun-toting figure. Southern Democrats in states such as South Carolina rallied around this cause under the banner of US nationalism, linking the 100th anniversary of the War for American Independence from Britain with an 1876 War of Southern Independence from black Republican rule. By the end of Reconstruction, sympathy from white northerners had waned for African American rights and Republican rule in the South. They began to view their southern counterparts' violent, revolutionary activities as noble and aligned with the aims of the nation's founding fathers against the British.[39]

In *The Birth of a Nation*, the fear of black armed militancy was captured in the climatic standoff between the African American federal troops and the Ku Klux Klan. After an altercation in Piedmont, the Cameron family is pursued by the African American federal troops. Ironically, two white soldiers who fought for the Union offer the family refuge in their cabin. Intertitles appear, asserting that "the former enemies of North and South are united again in common defense of their Aryan birthright (shot 1287)."[40] This scene is clearly a message to the audience about North and South reconciliation based on the need for white nationalism to suppress African American criminality. Subsequently, in the movie, a furious battle erupts among the encamped Camerons, the two white Union soldiers, and the African American federal army. Ben Cameron and the Ku Klux Klan ride off to defeat federal soldiers. African American soldiers are disarmed in Piedmont. In most scenes in *Birth*, armed African American federal troops are portrayed as criminals because they attack civilians. Thus the Klan (both in *Birth* as well as in reality during the era of Reconstruction) felt justified to use any means necessary (even violence) to defeat black Republican rule and return to the white-dominated social, economic, and political order of the antebellum South.

Although the film portrays African Americans during Reconstruction as the aggressors, in reality, the problem at the time was overwhelming white-on-black violence. Historian Kenneth W. Howell notes, for example, that in Texas, whites instigated the majority of violent racial incidents during the Reconstruction era.[41] Fearing social change and promoting hatred toward blacks, white southerners organized paramilitary organizations and rifle clubs such the Ku Klux Klan, the Red Shirts, and the White League, among others (many connected to the Democratic Party). The goal of these groups was to intimidate, assault, and murder African Americans and white Republicans who challenged the antebellum status quo. In 1868 in Arkansas, there were over 200 such politically connected murders. The media in Alabama (such as the *Selma Times* and the *Mobile Register*) encouraged whites to overthrow Reconstruction through violence.[42] A tragic illustration of such violence occurred on Easter Sunday in 1873 in Colfax, Louisiana. There had recently been a disputed gubernatorial election. On that Sunday, 150 African Americans were killed after a standoff against over 300 white paramilitary insurgents. The federal government ultimately intervened, declaring the Republican candidate the winner.[43] So while southern blacks during Reconstruction affirmed the right to bear firearms with independence and masculinity,[44] whites saw armed black men as a threat and went on a rhetorical and violent campaign to disarm and disenfranchise blacks.

Griffith's 1915 portrayal of armed blacks in *Birth*, based on his viewpoint of the Reconstruction era, left a lasting impression on its white viewers. The movie's image of armed black militants played on the fears of the white mainstream and justified racist violence.

Another half-century did little to change the mind of the mainstream. In 1966, Stokely Carmichael (1941–1998) popularized the phrase "Black Power." He was president of the Student Nonviolent Coordinating Committee (SNCC) and had participated with Dr. Martin Luther King Jr. in the March against Fear. The media subsequently juxtaposed the Black Power slogan against King's philosophy of non-violent resistance. Although Carmichael clearly articulated the philosophy of Black Power as political and economic self-sufficiency and self-defense,[45] the white main-stream imagined Black Power as violent and criminal.[46]

Although Carmichael coined the term *Black Power* in 1966,[47] armed self-defense was not a new concept to American blacks. In 1964, Tuscaloosa, Alabama, residents (primarily World War II veterans) organized a gun club and effectively protected themselves against police and Ku Klux Klan violence and intimidation in the wake of a nonviolent protest that went amok.[48] While their defense went relatively unnoticed by the national media and politicians, local whites (particularly the police and the Klan) were shocked that blacks had stepped out of the conventional model of social protest by successfully organizing armed defense groups (and thus were left alone).[49]

Similarly, in 1957, in Monroe, North Carolina, Robert Franklin Williams (1925–1996) organized a rifle club to protect the black community against Baptist evangelist and veteran James Cole (1924–1967) and Klan violence. Cole served as grand dragon of the KKK. Under his leadership, the Klan unleashed a series of rallies that attracted thousands of supporters. Speakers at the rallies employed rhetoric to incite fear of blacks. This incendiary speech resulted in numerous bombings of black homes and schools. Cole and his KKK members decided to target Dr. Albert Perry (1921–1972), a black doctor and veteran who they suspected was providing financial support to the NAACP, of which Perry was vice president in the late 1950s.

As a result, Perry received numerous death threats, which prompted the president of the local chapter of the NAACP, activist Robert Williams, to organize a Black Armed Guard that protected Dr. Perry's house. Williams, a US Army and Marine veteran who also served in leadership roles with the local NAACP, understood the strategic aspects of nonviolent protest. However, Williams was a realist and a pragmatist. He came to the conclusion that the power structure in Monroe would not negotiate and that it was up to black people to protect themselves against white-on-black violence.[50] In October 1957, following a Klan rally, a motorcade attacked Perry's house. However, when they arrived there, the Black Armed Guard returned fire and the Klan members dispersed in shock. This event led the city government of Monroe to ban Klan motorcades.[51] In his book *Negroes with Guns*, Williams spoke forcefully of the need for black people to protect themselves because government was failing them. The rhetoric of the Klan framed blacks as violent people who should be feared, yet as Williams shows, the violence they witnessed came from whites who were able to "practice violence with impunity."[52] When Williams assumed the presidency of the local branch of the NAACP in the late 1950s, he was rejected by the national leaders such as Roy Wilkins, Daisy Bates, and Thurgood Marshall. Moreover, New York governor Nelson Aldrich Rockefeller (1908–1979), seeking to discredit Williams and armed black militancy, addressed delegates at the 1959 NAACP national convention by congratulating them for "rejecting retaliation against terror."[53] Williams continued to practice armed self-defense and published his ideologies in the newspaper he edited, *The Crusader*. This forthrightness caught the attention of people in the mainstream Civil Rights movement, who pitted him against Martin Luther King Jr. Later, Williams and his revolutionary activities also caught the attention of the FBI, which ultimately discredited him as a criminal. He and his family fled the country after Williams was falsely accused of kidnapping in the wake of a 1961 civil rights protest in Monroe that went wrong. The CIA credited Williams for being the ideological leader of the Black Panther Party.[54] *Life* magazine reported that Williams's picture was "prominently displayed in extremist haunts in the big city ghetto."[55]

The vilification of Williams and others who have advocated for armed self-defense represents in many respects the "rebirth" of a nation in which a white mainstream maintains that armed self-defense by African Americans is the same as criminality.

FEAR OF BLACK ELECTED OFFICIALS

Perhaps the most significant legacy of the Reconstruction era was the enfranchisement and unprecedented election of African Americans to public office. From 1865 to 1877, approximately 2,000 African Americans were elected to state and federal office. Moreover, 21 African Americans were elected to the US Congress from 1870 to 1891.[56] Despite these monumental achievements, which created the potential for the nation to reach racial equality, there were groups that engaged in fear mongering in an effort to undermine these achievements. As mentioned earlier, African American elected officials were vilified as incompetent, corrupt, and incapable of self-rule. Many whites held that it was their birthright to rule and govern the Republic. They feared there would be black oppression of whites if African Americans were elected to public office. Furthermore, African Americans, in the eyes of many whites during the Reconstruction era, were viewed as inferior. Some whites even thought that if black people were granted the opportunity to govern, chaos and disaster would result.[57]

Those whites who used political mudslinging and smear campaigns sought to discredit African American elected officials. The media also discredited black elected officials during and after Reconstruction. One Maine journalist of that era, James S. Pike, questioned the behavior of African American elected officials and would go on to blame them (along with the Republican Party) for the failure of Reconstruction.[58]

In addition, political scientist John William Burgess (1844–1931) argued that the federal government made a grave error in enacting Reconstruction policies. Linking black skin with inferiority, Burgess suggested that African Americans derived from a race that had not made any contributions to civilization; thus they should never have been granted enfranchisement and the opportunity to govern.[59] Likewise, politicians such as US senator Benjamin Tillman sought to misrepresent black elected officials as corrupt and greedy. At the 1895 South Carolina Constitutional Convention (which overturned Reconstruction and disenfranchised African Americans), Tillman alleged that "black members of the Reconstruction state legislature had indulged in expensive and needless articles, such as 40 cent spittoons, 25 cent hat pegs, $4 looking glasses, $200 crimson plush sofas, champagne, $6,000 mirrors, in addition to defrauding the people with extravagant printing costs."[60] South Carolina congressman Thomas Miller (1890–1891) responded to Tillman in 1895, providing a more accurate representation of black elected officials during Reconstruction.[61] Miller stated, "We were eight years in power . . . We had built school houses, established charitable institutions, built and maintained the penitentiary system . . . rebuilt bridges, and reestablished the ferries. In short we had reconstructed the state and placed it on the road to prosperity."[62]

Despite political and personal danger, many African American elected officials in federal, state, and local offices made major contributions to this nation, served honorably, and used their influence to challenge white supremacy. In fact, African American elected officials in the state of South Carolina established a universal public school system.[63] Unbeknownst to their enemies, many black elected officials understood the political system and operated within it with diplomacy and effectiveness. For example, South Carolina congressman Joseph Hayne Rainey (1870–1879) supported a poll tax that generated funding that supported public education.[64] Most important, Rainey's first major speech on the floor of Congress addressed Klan and paramilitary terrorism against African Americans and their Republican allies in the South. Unfortunately, the passage of the Ku Klux Klan Act of 1871 was watered down and did not prevent Klan and paramilitary violence. Because of Rainey's outspoken condemnation of racist terrorism, he became a target of the Klan during his tenure in Congress.[65]

The contributions of African American elected officials would remain in the margins of history, overshadowed by racist rhetoric. Misrepresentation of their work was perpetuated by historians, politicians, and the media. In fact, D. W. Griffith's view of history was grounded in the literature of such scholars. The common view of the time was sympathetic to the "Lost Cause" and demonized African Americans and their Republican allies.

What was Griffith's answer to the controversy about racist propaganda in his film? Griffith said, "I gave to my best knowledge the proven facts, and presented the known truth about the Reconstruction period in the America South. These facts are based on an overwhelming compilation of authentic evidence and testimony."[66] His movie offered "proof" to a new generation of viewers that black citizens should not be elected to public office. Instead of pioneering black legislators who were trying to put their states back together after a devastating war, he showed viewers the fictitious character of Silas Lynch, a corrupt African American lieutenant governor in Reconstruction-era South Carolina. In the film, black elected officials are seen desecrating the US political system by passing controversial laws (such as those that permit miscegenation). They are also shown eating watermelon, drinking whiskey, taking off their shoes, and propping their feet up on their desks. Of course, Griffith's film has long been lambasted for its stereotypes. Yet racist propaganda and personal attacks against the nation's first African American president, Barack Hussein Obama, suggest that there are still many Americans who believe black people have no place in this country's government.

THE BLACK BEAST BARACK

On June 3, 2008, Barack Obama (b. 1961) secured enough delegate votes to be announced the presumptive nominee for the presidency on the Democratic Party ticket. One month later the *New Yorker*, a popular national magazine, published a controversial cartoon by Barry Blitt. Blitt depicted the future president as a Muslim in the Oval Office, "fist bumping" the first lady, who is sporting an afro and camouflage military pants while she carries an AK-47 over her shoulder. Her style is reminiscent of the stereotypical image of the female Black Power activist of the 1960s. Behind them is a portrait of Osama bin Laden, while the US flag is burning in the Oval Office's fireplace. This controversial editorial cartoon, known as "The Politics of Fear," brilliantly juxtaposes America's historical record of racism, xenophobia, and nationalism within the context of the twenty-first century. It reflects mainstream Americans' fear of blacks in public office—especially managing the highest office in the land.

In Obama's victory speech in Chicago in November 2008, he addressed the existence of such fears when he stressed that he did not intend to govern by aligning with any particular race or party. Instead, he wanted to be the president of all Americans. One could argue that in spite of the racial discourse and false narratives during the 2008 election, the engagement of young people in the electoral process should have resulted in a de-escalation of racial fear mongering. Yet that phenomenon did not take place. Instead of reducing fears of black public officials as a threat, it seemed that the country was enacting "Rebirth of a Nation," an updated version of the old movie that played on the fear of a black president. Obama won the election. However, he did not secure a majority white electorate.

An examination of the 2012 presidential election results reveals that Republican challenger Mitt Romney (b. 1947) won three out of five white votes. He won among white men and white women. Geographically, Romney did better in the South, but he also won a majority of white voters in forty-six of fifty states. Although Obama was credited with energizing young people to participate in the electoral process, Romney still won a majority of the white vote in every age cohort, including the very youngest.[67]

Law professor Ian Haney-López writes about the concept of "dog whistle politics," which are racially coded messages used by politicians to build on underlying racial tensions. In an interview with journalist Bill Moyers, Haney-López states, "On one level, like a dog whistle, it's silent. Silent about race—it seems race-neutral. But on another, it has a shrill blast, like a dog whistle, that can be heard by certain folks. And what the blast is, is a warning about race and a warning, in particular, about threatening minorities." He notes that some white politicians warn the public about the dangers minorities pose and that whites should fear a federal government that is de-centering whites. Haney-López locates Romney's significant advantage among whites as an example of a "dog whistle" narrative.[68]

Enter the character of Silas Lynch. In *Birth of a Nation*, Lynch (the mulatto leader of the blacks, a "symbol of his race") delivers a pronouncement that blacks shall have full equality. *Birth* then portrays whites being disenfranchised on Election Day. At the polling stations, signs that say "Equality" and "Forty Acres and a Mule" are strategically placed. Blacks vote in overwhelming numbers, win the election, and Lynch is elected lieutenant governor. With the black party in control of the state house, the black politicians are seen triumphantly drinking alcohol and eating fried chicken.

Although this film addresses a larger social issue within a historical time frame, it nevertheless sets the foundation for today's dog whistle narrative about race and race in politics. Who is trustworthy, who is decent, and who is law-abiding? In contrast, who is loathsome, who is diseased, and who is dangerous? The notions persist that blacks prefer welfare to work and that the federal government is using taxpayers' money to pander to blacks so their votes will keep their allies in power. Haney-López explains that while there are different cultural ideas that are expressed in dog whistle terms (such as the idea that Hispanics are dirty or the stereotype that undocumented immigrants breed crime), the primary cultural idea is race: "It's the primary cultural provocation that has been used by conservatives over the last fifty years. Race is special because it does so much damage not only to people of color, but in the way it restructures our society as a whole."[69]

Who is the contemporary representation of the film's Silas Lynch? In *Birth of a Nation*, there was a Black Party celebration, inducing black people to quit work. The implicit message was that black politicians such as Lynch would use taxpayers' money to take care of blacks who were not working. In contemporary America, Obama is called the "food stamp president." The message today is that white Americans should fear a president who takes their hard-earned money and gives it to healthy blacks who could work but choose not to because they are lazy. This construct was reiterated by Tom Coburn (b. 1948), then-senator from Oklahoma, who responded to a question about whether Obama wanted to destroy the United States. Coburn acceded that Obama is bright but that he had created more soci-etal dependency on the government because it had worked for him as a black male. Coburn stressed that this philosophy of dependency drives Obama's views on social policy. Likewise, Romney stated that 47 percent of the people would have voted for the former president (Obama) no matter what and that this percentage included people who are dependent on government, who believe they are victims, and who believe that government has a responsibility to care for them. Haney-López explains Romney's framing of this issue: "It's a dog whistle on one level because he's seeming to use the terms that are typically associated with minorities and he's attaching them to half the country. So in a way, you're getting the poor being racialized. So even when they're white, even when it's half the country, and he's talking about people who don't pay income tax, he's saying, these people are like minorities." Haney-López states that after the election, Romney held a conference call to explain to his major donors why he lost. His analysis was centered on Obama promising "gifts" to poor, young, black, and Hispanic people. Haney-López summarizes this tactic as "racism as a strategy. It's cold, it's calculating, it's considered, it's the decision to achieve one's own ends—here winning votes—by stirring racial animosity. And that's the decision that George Wallace made, that's the decision that Ronald Reagan made, that's the decision that Mitt Romney made. Modern society is structured around race, so race becomes the category through which people do a lot of their automatic thinking. The environment continually tells people that race is relevant."[70]

The contention about societal dependency of blacks generates considerable anxiety among whites and is meant to stoke fear in white taxpayers. *Birth* portrayed Lynch as a traitor who would build himself a throne. Similarly, Obama was framed as setting up an imperial presidency. Media host Glenn Beck (b. 1964) went so far as to say that Obama has a "deep-seated hatred for white people or the white culture."[71] A 2011 Tufts University study by Michael I. Norton and Samuel R. Sommers found that whites see racism as a zero-sum game. Revealed in this study was the public's belief that while discrimination against blacks has decreased, this change has increased discrimination against whites. The study participants believed that whites are now more discriminated against than blacks.[72] According to journalist Paul Rosenberg, "This perception is not simply mistaken, it's downright delusional, flying in the face of mountains of objective data." After an extensive examination of social science data, Rosenberg concluded that blaming blacks for being poor, uneducated, and outside mainstream society remains a consistent narrative—with discrimination left out of that narrative. White privilege is never acknowledged as a factor that stacks the deck against African Americans and other people of color.[73]

THE BLACK BEAST (IS A MUSLIM)

There is an explicit promotion of Christian ideology in *Birth*. For example, film scholar Clyde Taylor (b. 1968) highlights the film's theme of the loss and restoration of Eden, which "rehearses Christian eschatology in national terms." Taylor's analysis of the movie has an apocalyptic dimension, complete with a dark angel (Stoneman), martyrs (soldiers, Lincoln, Flora, and the South), Redeemers (Ben and the Klan), and a New Jerusalem (in the closing sequence). Griffith assumed that his audience would be Christian, so he used Christian symbolism both to evoke distinctions between good and evil and also to illustrate the working out of retributive justice. Griffith clearly viewed the United States as a Christian nation. The audience is meant to identify with the heroic Redeemer figures of the narrative—the Klan, whose symbols include the cross and their pure-white, priest-like robes.[74]

History professor Eric R. Schlereth explains that in the early United States, there were contentions regarding the role of diverse religious beliefs in politics; but eventually a compromise was reached, and "religious conflict became safe for American politics."[75] Was Griffith correct when he considered the country's religion to be Christian? According to former US Associate Supreme Court Justice David Brewer (1837–1910), the nation is Christian. In a college lecture devoted to the question, he asserted that the United States is "classified among the Christian nations of the world. It was so formally declared by the Supreme Court of the United States." (He was referring to the case of *Holy Trinity Church v. United States*, 143 US 471 (1892).) Brewer's lecture was printed in 1905 (around the time of the film). Brewer later clarified that Christianity is not the country's established religion, that its citizens are not compelled to support it, and that Americans are not all Christians or all named Christian. He said the country welcomed people of all religions; furthermore, "a profession of Christianity is not a condition of holding office or otherwise engaging in the public service, or essential to recognition either politically or socially."[76]

Nevertheless, the United States is often referred to as a leading Christian nation, based on its history. As Brewer notes, in 1606, the charter of Virginia vowed to profess the Christian religion. In 1620, the Pilgrims on the *Mayflower* made a compact to advance the Christian faith. The charters of New England, Massachusetts, Connecticut, Rhode Island, Carolina, and Pennsylvania had explicit references to Christianity, Jesus, or God. Brewer stressed that although Vermont's 1777 constitution granted people freedom to worship all forms of religion, Vermont still demanded that everyone observe the Sabbath. He observed, "It is not an exaggeration to say that Christianity in some of its creed was the principal cause of the settlement of many of the colonies, and cooperated with business hopes and purposes in the settlement of the others." In some of the colonies (for example, Maryland), a tax was levied for support of the Christian religion. In addition, the first colleges established in the colonies (Harvard, Yale, and William and Mary) all mentioned God.[77]

Brewer points out that in the US government, "whenever there is a declaration in favor of any religion, it is of the Christian."[78] Mohammad, Confucius, Buddha, and Judaism are not mentioned at government functions. For example, today, at the end of presidential inaugurations, the president is not obliged to say "so help me God" but usually does. In other examples, court witnesses swear their testimony by God, and an immigrant's acceptance of citizenship is an appeal to God. Brewer mentions that the 1890 Census showed that the majority of the organizations and buildings in the country had some connection to the church and that the majority of citizens had some connection to Christianity. Of course, not all citizens are active in a church. Nevertheless, at the turn of the twentieth century, the vast majority of the population still had some connection to Christianity. Thus Brewer maintained that calling the United States *a Christian nation* "is a recognition of a historical, legal, and social truth."[79]

Prior to Brewer, many other historians arrived at the same conclusion. Political economist and attorney Stephen A. Colwell (1800–1872) examined the constitutional provisions, judicial decisions, social bearings, and Christian education in public schools and advised that "it is not safe for Christians to infer that Christianity and Politics have no mutual relations. Ours are Christian political institutions." In 1835, French political analyst Alexis de Tocqueville (1805–1859) observed that for Americans, Christianity and liberty operate in tandem: "There is no country in the world where the Christian religion retains a greater influence over the souls of men than in America; and there can be no greater proof of its utility and of its conformity to human nature than that its influence is powerfully felt over the most enlightened and free nation of the earth . . . The Americans combine the notions of Christianity and of liberty so intimately in their minds that it is impossible to make them conceive [of] the one without the other."[80]

Because religion is political, it is central to the discourse of this chapter. In the 2008 presidential election, fearmongers were able to build panic and hatred around Obama's supposed Islamic religion. It is not that all citizens were Christian, but the majority were. For example, in that year, a Pew survey showed that 78.4 percent of adults followed a form of Christianity. In 2012 (Obama's second election), the Pew Research Center noted that the religious composition of the electorate was similar to that of 2008. During these elections, some of Obama's opponents attempted to plant fear in the voting public by implying (using the aforementioned dog whistle technique) that he is Muslim. The September 11, 2001, attacks in New York City and Washington, DC, had heightened citizens' apprehension about Muslims. The religion had become inseparable with terrorism in many people's minds. British public relations expert Martin A. Parlett (b. 1988) stressed that locating Obama within this Muslim frame was meant to generate profound anxiety among some American voters. In 2014, law professor Ian Haney-López made this observation about racial fear within the political group called the Tea Party: "They're obsessed about Muslims and Islam. And they really see this sort of threatening, this external threat in the form of the Middle East, but also ostensibly an internal threat of Muslims coming into the United States. For example, this is Kansas passing its law that there shan't be Sharia law in the courts of Kansas. Absurd, except that it triggers this racial fear."[81]

So, in comparison, did the public care about Romney's faith, which is Mormon? Not much. Although most Americans know little about the Mormon religion, voters in 2012 said they had limited interest in learning about Romney's faith. The vast majority of those who were aware of his faith said it did not concern them. According to a Pew survey, "Eight-in-ten voters who know Romney is Mormon say they are either comfortable with his faith (60%) or that it doesn't matter to them (21%)." Mormons overwhelming describe themselves as Christian, although half of non-Mormons do not describe them as such. Nearly half of all Mormons polled say they face discrimination because of their Mormon faith and that Americans do not see them as a part of the mainstream.[82]

Social scientist Jeffrey C. Alexander (b. 1947) contends that being successful in US politics is about being a member of the correct religion, class, and race. Although Romney received twice as much religion-related coverage as Obama, 82 percent of Americans said they learned "little or nothing" about the Mormon religion during Romney's presidential campaign. Despite the public's lack of knowledge about Mormonism, the Pew survey showed that public attitudes toward Mormons were positive and that participants surveyed used words such as "good people, honest, and dedicated" to describe Mormons.[83]

During the 2008 election, many Americans were convinced that Obama was Muslim. By July 2012, a Pew survey showed that even more Americans thought he was Muslim than thought so in 2008. One example of this type of thinking is represented by the public statements of Pastor Franklin Graham (b. 1952) in his efforts to create a moral panic that would sway people away from supporting Obama. Graham is a son of Billy Graham (1918–2018), the famous religious mentor of several sitting US presidents. In August 2010 the younger Franklin said, "We're going to see persecution, I believe, in this country, because our president is very sympathetic to Islam . . . because his father was a Muslim, gave him a Muslim name, Barack *Hussein* Obama, his mother married another Muslim man, they moved to Indonesia, he went to Indonesian schools. So, growing up, his frame of reference and his influence as a young man was Islam. It wasn't Christianity, it was Islam." Graham went on to say that Obama had hired Muslims in high-level government positions; as a result, Muslims were influencing America's foreign policy. By February 2012, Franklin did concede to the National Association for the Advancement of Colored People (NAACP) that Obama had said his faith was Christian; but Graham added that Obama's *policies* did not follow God's standards, implying that Obama did not follow biblical scripture.[84]

Because Obama has made it clear that his faith is Christian, why do these fear tactics persist, and who believes them? Journalism professor Barry A. Hollander's 2008 study (published in 2010) explored the factors that could predict who would maintain this misperception. The results showed that political and religious conservative views predicted a belief in Obama as a Muslim. Examples of these tactics abound even beyond presidential campaigns. For example, in 2013, at a Phoenix, Arizona, appearance by Obama, there were signs saying "Impeach the Half-White Muslim." A fall 2014 survey conducted by the Cooperative Congressional Election Study (of Harvard University) showed that 54 percent of Republicans believed Obama is a Muslim (i.e., this is what he believes deep down). In another example, in 2015, former New York mayor Rudy Giuliani (b. 1944) chided Obama for not loving America. Giuliani (who withstood, with his city, the terrorist attacks of 9/11) called into question Obama's foreign policy decisions when confronting terrorists; furthermore, he accused Obama on the one hand of chastising Christianity while on the other hand of refusing to say that some aspects of Islam are barbaric.[85] In 2016, Republican presidential nominee Donald Trump made covert statements regarding Obama being a secret Muslim. In the past, the film *Birth* used the incorporation of Christian symbolism to evoke distinctions between good and evil (which was also white dominance versus greater freedom for black Americans). Likewise, today, people still use religion to portray good and evil. *Birth of a Nation*'s symbolic language of racist fear, supposedly justified by God, has spawned propaganda down to the present day. There are clear links between Griffith's film and the moral panic surrounding Obama's campaign for public office and his presidential tenure in our present era.

CONCLUSION

There are several obstacles to transforming racial discourse. Many scholars contend that it is hard to find one generalized cause of racial conflict because racial feelings tend to be deep-rooted in a society. However, what is clear is that racial conflicts tend to be a result of systemic obstacles. Such conflicts are both state and local, and they require leadership and human agency. The systemic obstacles can be economic, social, and territorial.

Social obstacles are crucial to transforming racial conflict. One of most important social factors to consider is identity. Blacks are fighting to protect what they see as a loss of their identity as a result of continuous violence. They believe their very existence is at stake, and some even see themselves as victims.

During Reconstruction, African Americans were concerned about violence against themselves, their families and friends, and their communities. There was also a higher level of violence committed, threats piling up against a dream of social change that might make their lives less difficult and give them greater access to opportunities such as education, better-paying careers, property ownership, voting rights, and public office. Blacks went to work fearing that they might be lynched. During Obama's tenure and beyond more than a century later, black people are still apprehensive about violence in their communities. They drive to work fearing they will be harmed by police during a traffic stop. They are concerned about substandard schools and poor public service from fire-fighters and police departments in their neighborhoods. They are anxious about structural disenfranchisement at the local, state, and federal levels. What is the basis of their oppression? History professor Charles Pete T. Banner-Haley (b. 1948) defines black people's issues succinctly: "The most tenacious, and many would say most pernicious, is race."[86]

In a 2014 interview Bill Moyers (b. 1934) conducted with social justice advocate Angela Blackwell Glover, she had these insights into the results of racism: "Race has become so embedded, and baked in, that people can walk around feeling that they're not carrying racism in their hearts. But so long as they're okay with disproportionate incarceration, communities being left behind, children given no chance, this continues to be a society that is plagued by the legacy of the continuing impact of racism, right into today."[87]

The breadth of this critique defies easy summary. The existential challenges surrounding the creation of fear around race cannot be divorced from the epistemological and ontological understanding of the history of the United States. Several policies have been put in place to address the legacies of exclusion created by fear. It is clear that while policy prescriptions have "saved" the black community from social, economic, and political exclusion, blacks still lack agency because the cultural de-centering of whiteness and the intellectual unlearning of fear have yet to take place. As a result, the fearful rhetoric in *Birth* persists throughout the presidency of Barack Obama and beyond, although as Pulitzer Prize–winning journalist Nicholas D. Kristof (b. 1959) observed: "Barack Obama's political success could change global perceptions of the United States, redefining the American 'brand' to be less about Guantanamo and more about equality."[88] In the United States as well as in Europe, the notion of a post-racial country as a result of Obama's election was a popular narrative. Sadly, US society is still mired in the message of D. W. Griffith's controversial film.

Today, the world is like a giant sailing ship, facing immediate global problems. All hands are needed on deck. The ship's sails are unfurled. What is ahead—our failure or our success—cannot be known. Whether the world makes headway or not is up to us, the crew. This is no time to be in competition with or fearful of each other. Only with everyone's smarts, working together, can we slice through the rough seas that confront us all.

NOTES

1. Griffith, *The Birth of a Nation.*
2. Stokes, *D. W. Griffith's The Birth of a Nation.*

3. Stokes, *D. W. Griffith's The Birth of a Nation*, 9.

4. Barret, *Shooting the Civil War*, 129

5. "100 Years Later," narrated by Arun Ruth.

6. Dixon, *The Clansman*.

7. Griffith, *The Birth of a Nation*.

8. Stokes, *D. W. Griffith's The Birth of a Nation*, 8–9.

9. Ralls, "The Negro Problem," 55.

10. Kantrowitz, *Ben Tillman*.

11. Dray, *Capitol Men*, 234–244. Also see Emberton, *Beyond Redemption*, 208.

12. Emberton, *Beyond Redemption*.

13. Kantrowitz, *Ben Tillman*, 121.

14. Dixon, *100 Silent Films*, 14; Brown, "The Ku Klux Movement"; Cook, *Secret Political Societies*; Logue, "The Rhetorical Appeals of Whites to Blacks"; Maddex, *The Reconstruction of Edward A. Pollard*; Nolen, *The Negro's Image in the South*.

15. Anti-black political rhetoric by politicians and scholars such as Senator Benjamin Tillman and J. R. Ralls was reinforced by the surge of scientific racist scholarship in the early twentieth century. Lothrop Stoddard's 1920 *The Rising Tide of Color against White World* Supremacy and Madison Grant's 1922 *The Passing of the Great Race* were in line with scientific racism of the day. Both pieces emphasized white supremacy, the need for institutionalized racism, and, most important, the justification for the eugenics movement. D. W. Griffith's The Birth of a Nation reflected the socio-political issues of the day.

16. Stokes, *D. W. Griffith's The Birth of a Nation*, 174.

17. Stokes, *D. W. Griffith's The Birth of a Nation*, 5. Also see "100 Years Later," narrated by Arun Ruth.

18. Stokes, *D. W. Griffith's The Birth of a Nation*, 175–176.

19. Stokes, *D. W. Griffith's The Birth of a Nation*, 227–275.

20. Lenning, "Myth and Fact," 122.

21. Wise, *Between Barack and a Hard Place*.

22. Ward, *Unforgivable Blackness*, 121–126.

23. Romero, "There Are Only White Champions."

24. Feimster, *Southern Horrors*, 4–5; also see Hodes, *White Women, Black Men*.

25. Romero, "There Are Only White Champions," 31.

26. Runstedtler, *Jack Johnson*.

27. Guzman and Jones, *Negro Yearbook for 1952*, 275–279.

28. Perloff, "The Press and Lynchings of African Americans," 316–321.

29. Perloff, "The Press and Lynchings of African Americans," 326.

30. Madison, *A Lynching in the Heartland*.

31. Boyle, "The Kiss," 496–517.

32. Boyle, "The Kiss," 496–517.

33. Boyle, "The Kiss," 496–497.

34. *Brown v. Board of Education of Topeka*, 347 US 483, 1954.

35. Boyle, "The Kiss," 520.

36. Emberton, *Beyond Redemption*, 149.

37. Emberton, Beyod Redemption, 149–150.

38. Nye quoted in Emberton, Beyod Redemption, 153.

39. Emberton, Beyod Redemption, 198–202.

40. Stokes, *D. W. Griffith's The Birth of a Nation*, 209.

41. Howell, *Still the Arena of Civil War*, 19.

42. Barnes and Connolly, "Repression, the Judicial System, and Political Opportunities," 331.

43. Keith, *The Colfax Massacre*.

44. Emberton, *Beyond Redemption*, 150.

45. Chunnu-Brayda and Boyce, "Fear Factor," 60. Also see Blue and Murphee, "Stoke the Joke"; Lewis, *The Shadows of Youth*, 210.

46. Jeffries, *Bloody Lowndes*, 189.

47. Hamilton and Carmichael, *Black Power*.

48. Wendt, "God, Gandhi, and Guns."

49. Wendt, "God, Gandhi, and Guns," 47.

50. Dickson and Roberts, *Negroes with Guns*.

51. Dickson and Roberts, Negroes with Guns.

52. Williams, *Negroes with Guns*.

53. Tyson, "Robert F. Williams," 558.

54. Tyson, "Robert F. Williams," 559–567. Also see Dickson and Roberts, *Negroes with Guns*.

55. Quoted in Tyson, "Robert F. Williams," 566.

56. Lynch, "Introduction," xx.

57. Dean and Smith, *Reconstruction*.

58. Quoted in Lynch, "Introduction," xix.

59. Burgess, *Reconstruction and the Constitution*, 133.

60. Quoted in Dray, *Capitol Men*, 339–340.

61. Hahn, *A Nation under Our Feet*, 448.

62. Quoted in Hahn, A Nation under Our Feet, 448. Also see Boyce and Chunnu-Brayda, "I Shall Not Be Muffled Here."

63. Du Bois, *Black Reconstruction*.

64. Kladky, "Joseph Hayne Rainey," 137.

65. Kladky, "Joseph Hayne Rainey," 139–140.

66. Barret, *Shooting the Civil War*, 130–131.

67. Gallup, US Presidential Election Center.

68. Haney-López, *Dog Whistle Politics*, "The Dog Whistle Politics of Race."

69. Haney-López, *Dog Whistle Politics*.

70. Krehbiel, "Coburn Says Obama Not Out to Destroy Country"; Corn, "Secret Video"; Haney-López, *Dog Whistle Politics*.

71. Beck, "FOX and Friends."

72. Norton and Sommers, "Whites See Racism as a Zero-Sum Game."

73. Rosenberg, "It Is All Still about Race"; Loury, "Social Exclusion and Ethnic Groups," 18.

74. Taylor, "The Rebirth of the Aesthetic."

75. Schlereth, *An Age of Infidels*.

76. Brewer, *The United States*.

77. Schlereth, *An Age of Infidels*, 2; Brewer, *The United States*, 11, 12, 14, 18, 19 (quotation), 22, 20.

78. Brewer, *The United States*, 32.

79. Brewer, *The United States*, 46.

80. Brewer, *The United States*, 32, 37; Colwell, *The Position of Christianity,* 75; de Tocqueville, *Democracy in America,* vol. 1, chapter 17, Section "Indirect Influence of Religious Opinions," 308.

81. Pew Forum on Religion and Public Life, "US Religious Landscape Survey," 10; Parlett, *Demonizing a President*; Haney-López, *Dog Whistle Politics*.

82. Pew Forum, "Little Voter Discomfort."

83. Alexander, *The Performance of Politics*, xiii; Pew Forum, "Little Voter Discomfort."

84. Pew Forum, "Little Voter Discomfort"; Tashman, "Franklin Graham"; NAACP, "Franklin Graham Response."

85. Hollander, "Persistence in the Perception of Barack Obama," 55; Wang, "Obama Protesters Sing"; Samuelsohn, "Rudy Giuliani"; Alex Theodoridis, "Poll on Obama's Religion." The survey was part of the 2014 Cooperative Congressional Election Study by Harvard University, conducted by the survey firm YouGov in October and November. The sample size for this particular question about Obama's religion was 1,000. Respondents were interviewed online. http://projects.iq.harvard.edu/cces/home.

86. Banner-Haley, *From Du Bois to Obama*, 2.

87. Glover, "Is America a Post Racial Society?"

88. Kristof, "Rebranding the US with Obama."

BIBLIOGRAPHY

Alexander, Jeffery C. *The Performance of Politics: Obama's Victory and the Democratic Struggle for Power*. New York: Oxford University Press, 2010.

Ayers, Edward. *The Promise of the New South: Life after Reconstruction*. New York: Oxford University Press, 2007.

Banner-Haley, Charles Pete T. *From Du Bois to Obama: African American Intellectuals in the Public Forum*. Carbondale: Southern Illinois University Press, 2010.

Barnes, Donna A., and Catherine Connolly. "Repression, the Judicial System, and Political Opportunities for Civil Rights Advocacy during Reconstruction." *Sociological Quarterly* 40, no. 2 (Spring 1999): 327–345.

Barret, Jenny. *Shooting the Civil War: Cinema, History, and American National Identity*. London: I. B. Tauris, 2009.

Beck, Glenn. "FOX and Friends." *Fox News*, July 28, 2009. https://www.youtube.com /watch?v=MIZDnpPafaA.

Blue, Mary, and Vanessa Murphee. "'Stoke the Joke' and His 'Self-Appointed Critics': A Clash of Values on Network Television News, 1966–70." *Media History* 15, no. 2 (2009): 205–220.

Boyce, Travis D., and Winsome Chunnu-Brayda. "'I Shall Not Be Muffled Here': Thomas E. Miller, the Lost African American Congressman, 1890–1891." In *Before Obama: A Reappraisal of Black Reconstruction Era Politicians*, vol. 2: *Black Reconstruction Era Politicians: The Fifteenth Amendment in Flesh and Blood*, ed. Matthew Lynch, 265–283. Santa Barbara, CA: ABC-CLIO, 2012.

Boyle, Kevin. "The Kiss: Racial and Gender Conflict in a 1950s Automobile Factory." *Journal of American History* 84, no. 2 (September 1997): 496–523.

Brewer, D. J. *The United States, a Christian Nation*. Philadelphia: John C. Winston, 1905. https://archive.org/details/unitedstateschri00brew.

Brown, William G. "The Ku Klux Movement." *Atlantic Monthly* 87 (1901): 634–644.

Burgess, John William. *Reconstruction and the Constitution, 1866–1876*. New York: Charles Scribner's Sons, 1902.

Chunnu-Brayda, Winsome, and Travis D. Boyce. "Fear Factor: When Black Equality Is Viewed as Militant." In *Documenting the Black Experience: Essays on African American History, Culture, and Identity in Nonfiction Films*, ed. Novotny Lawrence, 57–72. Jefferson, NC: McFarland, 2014.

Colwell, Stephen A. *The Position of Christianity in the United States, in Its Relations with Our Political Institutions, and Specifically with Reference to Religious Instructions in the Public Schools*. Philadelphia, PA: Lippincott, Grambo, 1854. http://www.ebooksread .com/authors-eng/stephen-colwell/the-position-of-christianity-in-the-united-states-in -its-relations-with-our-pol-wlo.shtml.

Cook, Walter Henry. *Secret Political Societies in the South during the Period of Reconstruction: An Address before the Faculty of Friends*. Cleveland, OH: Western Reserve University, 1914.

Corn, David. "Secret Video: Romney Tells Millionaire Donors What He REALLY Thinks of Obama Voters." *Mother Jones*, September 17, 2012. http://www.motherjones.com /politics/2012/09/secret-video-romney-private-fundraiser.

Dean, Elizabeth, and Llewellyn Smith, directors/producers. *Reconstruction: The Second Civil War*. Hollywood, CA: PBS Home Video, 2004. DVD.

de Tocqueville, Alexis. *De la Démocratie en Amérique [Democracy in America]*, vol. 1, trans. Henry Reeve. London: Saunders and Otley, 1835. Revised printing, trans. Henry Reeve. New York: Colonial Press, 1899.

Dickson, Sandra, and Churchill Roberts, directors. *Negroes with Guns: Rob Williams and Black Power*. South Burlington, VT: California Newsreel, 2005. DVD.

Dixon, Bryony. *100 Silent Films*. London, United Kingdom: Palgrave Macmillan, 2011.

Dixon, Thomas F., Jr. *The Clansman: An Historical Romance of the Ku Klux Klan*. Part one of a trilogy, illus. Arthur I. Keller (Arthur Ignatius). New York: Doubleday, Page, 1905. http://docsouth.unc.edu/southlit/dixonclan/.

Dray, Phillip. *Capitol Men: The Epic Story of Reconstruction through the Lives of the First Black Congressmen*. Boston: Houghton Mifflin, 2008.

Du Bois, W.E.B. *Black Reconstruction: An Essay toward History of the Part Which Black Folk Played in the Attempt to Reconstruct Democracy in America, 1860–1880*. New York: Harcourt, 1935.

Emberton, Carole. *Beyond Redemption: Race, Violence, and the American South after the American Civil War*. Chicago: University of Chicago Press, 2013.

Feimster, Crystal N. *Southern Horrors: Women and the Politics of Rape and Lynching*. Cambridge, MA: Harvard University Press, 2009.

Gallup. US Presidential Election Center. http://www.gallup.com/poll/154559/us -presidential-election-center.aspx.

Glover, Angela Blackwell. "Is America a Post Racial Society?" Moyers and Company, March 6, 2014. http://billmoyers.com/2014/03/06/is-america-a-post-racial-society/.

Griffith, D. W., director. *The Birth of a Nation*, 1915. New York: Kino on Video, 2002. DVD.

Guzman, Jessie Parkhurst, and Lewis Ward Jones, eds. *Negro Yearbook for 1952*. Tuskegee, AL: Wm. H. Wise 1952. Modern ed. Whitefish, MT: Literary Licensing, 2012.

Hahn, Steve. *A Nation under Our Feet: Black Political Struggles in the Rural South from Slavery to the Great Migration*. Cambridge, MA: Belknap Press of Harvard University Press, 2003.

Hamilton, Charles V., and Stokely Carmichael. *Black Power, the Politics of Liberation in America*. New York: Random House, 1967.

Haney-López, Ian. *Dog Whistle Politics: How Coded Racial Appeals Have Wrecked the Middle Class*. Oxford: Oxford University Press, 2014.

Haney-López, Ian. "The Dog Whistle Politics of Race, Part I." Moyers and Company, February 28, 2014. http://billmoyers.com/episode/ian-haney-lopez-on-the-dog-whistle-politics-of-race/.

Hine, William C. "Civil Rights and Campus Wrongs: South Carolina State College Students Protest, 1955–1968." *South Carolina Historical Magazine* 97 (October 1996): 310–331.

Hodes, Martha. *White Women, Black Men: Illicit Sex in the 19th-Century South*. New Haven, CT: Yale University Press, 1997.

Hollander, Barry A. "Persistence in the Perception of Barack Obama as a Muslim in the 2008 Campaign." *Journal of Media and Religion* 9, no. 2 (2010): 55–66.

Howell, Kenneth W. *Still the Arena of Civil War: Violence and Turmoil in Reconstruction Texas, 1865–1874*. Denton: University of North Texas Press, 2012.

Jeffries, Hasan K. *Bloody Lowndes: Civil Rights and Black Power in Alabama's Black Belt*. New York: New York University Press, 2009.

Kantrowitz, Stephen. *Ben Tillman and the Reconstruction of White Supremacy*. Chapel Hill: University of North Carolina Press, 2000.

Keith, LeeAnna. *The Colfax Massacre: The Untold Story of Black Power, White Terror, and the Death of Reconstruction*. New York: Oxford University Press, 2008.

Kladky, William P. "Joseph Hayne Rainey and the Beginnings of Black Political Authority." In *Before Obama: A Reappraisal of Black Reconstruction Era Politicians*, vol. 2: *Black Reconstruction Era Politicians: The Fifteenth Amendment in Flesh and Blood*, ed. Matthew Lynch, 123–157. Santa Barbara, CA: ABC-CLIO, 2012.

Krehbiel, Randy. "Coburn Says Obama Not Out to Destroy Country." *Tulsa World*. August 17, 2011. http://www.tulsaworld.com/archives/coburn-says-obama-not-out-to-destroy-country/article_935045bc-3f66-5d8a-929c-dd66dcc09f00.html.

Kristof, Nicholas. "Rebranding the US with Obama." *New York Times*, October 22, 2008. http://www.nytimes.com/2008/10/23/opinion/23kristof.html?_r=0.

Lenning, Arthur. "Myth and Fact: The Reception of *The Birth of a Nation*." *Film History* 16, no. 4 (2004): 117–141.

Lewis, Andrew B. *The Shadows of Youth: The Remarkable Journey of the Civil Rights Generation*. New York: Hill and Wang, 2009.

Logue, Cal M. "The Rhetorical Appeals of Whites to Blacks during Reconstruction." *Communications Monographs* 44, no. 3 (August 1977): 241–251.

Loury, Glenn C. "Social Exclusion and Ethnic Groups: The Challenge to Economics." Boston: Boston University, 2000. http://www.bu.edu/irsd/files/social_exclusion.pdf.

Lynch, Matthew. "Introduction." In *Before Obama: A Reappraisal of Black Reconstruction Era Politicians*, vol. 2: *Black Reconstruction Era Politicians: The Fifteenth Amendment in Flesh and Blood*, ed. Matthew Lynch, xix–xxviii. Santa Barbara, CA: ABC-CLIO, 2012.

Maddex, Jack P., Jr. *The Reconstruction of Edward A. Pollard: A Rebel's Conversion to Postbellum Unionism*. Chapel Hill: University of North Carolina Press, 1974.

Madison, James H. *A Lynching in the Heartland: Race and Memory in America*. New York: Palgrave Macmillan, 2003.

NAACP. "Franklin Graham Response to NAACP Faith Leaders." NAACP, February 28, 2012. http://www.naacp.org/pages/franklin-graham-response-to-naacp-faith-leaders.

Newton, Michael. *White Robes and Burning Crosses: A History of the Ku Klux Klan from 1866*. Jefferson, NC: McFarland, 2014.

Nolen, Claude H. *The Negro's Image in the South: The Anatomy of White Supremacy*. Lexington: University of Kentucky Press, 1967.

Norton, Michael I., and Samuel R. Sommers. "Whites See Racism as a Zero-Sum Game That They Are Now Losing." *Perspectives on Psychological Science* 6 (2011): 215–218. doi: 10.1177/1745691611406922. http://ase.tufts.edu/psychology/sommerslab/documents /raceinternortonsommers2011.pdf, and http://pps.sagepub.com/content/6/3/215.

"100 Years Later, What's the Legacy of *Birth of a Nation*?" Arun Ruth, narrator. *All Things Considered*. National Public Radio, February 8, 2015. http://www.npr.org/blogs /codeswitch/2015/02/08/383279630/100-years-later-whats-the-legacy-of-birth-of-a -nation.

Parlett, Martin A. *Demonizing a President*. Santa Barbara, CA: Praeger, 2014.

Perloff, Richard M. "The Press and Lynchings of African Americans." *Journal of Black Studies* 30, no. 3 (January 2000): 316–330.

Pew Forum. "Little Voter Discomfort with Romney's Mormon Religion." July 26, 2012. http://www.pewforum.org/2012/07/26/2012-romney-mormonism-obamas-religion/.

Pew Forum on Religion and Public Life. "US Religious Landscape Survey, Religious Affiliation: Diverse and Dynamic." February 2008, 10. http://religions.pewforum.org /pdf/report-religious-landscape-study-full.pdf.

Ralls, J. R. "The Negro Problem. An Essay on the Industrial, Political, and Moral Aspects of the Negro Race in the Southern States as Presented under the Late Amendments to the Federal Constitution." Atlanta: James P. Harrison, 1877. Reprinted in *Racist Southern Paternalism*, ed. John David Smith. New York: Garland, 1993. http://babel .hathitrust.org/cgi/pt?id=nc01.ark:/13960/t48p6j64s;view=1up;seq=5.

Romero, Francie Sanders. "'There Are Only White Champions': The Rise and Demise of Segregated Boxing in Texas." *Southwestern Historical Quarterly* 108, no. 1 (July 2004): 27–34.

Rosenberg, Paul. "It Is All Still about Race: Obama Hatred, the South, and the Truth about GOP Wins." *Salon*, November 4, 2014. http://www.salon.com/2014/11/04/it_is _all_still_about_race_obama_hatred_the_south_and_the_truth_about_gop_wins/.

Runstedtler, Theresa. *Jack Johnson, Rebel Sojourner*. Oakland: University of California Press, 2013.

Samuelsohn, Darren. "Rudy Giuliani: President Obama Doesn't Love America; the Former New York Mayor Makes His Remarks at a Scott Walker Event." *Politico*, February 18, 2015. http://www.politico.com/story/2015/02/rudy-giuliani-president -obama-doesnt-love-america-115309.html.

Schlereth, Eric R. *An Age of Infidels: The Politics of Religious Controversy in the Early United States*. Philadelphia: University of Pennsylvania Press, 2013.

Shuler, Jack. *Blood and Bone: Truth and Reconciliation in a Southern Town*. Columbia: University of South Carolina Press, 2012.

Stokes, Melvyn. *D. W. Griffith's The Birth of a Nation: A History of the Most Controversial Motion Picture of All Time*. New York: Oxford University Press, 2007.

Tashman, Brian. "Franklin Graham: Muslims Who 'Hate Israel and Hate Christians' Run the White House." *Right Wing Watch*, March 2, 2015. http://www.rightwingwatch.org /content/franklin-graham-muslims-who-hate-israel-and-hate-christians-run-white -house.

Taylor, Clyde. "The Rebirth of the Aesthetic." In *The Birth of Whiteness: Race and the Emergence of US Cinema*, ed. Daniel Bernardi, 15–37. New Brunswick, NJ: Rutgers University Press, 1996.

Theodoridis, Alex. "Poll on Obama's Religion." 2014 Cooperative Congressional Election Study by Harvard University. Survey firm YouGov. October and November 2014. http://projects.iq.harvard.edu/cces/home.

Tyson, Timothy B. "Robert F. Williams, 'Black Power,' and the Roots of the African American Freedom Struggle." *Journal of African American History* 85, no. 2 (September 1998): 540–570.

Wang, Nick. "Obama Protesters Sing 'Bye Bye Black Sheep,' Rail against 'Half-White Muslim' in Arizona." *Huffington Post*, August 7, 2013. http://www.huffingtonpost.com /2013/08/07/obama-protesters-arizona_n_3719050.html.

Ward, Geoffrey C. *Unforgivable Blackness: The Rise and Fall of Jack Johnson*. New York: A. A. Knopf, 2004.

Wendt, Simon. "God, Gandhi, and Guns: The African American Freedom Struggle in Tuscaloosa, Alabama, 1964–1965." *Journal of African American History* 80, no. 1 (Winter 2004): 36–56.

Wiggins, William H. "Boxing's Sambo Twins: Racial Stereotypes in Jack Johnson and Joe Louis Newspaper Cartoons, 1908–1938." *Journal of Sport History* 15, no. 3 (Winter 1988): 242–254.

Williams, Robert F. *Negroes with Guns*. Detroit: Wayne State University Press, 1998 (reprint).

Wise, Tim. *Between Barack and a Hard Place: Racism and White Denial in the Age of Obama*. San Francisco: City Lights Books, 2009.

How Fear, Once Created and Spread,
Is Used for Political Ends

8

A Pharmacological Gulf of Tonkin

The Myth of the Addicted Army in Vietnam and the Fear of a Junkie Veteran

Łukasz Kamieński

Psychopharmacology has fueled war and sustained soldiers in combat in remarkable ways. Although drug addiction among soldiers returning home from wars has been limited to a minimum of cases, sensationalized myths of large numbers of drug-addicted veterans who might present a threat to society upon their return have been disseminated in some notable instances. These myths have been used in efforts to enact both anti-drug regulations that apply to the military and anti-drug laws that apply to society.

Throughout the centuries, psychoactive substances have been used in war for two general purposes. First, drugs have been "prescribed" to soldiers by military authorities for improving fighting effectiveness. Stimulants (such as amphetamines and cocaine) have been issued by troops, prior to battle or during fighting, to enhance combat performance. These drugs—by improving stamina, empowering the body, increasing alertness, and boosting fighting spirit—have been significant force multipliers. Sedatives, such as alcohol, marijuana, and opiates, have been administered after the actual fighting to cure or prevent the effects of war from damaging soldiers' psyches. Because combat trauma might make soldiers less fit for future fighting, downers helped calm their shattered nerves. Second, drugs have been self-prescribed by combatants. Men-at-arms have always taken various intoxicants recreationally, both stimulants and depressants. Although not officially approved, such unauthorized self-medication was often accepted so long as it did not affect combat effectiveness, unit cohesion, and troop morale.

DOI: 10.5876/9781646420025.c008

The following examples illustrate how battlefield intoxicants have been both perennial and universal. In Greek civilization, opium was commonplace. In the *Odyssey*, Homer describes how grief over the loss of companions in the Trojan War was alleviated by *nepenthe*, or the "drink of oblivion"—a mixture of wine and opium.[1] The warriors of the Siberian tribes of Chukchi, Kamchadals, Khanty, Koryaks, and Yakuts traditionally used *Amanita muscaria*, a mushroom also known as "fly agaric," which has both hallucinogenic and stimulating effects. Legends say that the people who consumed the fungus were fierce and brutal "mushroom warriors." The use of *Amanita muscaria* in combat was not, however, limited to Siberia. During the war between Sweden and Norway in 1814, some Swedish soldiers got high on it and fought in "a raging madness, foaming at the mouth."[2] From about the 1620s, the Rajputs, members of a Hindu warrior class, were regular opium eaters. Moderate use of opium in India was assumed to be essential for good combat.[3] Conversely, in nineteenth-century China, the uncontrolled consumption of opium led to the deterioration of the armed forces. Approximately 70 percent of soldiers there were addicts. Thus the Chinese Army was unable to defend the country against the flow of opium in the Opium Wars of 1839–1842 and 1856–1860. To take another example, during the Anglo-Zulu War of 1879, the British were astonished by the bravery and fearlessness of the enemy. But traditional bellicosity apart, the Zulus had been fortified with herbal stimulants, mainly *dagga*, a South African variety of *Cannabis*.[4] West African peoples, in turn, consumed mildly stimulating cola nuts, which contain caffeine and theobromine. Or take the case of the Andean tribes who chewed coca leaves, a mild stimulant that enhanced their combat performance. World War I brought cocaine, derived from coca leaves, to the frontline. Soldiers were not only issued the drug to enhance their performance but also took it recreationally to calm their nerves. Inevitably, the war left hundreds of thousands of veterans addicted to cocaine.

The drug of choice during World War II was amphetamines.[5] The German blitzkrieg was significantly fueled by a methamphetamine "attack pill" called Pervitin. From 1939 to 1945, the Wehrmacht soldiers were issued 200 million meth pills. Great Britain, the United States, and Japan followed suit by providing amphetamines to their troops. It is estimated that British soldiers consumed 72 million Benzedrine tablets and that American troops used between 250 million and 500 million Benzedrine pills during the war. The Japanese Army regularly administered methamphetamine to its soldiers for the purpose of "boosting fighting spirit." During the Korean War (1950–1953), the administration of dextroamphetamine (Dexedrine) to American troops became commonplace. Servicemen were also given amphetamine injections and had access to methamphetamine. Soldiers self-prescribed intoxicants, too. After soldiers discovered that heroin increases the effects of amphetamine, they began injecting a mixture of the two drugs known as *speedballs*, though today the term is used to describe the mix of heroin and cocaine.[6]

What the majority of the aforementioned examples illustrate is that most of the effects of psychoactive substances, especially stimulants, have been highly desired for increasing military effectiveness. These substances have helped provide what every military organization has tried to achieve through training, in that stimulants enhanced performance, reduced stress, eliminated hunger, fueled courage, induced numbness, and boosted morale. Most important, many intoxicants and their cocktails produced the majority of these effects all at once. Because these drugs enable better training and better fighting, combatants have eagerly used them.

However, as history reveals, the military use of drugs has often led to substance dependency. And at times, politicians, mass media, and anti-drug activists have constructed an intimidating image of addicted returning soldiers as ferocious "others" who would spread narcotic epidemics and threaten the social order. This atmosphere of fear sometimes led to the rise of moral panics, which were often used instrumentally by policymakers in their efforts to enact national anti-narcotic measures.

Throughout American history, substance dependence and its associated dangers have been traditionally linked to the category of the *stranger*: a foreigner, an immigrant, or a member of an ethnic minority group. Drugs have been connected with a specific other. Thus a fear of opium smoking in the United States has been associated with Chinese immigrants. A fear of cocaine, which was used in the South by black workers who commonly used the drug to help themselves perform hard work in ports, at construction sites, and so forth, has been associated with black workers. A fear of marijuana brought by immigrants from Mexico has been associated with Mexican immigrants. In sum, American attitudes toward illegal drugs and the discourse on the threats the drugs pose to traditional white society have been shaped largely through the prism of the stranger.[7]

This chapter looks at one of the cases of "othering" through the creation of a moral panic over the issue of drugs: American soldiers who served in the Vietnam War were stigmatized as strangers for being excessive drug users. In the early 1970s, heroin was closely associated with a new type of other—a returning Vietnam soldier who was a junkie. The fear of addicted veterans was used by the Nixon administration to help justify launching a war on drugs in 1971. The construct of a junkie veteran, embodied as an "other" who poses a considerable threat to society, had been used before by other governments in their drives to enforce specific drug-control regimes. One such example is the "cocaine panic" generated by mass media and politicians in Great Britain during World War I. People assumed that cocaine used by British soldiers had been supplied by Germany, not only to harm the combat effectiveness of British troops but also to undermine the British Empire. A national

sense of fear led to the passing of the Defense of the Realm Act of 1916, which introduced anti-narcotics regulations in the army that were later extended to the entire
nation under the Dangerous Drugs Act of 1920.

THE NARCOTIC "CONDITION" IN VIETNAM

The Vietnam War (1954–1975) is sometimes referred to as the first "pharmacological war" because the consumption of psychoactive substances by American military
personnel reached alarming proportions. According to the Department of Defense
(DOD), in 1968, as many as half of American men deployed in Vietnam took some
kind of illicit drug. In 1970, this rate increased to 60 percent; in 1973, the year of
the US withdrawal from the war, 70 percent of soldiers there used narcotics. In 1971,
50.9 percent smoked marijuana; 28.5 percent took hard narcotics, mostly heroin
and opium; and 30.8 percent used psychedelic drugs.[8] These disturbing statistics
gave rise to the widespread premise that the majority of American servicemen in
Indochina were habitual users.

Egil Krogh Jr. was President Richard Nixon's liaison to the Bureau of Narcotics
and Dangerous Drugs. On Krogh's return from a fact-finding trip to Vietnam, he
reported, "Mr. President, you don't have a drug problem in Vietnam; you have a
condition. Problems are things we can get right on and solve. Conditions we have
to ameliorate as best we can. I don't think we can solve this short of bringing everybody home."[9] Conditions cannot be tackled and resolved like problems; rather, they
must be managed. This chapter will examine how this narcotic "condition" came
about, explore the measures employed to treat it, and consider the consequences of
"bringing everybody home" with the gradual American withdrawal from Vietnam.

DRUGS PRESCRIBED BY THE MILITARY

The history of massive pill popping by American troops dates back to World
War II, when soldiers might have used as many as 500 million amphetamine pills.[10]
However, the regular prescription of uppers was authorized only during the Korean
War, when the administration of dextroamphetamine became commonplace.
Hence, to enhance soldiers' wakefulness and performance in Vietnam, the military
issued amphetamine stimulants, also known as *speed*. Elton Manzione, a member
of a long-range reconnaissance platoon (known as a Lurp), revealed that "we had
the best amphetamines available and they were supplied by the US government."
He also quoted a US Navy commando: "When I was a SEAL team member in
Vietnam, the drugs were routinely consumed. They gave you a sense of bravado
as well as keeping you awake."[11] Pills were usually distributed to men leaving on

long-range reconnaissance missions and ambushes. The opening lines of *Dispatches*, the acclaimed book by Michael Herr, a war correspondent for *Esquire* magazine, bring this out superbly: "Going out at night the medics gave you pills. Dexedrine breath like dead snakes kept too long in a jar."[12]

Because amphetamines were issued, as one veteran put it, "like candies," with no attention given to recommended dose or frequency of administration, American troops consumed a massive amount of speed. In 1971, a report by the House Select Committee on Crime revealed that from 1966 to 1969, the US armed forces used 225 million tablets.[13] Statistically, consumption averaged thirty or forty 5 mg Dexedrine pills per fighting man per year.[14] A study revealed that 3.2 percent of soldiers arriving in Vietnam were heavy amphetamine users; after one year "in country," this rate increased to 5.2 percent.[15] Further studies revealed that 7 percent of servicemen were heavy amphetamine abusers. In summary, the administration of drugs by the military contributed to the spread of the amphetamine habit.

Drugs were issued not only for boosting soldiers' performance but also to reduce the harmful impact of combat on their psyches. To prevent soldiers' mental breakdowns and suffering from war traumas, the DOD employed sedatives and neuroleptics. For the first time in military history, the prescription of potent antipsychotic drugs became routine. By and large, Vietnam was "the first war in which the forces of modern pharmacology were directed to empower the battlefield soldier."[16]

DRUGS SELF-PRESCRIBED BY SOLDIERS

What made Vietnam the first pharmacological war was not only the official administration of psychoactive substances but, most of all, the prevalence of self-medication by soldiers. The unauthorized use of drugs is often described in Vietnam War literature. Take, for example, Tim O'Brien's fictional story, "The Lives of the Dead": "Ted Lavender had a habit of popping four or five tranquilizers every morning. It was his way of coping, just dealing with the realities, and the drugs helped to ease him through the days."[17] Michael Herr reported an account of a Lurp "who took his pills by the fistful, downs from the left pocket of his tiger suit and ups from the right, one to cut the trail for him and the other to send him down it."[18] Such pharmacological cocktails of downers and uppers both calmed the soldiers and sharpened their senses.

Anything that would help mitigate the consequences of being in Vietnam could be taken for self-medication. Table 8.1 shows the most popular self-prescribed drugs. Alcohol was the most common intoxicant, followed by marijuana, opium, heroin, amphetamines, and barbiturates. Other popular drugs used by servicemen included morphine (popular among medics) and hallucinogens (mostly LSD).

TABLE 8.1. The most common drugs used by American servicemen in Vietnam*

	Percentage reporting use (%)
Alcohol	92
Marijuana	69†
Opium	38
Heroin	34
Amphetamines	25
Barbiturates	23

* Based on interviews, general sample = 451.
† Estimated.
Source: Robins, *The Vietnam Drug User Returns: Final Report*, 29.

Marijuana was the most common non-alcoholic drug. It was ridiculously cheap, as a carton of ready-made marijuana cigarettes could be purchased for five dollars or exchanged for a pack of American cigarettes. Marijuana was also easily available, as a military psychiatrist affirmed: "The drug is everywhere. All a person has to do to get the drug in any village hamlet or town is say the word Khan Sa."[19] In short, Vietnam was a paradise of psychoactive substances, with almost any intoxicant available at one's fingertips.

ANTI-NARCOTIC MEASURES

At first, the army ignored the widespread use of marijuana in its ranks. In 1968, however, after a number of alarming media reports presented marijuana use as a plague that was debilitating American troops in Vietnam, action was taken. Educational programs were introduced in the forms of compulsory lectures, radio broadcasts, pamphlets, and so forth, informing troops of marijuana's harmful and habit-forming effects. When these efforts proved ineffective, the army undertook more penitentiary actions, which were also doomed to failure. In 1969, it was estimated that 30 percent of soldiers had smoked marijuana prior to their departures to Vietnam; after being deployed in Vietnam, 60 percent of men did so.[20] A DOD-commissioned survey revealed that in 1971, almost 51 percent of army personnel in Vietnam used marijuana.[21] The army's more restrictive policy on marijuana had a serious unintended consequence: heroin use among soldiers quickly gained popularity. It was soon realized that marijuana, which would remain the more popular drug of choice, was not a problem at all.

Numerous laboratories in Vietnam produced cheap and powerful heroin of 94–98 percent purity in a smokable form known as *white snow*. These laboratories flooded the country with the "white junk" to meet the rising demand of US troops.[22] The remarkable purity of this heroin, which enabled its oral ingestion instead of intravenous application, made it an extremely attractive drug of choice among soldiers. They smoked it like cigarettes, mixed it with tobacco or marijuana, inhaled its heated fumes, or snorted it like cocaine.[23] Unlike marijuana, the use of odorless heroin was hard to detect without urine tests or blood samples. Some soldiers did not even bother to hide their habits, which were, at times, almost as common and ordinary as puffing cigarettes. Taking illicit drugs became so overt an activity that soldiers (dubbed GIs) engraved their Zippo lighters with sayings such as "Say Hi! If you're high."[24]

Approximately 79 percent of all soldiers who tried any narcotic in Vietnam used heroin.[25] In the spring of 1971, military doctors estimated that 25,000 to 37,000 soldiers, or 10 percent to 15 percent of troops in Vietnam, were addicted to heroin. In some units, almost 20 percent of troops were addicted to the drug. Surveys and studies showed that 85 percent of all American servicemen in Vietnam had been offered heroin; of these servicemen, 35 percent tried heroin and 19 percent became habitual users.[26] In 1973, the DOD confirmed that about one third of soldiers used heroin and 20 percent became habitual users.[27] In the final stages of the war, the use of drugs was omnipresent; on some bases the problem was so severe that commanders allowed prostitutes to go to soldiers' barracks, with the goal of deterring soldiers from going to downtown brothels where they usually got supplied with dope.[28]

THE MYTH OF THE ADDICTED ARMY

The drug problem gave rise to the myth of a weak, degenerated, and addicted US Army in Vietnam. According to one widespread view, narcotics had made soldiers unfit for combat, hampered units' fighting power, broken down military discipline, destroyed troops' morale, and resulted in the collapse of the entire war effort. A popular myth of the "junkie army," which was persistently reinforced by gloomy press reports and politicians' public statements, implied that drugs and addiction were among the main reasons for the US inability to win the war.

Myriad hyperbole and false stories emerged about the use of intoxicants in Vietnam. Jeremy Kuzmarov traced the spuriousness of such stories and deconstructed "the myth of the addicted army"—the army that allegedly lacked a fighting spirit and combat effectiveness. The myth was propagated by John Steinbeck IV, the son of the famous writer, who upon his return from Vietnam, where he had served as a war correspondent, published an article titled "The Importance of Being Stoned in Vietnam" in the January 1968 issue of *Washingtonian Magazine*.

Kuzmarov noted that "by his own admission, Steinbeck overdramatized the nature of drug abuse in Vietnam for political purposes," claiming, for example, that 75 percent of soldiers got high regularly.[29]

Other media outlets quickly struck a similar tone and helped foster the myth to the extent that it reached an absurd and apocalyptic peak. A headline in *US News and World Report* read "Marijuana—the Other Enemy in Vietnam." On May 24, 1971 *Newsweek* published a photo of a syringe hitting a soldier's helmet.[30] In the same issue Stewart Alsop claimed that "the drug epidemic" was "horrifying... worse even than My Lai."[31] The columnist presented emotional and populist arguments strikingly similar to the myths peddled in Great Britain during the cocaine panic, when the *Times* of London hailed cocaine as a threat "more deadly than bullets," not only to British soldiers on battlefronts but also to the British Empire.[32] The cover of the July 5, 1971, issue of *Newsweek* featured an image of a civilian junkie shooting up heroin with the blazing headline "The Heroin Plague: What Can Be Done?" The lead story described the spread of addiction from "the back alleys of Long Binh and Saigon" to "Middle-American towns and neighborhoods."[33] The authors went on to somehow demonstrate with exaggeration that "heroin has exploded on us like an atom bomb. Ten years ago, even three years ago, heroin was a loser's drug, an aberration afflicting the blacks and long-haired minorities. Now all this has changed. Nice Jewish boys are coming out of the woodwork as well as Mormon kids, Japanese Americans and all other exemplars of hard-working middle-class ideals."[34] The simile to Americans is neither as dark nor as grotesque as a non-native English speaker might think. The parallel was as inappropriate as a comparison sometimes drawn by antiwar activists between the My Lai massacre and Nazi atrocities.[35] Without commonsense limits, some media outlets inflated the problem of the so-called drug epidemic in the military so much that it was compared to medieval plagues. These hyperbolic analogies were accompanied by unreliable statistics equating substance use with abuse. Thus the category of "addict soldiers" usually encompassed those who merely tried drugs and never turned into habitual users. Antiwar activists used images of Nazi atrocities to link the United States with the perpetrators of the Holocaust, equating the soldiers at My Lai with storm troopers.

At the same time, some media outlets and politicians resorted to rhetoric that closely resembled the language of the World War I panic in Great Britain, when cocaine was perceived as a weapon used by the Germans to undermine the British war effort. Half a century later, heroin was seen as a vile weapon used by the communists to impair American forces in Vietnam. In November 1967, Walter Cronkite, then editor and host of the *CBS Evening News*, introduced a report by correspondent John Laurence with this comment: "The Communists are battling American troops not only with fire power, but with drugs."[36]

The myth of the addicted army, as Kuzmarov points out, turned "attention away from the escalation of American atrocities and the ravaging of the Vietnamese countryside."[37] Long before Kuzmarov, however, Thomas Szasz, a prominent psychiatrist in the 1960s, disputed the myth of the addicted army and ridiculed notions that junkie veterans returning home posed a vital threat to public safety and national security. Szasz claimed that soldiers who abused drugs were being made scapegoats for the total fiasco of the American strategy in Vietnam and were being turned into national antiheroes of a "pharmacological Gulf of Tonkin." He noted: "Like the Germans after World War I who claimed that their troops were stabbed in the back by pacifists and other 'unpatriotic elements' at home, we claim that our troops are being stabbed in the back by heroin and the pushers responsible for supplying it to them. As we de-escalate against the 'Vietcong,' we will escalate against heroin. No doubt we shall find it easier to control Americans who shoot heroin than Vietnamese who shoot Americans."[38] As Szasz saw it, Nixon's war on drugs was a curveball used to distract public attention from the US strategic failure in Vietnam.

Szasz was correct: the full story of drug use in Vietnam was far different from the popular view. A survey commissioned by the army revealed that even soldiers who were addicted to heroin could conduct their normal duties. Drug use was not necessarily an obstacle to fighting efficiency, and intoxication did not render troops inoperable.[39] Michael Herr described the January–July 1968 siege of Khe Sanh, during which GIs voluntarily stopped smoking marijuana simply because they did not want to risk their lives.[40] There is plenty of evidence of such self-disciplining behavior among troops. Soldiers usually reached for drugs when it was not too risky to get stoned; that is, when they were in the rear, after they had completed a mission, or when they were between patrols. They did not carelessly go into action intoxicated in defiance of their natural instincts for self-preservation. As noted social psychologist Lieutenant Colonel Larry H. Ingraham observed: "Soldiers are not fools. They know the dangers of working around heavy equipment or going into combat unable to function. Individuals who threaten the lives of others are oftentimes violently excluded from the combat group. In Vietnam, during 1970–71, there were performance problems which resulted from heroin *withdrawal*, but not from heroin addiction per se."[41] Less effective soldiering might be caused not so much by drug usage but by drug withdrawal and its poignant psychophysical symptoms. To sum up, contrary to the myth of an addicted army, drug use did not seriously interfere with combat performance.

THE OUTBREAK OF MORAL PANIC

By 1970, more reports of a dramatic rise in opiate consumption by troops in Vietnam were reaching the American public. On May 27, 1971, two US congressmen,

Morgan F. Murphy and Robert H. Steele, presented an influential report, "The World Heroin Problem," to the Foreign Affairs Committee of the US House of Representatives. In their report, it was estimated that 25,000 to 37,000 servicemen serving in Vietnam, or roughly 10 percent to 15 percent of the troops, were addicted to heroin. Although these figures approximated statistics gathered previously by military doctors, the public release of the figures in this report prompted a media frenzy and an atmosphere of moral panic.

Because this media coverage created general anxiety within US society, President Nixon felt obliged to make a firm response. In a special message to Congress on June 17, 1971, he stated that "public enemy number one in the United States is drug abuse" and announced measures for "a full-scale attack on the problem."[42] The president declared a "War on Drugs." Nixon acknowledged that "while by no means a major part of the American narcotics problem, an especially disheartening aspect of that problem involves those of our men in Vietnam who have used drugs."[43]

Apart from domestic policing and treatment programs, the core measures of Nixon's initial anti-drug abuse efforts were the screening of all servicemen returning from Indochina, their detoxification, and adequate drug and psychological treatment programs. This action was thought to be essential to prevent a narcotics epidemic from spreading across the United States. With the Vietnamization of the war and the gradual withdrawal of American troops from Vietnam, nearly 1,000 soldiers were returning to the United States every day. If one were to assume that up to 25 percent of these soldiers were heroin addicts, this number was considered a serious threat to American society. Preventive measures were therefore needed. It was feared that veterans would commit crimes to obtain the quantities of heroin they needed to bring on intoxicating effects similar to those they had experienced in Vietnam. The heroin that was available in the United States was not only much more expensive than that in Indochina but also much weaker and less pure. Nixon warned that "a habit which costs $5 a day to maintain in Vietnam can cost $100 a day to maintain in the United States, and those who continue to use heroin slip into the twilight world of crime, bad drugs, and all too often a premature death."[44] This was not only a gross exaggeration but also a harmful one. The president was frightening society not with a threat (a real danger) but with a risk (a probable danger). He presented the risk as if it were a threat. Thus the president was creating a fear of an addicted veteran returning home and endangering the orderly civilian world. A new "other" was created.

To thwart this risk, preventive actions were required to create a sort of *cordon sanitaire* (a barrier to stop the spread of disease). Nixon demanded swift action from Secretary of Defense Melvin R. Laird for the identification and detoxification of drug-using servicemen departing from Vietnam.[45] The military responded promptly, and in mid-July 1971 the program, under the name Operation Golden Flow, was launched. The program required that all American servicemen submit to a compulsory urine test for the presence of heroin before leaving Vietnam. Only those who tested negative could return to the United States without delay. Those who tested positive had to undergo a compulsory five- or seven-day methadone detoxification. Soldiers who passed a second test were allowed to return to the United States, but those who tested positive twice in a row (approximately 1,000 to 2,000 cases a month) were processed for dishonorable discharges and then sent back home.[46] Such discharges often worsened these veterans' drug problems, as only 5 percent of those who needed professional assistance were given any medical treatment. According to a report by Jerome Jaffe, the director of the newly established Special Action Office for Drug Abuse Prevention (SAODAP), as many as 5.2 percent of soldiers tested positive for heroin through September 1971; in March 1972, the percentage of those who tested positive fell to less than 2 percent.[47] Overall, under Operation Golden Flow, only 4.5 percent of personnel tested positive. However, the urinalysis was not a credible indicator of drug abuse. The research carried out by Lee N. Robins of Washington University in St. Louis on a sample group of veterans proved that 3 percent of soldiers who tested positive claimed they had not taken heroin while 3 percent of those who tested negative admitted to using the drug.[48] One method of distorting results was to get heavily drunk before the urinalysis; another was to submit a sample of pure urine bought on a "black market for clean urine" that developed among soldiers. The rationale behind Operation Golden Flow was less to help addicted soldiers and more to clear the consciences of politicians and the military and to address an imagined and exaggerated national emergency.

A PAINFUL HOMECOMING AND OTHERING OF VETERANS

Following David Campbell's postmodern analysis of foreign policy, the myth of the addicted army can be perceived in the context of the formulation and implementation of US foreign policy. In the book *Writing Security*, Campbell demonstrates how national identity is continuously constructed by the perception of threat.[49] Foreign policy becomes a grand, nonobjective discourse on the dangers posed by aliens or others. As the title of his book implies, security is "written," meaning it is continuously constructed and created rather than grounded in objective, fixed, and unchangeable factors. The politicians and influence groups who shape public opinion choose some aspects of reality and describe them as dangerous threats to the state and to society's security. For Campbell, the aim of a national security strategy is, first and foremost, to define and uphold the identity of a state and its nation. Identity is always relational—it is created by establishing borders between us and them (meaning an other or a stranger). The perception and interpretation of specific factors, groups, and phenomena, in terms of threats, help to highlight the hallmarks of a society and to reinforce feelings of belonging, identification, attachment, and solidarity.

When American soldiers are viewed from Campbell's perspective, they were returning from Vietnam and were othered by politicians and society. Because they were presented as excessive drug abusers, they were unjustly regarded as potential disturbers of the social order. Veterans were portrayed as threats to American identity as well as to society's security. The mass media and politicians sustained this atmosphere of fear, with President Nixon at the forefront. The comparison of drug addiction to a plague, to a fatal contagious disease that develops like a cancer, that debilitates armed forces and then invades homes and threatens our children, was a useful analogy for constructing the image of the hostile other and heightened a sense of insecurity. The use of metaphors of poison or disease has always been a common means of differentiating between us and them. Thus the boundary was drawn between normal, healthy Americans and unhealthy, filthy drug users.[50] A similar demarcation was also made between the forces of modernity and non-modernity.

Addiction is, by its nature, non-modern because it cuts an addict off from society and alienates him or her from the social and cultural mainstream of community activities.[51] Addiction is a negation of modernity in that it turns users into economically unproductive and socially dysfunctional individuals. Substance abuse is also non-modern because it is irrational in the sense that by providing artificial and inauthentic pleasures, it detaches a person from reality. Pleasures derived from drugs go beyond the category of delight allowed by law and society. By depriving addicts of free will, drug addiction undermines the essence of individual freedom, which is one of the pillars of American identity. While modernity frees people from old social, mental, economic, and customary limitations, drugs enslave people in a novel and toxic way. Addiction can be seen as a force that destroys the fruits of modernity that give people a chance and a right to better their economic status and make self-improvements. Addiction degrades and consumes and can turn life into a painful experience, all of which conflicts with the American credo that praises pragmatism, efficiency, productivity, in-group solidarity, and individual freedom.

Looking upon the Vietnam veteran as the other, as a potential threat to American identity, contributed significantly to the development of a post-Vietnam syndrome. The service members who had risked their lives in defense of American values and identity, on their return home, were considered a severe challenge to Americanness. Homecoming is always a momentous experience, both for the returning soldiers and their society. Young people who had been called to serve in a hostile land and who turned to drugs to stay sane and cope with the reality of war came to be portrayed as fearsome addicts. They were stigmatized and victimized by politicians, mass media, and society.

In his book *The Drugged Nation*, John Finlator, a former agent of the Federal Bureau of Narcotics, expressed a popular sentiment of the day—the fear of a narcotics plague that would flood America. He issued this warning in a hysterical tone: "The junkman has descended on us like the Vandals upon Rome . . . assaulting an unsuspecting and unprepared people." Soldiers returning from Vietnam were "the Vandals" who endangered the very spirit of America—in effect, another Rome.[52] It was feared, as President Nixon implied in June 1971, that junkie veterans would turn to something like Vandal violence, exacerbating domestic crime rates and spreading disorder.

Of course, the apocalyptic visions were not fulfilled. However, unlike the myth of addicted armed forces, the problem of drug abuse among veterans was not a fabrication. The drug use had been vastly exaggerated, and the image of a maladjusted, addicted vet persisted through the 1990s. This lingering image was largely a result of pop culture references, in movies in particular. For example, in *Born on the Fourth of July* (1989), the scale of addiction was depicted by showing vets doing drugs in the back of a veterans' center. The US withdrawal from Vietnam did not mark the end of the narcotics problem because heroin arrived in the United States along with returning soldiers. Many people brought stashes of drugs with them; many had sent drugs home in advance of their returns. For example, one veteran confessed that a year before his date of return, he smuggled opiates in a stereo set he had sent to his father in the United States. Soldiers arranged special transfers of heroin from Vietnam, which they shared after returning home.[53] The Office of Veterans Action in New York estimated that in 1971, between 30,000 and 45,000 heroin-addicted Vietnam veterans lived in the city.[54]

A survey of veterans who returned home in September 1971, commissioned by SAODAP and conducted by a team led by Lee N. Robins, revealed that the majority of interviewees were not habitual users of drugs. The results were startling: 43 percent of veterans reported the use of narcotics in Vietnam, but only 10 percent reported narcotics use after returning home (see table 8.2). The percentage of veterans reporting narcotic use since returning from Vietnam actually dropped below the percentage of those who reported any narcotic use *before* going to Vietnam. Many soldiers had quit by the time they left for home: 75 percent of those who had used narcotics before departing for Vietnam and continued to use them there quit before leaving for home, and 80 percent of soldiers who used drugs for the first time in Vietnam quit before returning home: "More than 60 percent of detected addicts stopped all narcotic use as they left Vietnam and did not resume it after their return to the United States."[55]

TABLE 8.2. Narcotic consumption by American soldiers in three time periods*

	Since Return (%)	In Vietnam (%)	Before Vietnam (%)
Any narcotic use	10	43	11
Any heroin use	7	34	2
Narcotics use more than weekly for a month or more	4	27	1
Addicted to narcotics at any period	1	20	< 0.5
Urine positive for narcotics	1	10.5	—

* General interview sample = 451.
Source: Robins et al., "How Permanent Was Vietnam Drug Addiction," 39.

These findings were so astonishing and so severely undermined prevailing views on the topic that some commentators assumed that the survey results had been fabricated at the request of authorities. The truth, however, is that drug use in Vietnam was contextual—it resulted from extreme conditions and the nature of combat. When the factors and conditions that led soldiers to take drugs were no longer present, most of them gave up the habit. Another reason for a high rate of remission was that soldiers were averse to the intravenous application of heroin. If they wanted to continue "hitting the stuff," they would have to forget about smoking heroin and inject it instead. Operation Golden Flow also contributed to this effect because the threats of a delayed return home, dishonorable discharge and court-martial seemed to be effective deterrent measures for some soldiers.

Commenting on this paradoxical tendency in drug use, Richard Davenport-Hines wrote, "The fact that US servicemen had experimented with heroin as a result of alcohol and marijuana prohibition, voluntarily renounced its use[,] and did not relapse undermined most assumptions of US drug policy."[56] It also punctured the myth of the veteran as a dangerous other. An important conclusion that can be drawn from Robins's findings is that there was nothing exceptionally distressing about the homecoming "junkie soldiers" that the American public should have to fear.

CONCLUSION

Looking back, war not only favored the rise of drug consumption but at times was also a critical factor in the fostering of narcotic-control regulations. The othering of homecoming soldiers, who were depicted as dangerous junkies, was often decisive for the implementation of such regulations. Scapegoating soldiers, then, served political purposes.

What happened to Vietnam War veterans in this regard had its analogy in American history. Although the massive medical use of opiates during the Civil War left many veterans hooked on morphine and opium, it did not lead to a social problem of narcotism.[57] The notion of a "soldiers' disease" or "army disease" (i.e., the opiates habit) exhausting veterans and their families appeared as late as the 1910s. This modern myth was constructed and used as a means to attract public support for the 1914 Harrison Act, which put most psychoactive substances under government control. This legislation became the basis of US drug policy until Nixon's "War on Drugs" in the 1970s. The heated debate on the "soldiers' disease" did not simply overlap coincidentally with the campaign for the Harrison Act. In 1915, Yale University professor Jeannette Marks warned: "Did you know that there is practically no old American family of Civil War reputation which has not had its addicts? Did you know that it was called 'the army disease' because of its prevalence? Did you know that with the war which now hangs over us, the drug evil will spring into a gigantism of even more terrible growth than the present?"[58] President Nixon spoke in a similar vein.

It was German philosopher and political theorist Carl Schmitt who introduced the modern meaning of the other, or stranger, as a description of the enemy. The enemy is someone who "intends to negate his opponent's way of life," so he "must be repulsed or fought."[59] The veterans of both the Civil War and the Vietnam War were presented as others, not so much in Schmitt's understanding as a political enemy. They were othered, rather, in terms of an imagined challenge to the social order, as a threat to a peaceable way of life.

NOTES

1. Homer, *The Odyssey*, 219–227, 127.
2. Wasson and Wasson, *Mushrooms, Russia, and History*, 192.
3. Courtwright, *Forces of Habit*, 140.
4. Kan, *Drugs and Contemporary Warfare*, 47.
5. See Rasmussen, *On Speed*, 53–85.
6. Rasmussen, *On Speed*, 53–85.
7. Musto, *The American Disease*, 5–8.
8. Lewy, *America in Vietnam*, 154.
9. Krogh, "Heroin Politics and Policy," 40.
10. Rasmussen, *On Speed*, 84.
11. Quoted in Gray, *Postmodern War*, 209.
12. Herr, *Dispatches*, 5.
13. *US House Report 91-1807*, quoted in Iversen, *Speed, Ecstasy, Ritalin*, 72.

14. Rasmussen, *On Speed*, 190.

15. Rasmussen, *On Speed*, 191.

16. Grossman, *On Killing*, 270.

17. O'Brien, "The Lives of the Dead," 230.

18. Herr, *Dispatches*, 5.

19. Quoted in Kuzmarov, *Myth of the Addicted Army*, 17.

20. Dubberly, "Drugs and Drug Use," 180.

21. Lewy, *America in Vietnam*, 154.

22. Booth, *Opium: A History*, 270–271.

23. Baker, "US Army Heroin Abuse," 857; Davenport-Hines, *The Pursuit of Oblivion*, 423.

24. Quoted in Booth, *Opium: A History*, 272.

25. Robins et al., "How Permanent Was Vietnam Drug Addiction," 39.

26. Booth, *Opium: A History*, 272.

27. Buzzanco, *Vietnam and the Transformation of American Life*, 114.

28. Buzzanco, *Vietnam and the Transformation of American Life*, 114.

29. Kuzmarov, *Myth of the Addicted Army*, 4–5.

30. Weimer, "Drugs-as-a-Disease," 269.

31. Alsop, "Worse than My Lai," 108.

32. Quoted in Streatfeild, *Cocaine: An Unauthorized Biography*, 158.

33. Kuzmarov, *Myth of the Addicted Army*, 44.

34. Kuzmarov, *Myth of the Addicted Army*, 44.

35. Dove, "The Holocaust."

36. Quoted in Pach, "TV News," 460.

37. Kuzmarov, *Myth of the Addicted Army*, 189.

38. Quoted in Kuzmarov, *Myth of the Addicted Army*, 71.

39. Epstein, *Agency of Fear*, 181.

40. Herr, *Dispatches*, 181.

41. Ingraham, "Sense and Nonsense," 61.

42. Nixon, "Remarks about an Intensified Program"; Nixon, "Special Message"; original emphasis.

43. Nixon, "Special Message."

44. Nixon, "Special Message."

45. Musto and Korsmeyer, *Quest for Drug Control*, 98–99.

46. Brush, "Higher and Higher."

47. Baker, "US Army Heroin Abuse," 859; Jaffe, "One Bite of the Apple," 48.

48. Robins, *The Vietnam Drug User Returns*, 36.

49. Campbell, *Writing Security*.

50. Weimer, "Drugs-as-a-Disease," 266.

51. Weimer, "Drugs-as-a-Disease," 267.
52. Finlator, *Drugged Nation*, 8.
53. Vietnam veteran Yoshia Chee quoted in Mauer, *Strange Ground*, 364.
54. Mauer, *Strange Ground*, 364.
55. Robins et al., "How Permanent Was Vietnam Drug Addiction," 40.
56. Davenport-Hines, *The Pursuit of Oblivion*, 423.
57. Quinones, "Drug Abuse."
58. Marks, "Curse of Narcotism," 315.
59. Schmitt, *Concept of the Political*, 27.

BIBLIOGRAPHY

Alsop, Stewart. "Worse than My Lai." *Newsweek*, May 24, 1971, 108.

Baker, Stewart L., Jr. "US Army Heroin Abuse Identification Program in Vietnam: Implications for a Methadone Program." *American Journal of Public Health* 62, no. 6 (1972): 857–860.

Booth, Martin. *Opium: A History*. New York: St. Martin's, 1998.

Brush, Peter. "Higher and Higher: Drug Use among US Forces in Vietnam." *Vietnam* 15, no. 5 (2002): 46–53, 70. http://archive.is/BpHU.

Buzzanco, Robert. *Vietnam and the Transformation of American Life*. Oxford: Blackwell, 1999.

Campbell, David. *Writing Security: United States Foreign Policy and the Politics of Identity*. Minneapolis: University of Minnesota Press, 1992.

Courtwright, David T. *Forces of Habit: Drugs and the Making of the Modern World*. Cambridge, MA: Harvard University Press, 2001.

Davenport-Hines, Richard. *The Pursuit of Oblivion: A Social History of Drugs*. New York: W. W. Norton, 2004.

Dove, Laura, "The Holocaust in the American Imagination 1945–1978." In *Memory Made Manifest: The United States Holocaust Memorial Museum, 1995*. http://xroads.virginia.edu/~cap/holo/image.html.

Dubberly, Benjamin C. "Drugs and Drug Use." In *Encyclopedia of the Vietnam War: A Political, Social, and Military History*, edited by Spencer C. Tucker, vol. 1, 179–180. Santa Barbara, CA: ABC-CLIO, 1998.

Epstein, Edward Jay. *Agency of Fear: Opiates and Political Power in America*. London: Verso, 1990.

Finlator, John. *The Drugged Nation: A "Narc's" Story*. New York: Simon and Schuster, 1973.

Gray, Chris Hables. *Postmodern War: The New Politics of Conflict*. New York: Guilford, 1997.

Grossman, David. *On Killing: The Psychological Cost of Learning to Kill in War and Society.* Boston: Little, Brown, 1995.

Herr, Michael. *Dispatches.* London: Picador, 2004.

Homer. *The Odyssey.* Translated by Rodney Merrill. Ann Arbor: University of Michigan Press, 2002.

Ingraham, Larry H. "Sense and Nonsense in the Army's Drug Abuse Prevention Effort." *Parameters* 11, no. 1 (1981): 60–70.

Iversen, Leslie. *Speed, Ecstasy, Ritalin: The Science of Amphetamines.* Oxford: Oxford University Press, 2008.

Jaffe, Jerome H. "One Bite of the Apple: Establishing the Special Action Office for Drug Abuse Prevention." In *One Hundred Years of Heroin*, edited by David F. Musto, 43–53. Westport, CT: Auburn House, 2002.

Kan, Paul Rexton. *Drugs and Contemporary Warfare.* Washington, DC: Potomac Books, 2009.

Krogh, Egil, Jr. "Heroin Politics and Policy under President Nixon." In *One Hundred Years of Heroin*, edited by David F. Musto, 39–53. Westport, CT: Auburn House, 2002.

Kuzmarov, Jeremy. *The Myth of the Addicted Army: Vietnam and the Modern War on Drugs.* Amherst–Boston: University of Massachusetts Press, 2009.

Lewy, Gunter. *America in Vietnam.* Oxford: Oxford University Press, 1980.

Marks, Jeannette. "The Curse of Narcotism in America, a Reveille." *American Journal of Public Health* 5, no. 4 (1915): 314–322.

Mauer, Harry. *Strange Ground: An Oral History of Americans in Vietnam, 1945–1975.* New York: Da Capo, 1998.

Murphy, Morgan F., and Robert H. Steele. "The World Heroin Problem." Report of the Special Study Mission, 92nd Cong., 1st sess., May 21, 1971, Washington, DC.

Musto, David F. *The American Disease: Origins of Narcotic Control.* New Haven, CT: Yale University Press, 1973.

Musto, David F., and Pamela Korsmeyer. *Quest for Drug Control: Politics and Federal Policy in a Period of Increased Substance Abuse, 1963–1981.* New Haven, CT: Yale University Press, 2002.

Nixon, Richard. "Remarks about an Intensified Program for Drug Abuse Prevention and Control." June 17, 1971. Collection: Public Papers of the Presidents, Richard Nixon 1971. The American Presidency Project. http://www.presidency.ucsb.edu/ws/?pid=3047.

Nixon, Richard. "Special Message to the Congress on Drug Abuse Prevention and Control." June 17, 1971. Collection: Public Papers of the Presidents, Richard Nixon 1971. The American Presidency Project. http://www.presidency.ucsb.edu/ws/?pid=3048.

O'Brien, Tim. "The Lives of the Dead." In *The Things They Carried*, ed. Tim O'Brien, 225–246. New York: Broadway, 1998.

Pach, Chester J., Jr. "TV News, the Johnson Administration, and Vietnam." In *A Companion to the Vietnam War*, edited by Marilyn B. Young and Robert Buzzanco, 450–469. Oxford: Blackwell, 2006.

Quinones, Mark A. "Drug Abuse during the Civil War (1861–1865)." *International Journal of the Addictions* 10, no. 6 (1975): 1007–1020.

Rasmussen, Nicolas. *On Speed: The Many Lives of Amphetamine*. New York: New York University Press, 2008.

Robins, Lee N. *The Vietnam Drug User Returns: Final Report*. Washington, DC: Special Action Office for Drug Abuse Prevention, 1974.

Robins, Lee N., Darlene H. Davis, and David N. Nurco. "How Permanent Was Vietnam Drug Addiction?" *American Journal of Public Health* 64, Supplement (1974): 38–43.

Schmitt, Carl. *The Concept of the Political*. New Brunswick, NJ: Rutgers University Press, 1976.

Streatfeild, Dominic. *Cocaine: An Unauthorized Biography*. London: Virgin, 2002.

Wasson, Valentina Pavlovna, and R. Gordon Wasson. *Mushrooms, Russia, and History*, vol. 1. New York: Pantheon Books, 1957.

Weimer, Daniel. "Drugs-as-a-Disease: Heroin, Metaphors, and Identity in Nixon's Drug War." *Janus Head* 6, no. 2 (2003): 260–281.

9

The Strategies of Fear, the Commercialization of Society,
and the Rise of the Factory System in the Low Countries
during the Eighteenth and Nineteenth Centuries

Jelle Versieren and Brecht De Smet

The Smithian myth of a peaceful commercial transition to capitalism still looms large among historians. Adam Smith (1723–1790) is a well-known Scottish economist. Nonetheless, Smith's forgotten Scottish contemporary, James Steuart (1713–1780), contended that fear accompanied the creation of British English markets in commodities. Starting from a critique of the contemporary ideological image of Great Britain as the forerunner of a free liberal society, a sketch of the labor history of the Low Countries also appears to be highly ambiguous regarding fear and freedom in the economic and political transformation of capitalism. When comparing the changing power relations between elites and common people in the two socio-geographic settings, fear surfaces in dissimilar contexts and at different times.

TWO EIGHTEENTH-CENTURY MODES OF CONCEPTUALIZATION OF THE TRANSITION TO CAPITALISM: JAMES STEUART AND ADAM SMITH, BETWEEN FEAR AND FREEDOM

Between the sixteenth and eighteenth centuries, the British social formation underwent a deep and fundamental transformation. Until the ascension of Elizabeth I, England (and in the eighteenth century, Great Britain) could be described as a semi-peripheral economy within the sphere of western Europe. The country lacked the financial resources needed to vie with France or Spain on the battlefield or to compete economically with the Low Countries in the sector of the high-quality wool

DOI: 10.5876/9781646420025.c009

industry.[1] The political situation was highly volatile and detrimental to England's trade interests when commercial and feudal elites fought against each other and among themselves.

Elizabeth decided to devote the limited resources available to the centralization of state-building abilities, the fusion of political communities, the pacification of disgruntled elites, the development of naval power, the support of chartered joint-stock companies, and a stable expansion of mostly petty production of wares in the English home market.[2]

In the seventeenth century, an oligarchic constitutional monarchy replaced the absolutist king. In the eighteenth century, according to the dominant thesis, a full-fledged market society of consumers surfaced in which the middle classes obtained a higher social and political status. The dominant historiographical narrative of a peaceful market society consisting of a flourishing middle class resembles a vulgar Whiggish fable from the late eighteenth century. This narrative comes with two main fallacies. First, it presumes a teleological development from the commercialization of British society to a modern capitalist society. Second, the commercialization of Great Britain was also based on coercive and exploitative practices entailing fear and submission. Between the fifteenth and eighteenth centuries, common people continually fought against the oligarchic state and the elites. The ensuing revolts were the result of a long process over several centuries of primitive accumulation of capital—the coercive separation of independent rural producers from their means of production—and the proletarianization of both rural and urban laborers. The enrichment of the elites and the higher middle class occurred in a context of a distributional polarization in which a considerable group of people had no hope of retaining the status of a respectable independent producer—the freeborn Englishman. Being a wage laborer implied social degradation to a relation of dependence on a master. Before the Industrial Revolution, wages did not cover the daily costs of the means of subsistence. In addition, with the loss of control over his work, the laborer could no longer live according to a traditional life cycle of marriage, acquisition of property, and securing the prospect of offspring. Furthermore, the laborer's master could rely on the visible iron hand of the law when he could not fulfill the agreement of servitude to deliver a certain amount of goods or services. Vagrants, beggars, and paupers were arrested and sent to workhouses to live their lives in unpaid slavery.[3]

Until the 1970s, historians and experts in the history of economic thought asserted that the principles of the nascent discourse of a modern market society could be discerned in the contributions of the Scottish Enlightenment philosophers. In particular, the representation of Adam Smith's economic thought has been the subject of many contradictory interpretations. Today, the contention that Smith was a theorist and defender of unbridled free-trade capitalism is unten-able.[4] He wrote his *Wealth of Nations* in a time when industrialization and social capital–wage labor relations were still undeveloped.[5] Although he embraced the achievements of the relatively new constitutional monarchy and the commercial-ization of the economy, he criticized other aspects and practices of the British econ-omy.[6] His work contained a harsh critique of the oligarchic politics of the British state and the manifold late feudal asymmetric power relations it perpetuated. He denounced the extensive political and economic coercion of landlords, merchants, and rich master craftsmen and coercion's impact on the daily lives of common peo-ple. Furthermore, his book should be considered a part of his overall moral philoso-phy and science of humanity. In his *four stages* theory of history, Smith portrayed commercial society in a broad and pervasive manner as the result of a slow and partial realization of the ideal natural order.

Smith warned that history represents a trial-and-error process—people only pos-sess a limited sense of rationality and are prone to many forms of self-deception—in which humankind did not actively follow a preconceived design or plan.[7] However, in his many shifts to a normative evaluation of the feudal and commercial aspects of British society, he explained how a philosophical contemplation could add something to the secret linear progression of human conduct. The commer-cial society, once achieved, is irreversible because people recognize its benefits. Commercialization lowers the sense of a permanent state of fear. When people obtain a certain degree of natural liberty—that is, the liberty to pursue personal welfare under non-specified political conditions—they no longer have to fear the arbitrary exercise of authority of those in power. Our first step toward a state of opulence and natural liberty entailed the enhancement of our personal security by political and moral means. The state needed to be impartial and to represent this impartiality through the promotion of the virtue of justice.[8] Each person has been endowed with equal formal rights, and Smith posited a limited intervention of the state to ensure that economic polarization between common people and elites could be contained. Furthermore, the impartial state and the legal apparatus should replace traditional common-law institutions based on arbitrariness and the monop-olization of power by local and national elites. Smith, expressing a remarkably pro-pitious opinion about the social worth of the toil and trouble of jobbing workers, condemned the bondages of dependence between the small independent skilled producers, apprentices, and journeymen (or day laborers) and the privileged group of rich master craftsmen and merchant traders who prohibited the free choice of work occupations.[9] In the eighteenth century, an apprentice was still subject to personal violence and maltreatment by his master. Journeymen and casual laborers lacked bargaining power concerning piece-rate payments and other remunerations because the corporative guild institutions sided with master craftsmen.[10] Local city councils and government institutions functioned as the political means of protection of the interests of the oligarchic elites.

Smith claimed that to be free of fear of arbitrary domination, individuals could only assert their independence when they acknowledged that their interdependent social relations translated into duties and shared virtues. He emphasized that a commercial society promoted the idea of individual autonomy but at the same time gave ground to its dissolution: capitalists tended to immerse themselves in a pool of greed, and workers degenerated into mindless beasts.[11] Other values are needed to complement the ideal of the exchange of goods between independent producers: a parochial moral economy and civic virtues of republican humanism. James Steuart, the most prominent contemporary disputant of Smith, also welcomed a society without fear of arbitrary coercive domination by an oligarchic elite. Likewise, Steuart supported the idea of "managed markets," the utmost importance of sufficient demand in the home market, and "the science of a legislator" and its ideal of the impartial state.[12] Whereas Smith asserted that popular sovereignty, the rule of law, and communal ties were grounded in the individual rights of freeborn men, Steuart maintained, in agreement with William Petty, that individual self-interests collated with state decision-making capabilities: the individual depends on a strong and wealthy nation.[13]

The biggest divergence from Smith's descriptive and normative analysis of commercialized British society can be found in Steuart's version of a stages theory of history. Smith presumed that humans' natural disposition to exchange goods created the necessary space for natural liberty and opulence. Production exists because symbols of wealth—money, goods, and labor—are circulated. Exchange of goods and the division of concrete labor are the reasons for long-term growth. Steuart regarded the existence of a commercial society (a developed space of exchange of use values) as the result of the intensification of labor productivity. He viewed the clustering of concrete labor activities as the means of the accumulation of wealth—both money and goods. Steuart described what Marx would later call "primitive accumulation": the separation between rural farmers and their means of production and the direct appropriation of their means of subsistence.[14] This separation resulted in the destruction of a self-sufficient household economy. Primitive accumulation had been supported by the forceful hand of the state to secure the procurement of a constant supply of goods for a small group of rich merchants. Steuart vacillated between two ideas. He could claim, on the one hand, that commercial society abolished the relations of fear and domination between peasants and lords. On the other hand, he could say that prosperity by trade only occurs when idle hands are forcefully set to work.

Idleness could not only be found in the enlarged pool of paupers and proletarianized day laborers. Steuart, pace Smith, also observed that the household economy encouraged indolent behavior. If landlords and rich yeomen succeeded in implementing modern husbandry through the concentration of farmland, a more efficient mode of exploitation could induce growth for the entire nation, and labor reserves could be mobilized toward manufacturing activities.[15] Initially, only a class of merchants reaped the benefits of the exchange of produced goods, but Steuart hoped the "secrets of trade" would become public knowledge after a period of time.[16]

Smith's stages of history theory expressed moderate optimism about the linear progression of a free commercial society. Such a society would lead to a community without fear because relations of bondage and servitude would be dissolved. Steuart asserted that particular forms of fear are a necessary ingredient for economic growth: the uncertainty of permanent subsistence of the common worker in the commercial society is the most direct incentive for parsimoniousness and productive conduct. The state had the duty to intervene when idleness persisted among its citizens.

When comparing these two models to historical data and archival sources, it appears that both thinkers were partly right. Between the sixteenth and eighteenth centuries, English and ensuing British society "drifted into the waters of a formally free market by default. In the course of the revolution [Cromwell], the executive government lost its arbitrary powers over local authorities. The dismantling of the prerogative courts made economic regulation a matter for Parliament. But Parliament, in contrast to the Privy Council, proved too unwieldy a body to pass significant bills of regulation for the country as a whole. The tortuous history of legislation after the Restoration shows that corporate regulation ended not because of a growing alliance to laissez-faire but as a result of the deadlock between diverse commercial interests."[17]

This process did not result in a modern labor market in which labor could be contractually bought and sold. The promulgation of new laws only sanctified political rights of the legal category of free craftspeople. Produced goods could be exchanged without any governmental or corporative restrictions; but day laborers, wage workers, and servants did not receive legal recognition of their particular precarious occupational situations. When they failed to fulfill their obligations to an employer, which legally meant a failure to deliver a certain amount of exchangeable goods, the latter could invoke the harsh and inflexible long arm of the law to impose fines or a direct sentence of imprisonment. De jure wage laborers were treated as independent producers; de facto, they lost all social status, along with "their birthright and claim to freedom . . . They no longer had the right to exclude others from the use and enjoyment of their labor power, and so they had forfeited their property in it altogether."[18]

Fear was a constant element in the patriarchal relation between employer and wage laborer, whether the latter worked under the same roof or functioned within a subcontracting or putting-out network. In the eighteenth century, this form of legal servitude would enable employers to physically lock up their workers in textile mills. When a day laborer lacked personal income, being sent to a workhouse was an imminent and permanent threat to his personal well-being. Private and public poor relief, almost absent, had been inscribed in the same tradition of contempt for impoverished workers.[19] The industrial class obtained political power through the 1832 Reform Act, which allowed it to introduce new Poor Laws and the laissez-faire re-conversion of the labor market. These Whiggish reforms unintentionally allowed the Chartist movement and early socialists to promote the promulgation of social reform laws and the creation of formal liberty of contract between employer and worker. At the same time, workers emphasized the communal values of a traditional economy in an effort to make employers more attentive to their social obligations.[20]

COMMERCIALIZED WORKSHOPS, MANUFACTURES, AND POLITICAL REFORMS: BETWEEN FEAR AND COMMUNITY

From structural and comparative perspectives, the historical conditions for the emergence of wage labor and the commodity market differed significantly between Great Britain and the Low Countries—especially the southern region. Feudalistic rural relations and corporative urban regulations still existed until the arrival of the French Jacobins and Napoleonic armies. At the end of the eighteenth century, both France and the Low Countries abolished the old privileges and customs (such as the overlapping local courts and competing legal institutions, the guild organizations, and the complex electoral procedures of appointing magistrates). The sudden collapse of both the feudal state system—within or without early reforms—and the absolutist monarchist regime has many explanations. The simplistic model of an inevitable eclipse of the Ancien Régime and the unstoppable rise of laissez-faire capitalism requires fundamental revision. The continental pre-modern commercialized society had been characterized by a slow but steady rise of rural productivity and demographic growth. However, in the second half of the eighteenth century, both the United Provinces and France suffered recurrent short-term cycles of recession combined with stagnant governmental tax revenues, which curbed their state-building abilities. General public opinion regarded these situations as a secular decline of the standard of living (when looking backward to an ideologically constructed past of prosperity and wealth). In fact, however, the intensified exploitation of labor allowed for a growth of national income.[21] The inequality of incomes between elites and the common people rose, which caused an alarming growth of beggary and pauperism.

Politically, in France the absolutist state could no longer mediate the ongoing conflicts between urban merchants and the bourgeoisie, financial speculators, independent farmers, and dominant aristocracy. In the United Provinces, the old factional fights within the aristocratic and mercantile oligarchy—the regents and the Orangists—undermined their legitimacy as the guardians of the body politic. The French Jacobins and their Dutch associates, the Patriots, developed new and discursive political practices that interpellated the common people as civilians of a unitary nation, transcending particularist interests and local communal identities. They regarded popular sovereignty and the idea of the public interest as pivotal in reviving an industrious and mercantile spirit.[22] Nonetheless, for a long time, these modernist ideas struggled to become ascendant.[23]

Hitherto, social conflicts could be mediated by a complex set of changing strategic combinations between different elites. In late medieval and early modern times, the urban bourgeoisie played a distinctive role in the cycles of centralization and decentralization of late feudal–era state power. Urban centers became an important base for levying taxes for the central government, and the bourgeoisie relied on the continuing expansion of offices to secure their social status and place in the political networks.[24] The degree of imposition of the particular interests of elites depended on the overall configuration of the accumulation of political power. Furthermore, the pre-modern bourgeoisie consisted of numerous class factions with contradicting agendas, whose determination depended on local political networks, professional status, labor activities, rental properties, and so on. It was only when the capital–wage labor relation came to the fore that the industrial bourgeoisie could subsume the interests of other factions under its economic leadership.

The best-known case of contradicting interests within the heterogeneous bourgeoisie entailed the recurring collisions among urban wholesaling merchants, retailers, and independent craftsmen in all western European cities over the right to engage in specific commercial activities.[25] These conflicts expressed a pre-modern rationality that defined the regulated boundaries between the circulation of goods and the concrete division of craft labor. Each corporative organization articulated a shared discourse about the common right to protect its collective livelihood and the necessity of economic coordination to avoid various sorts of manipulation or corruption. Moreover, rich trade guilds, from late medieval times until their abolition, attempted to institutionally incorporate smaller crafts in their quest for accumulation of political power. Furthermore, the very profitable wool industry in the Low Countries presents the best example of the tendency toward a vertical production chain of subcontracting craftspeople. At the top of the chain, master craftspeople weavers and merchants organized the workflow processes between different guilds and the exchange of final goods and then siphoned off a much-contested rent-seeking premium.

In addition to exercising their political and economic dominance, these weavers and merchants introduced new disciplinary rules upon their subordinates and relied in part on city officials for help with enforcement. While apprentices and journeymen of small masters were tied to the reciprocal corporative social codes, day laborers in larger workshops were brought to submission through the exertion of direct economic control. These workshops introduced the first forms of time management. Also, workshop masters emphasized the communal importance of their enterprises, which gave them authority to close the door or gate at the beginning and end of each workday. Latecomers were refused work.[26] Next to the uncommon use of corporeal punishment for the worst cases of misconduct, casual laborers feared the master's overwrought act of symbolic exclusion from the workplace. Aside from the deprivation of remunerations for buying the means of subsistence, workers risked being exposed as disloyal to the *bonum commune* of the city, thus putting themselves at risk of becoming unwanted paupers. In an upward economic cycle, these hands could be called "attached," in the sense that even day laborers were identified as the outer part of the social circle of a well-reputed employer. In the context of a downward economic cycle, fear of social exclusion was constant for people who lacked corporative rights.[27] Unskilled laborers, mostly newly arrived immigrants, lived on occasional earnings and did the most toilsome work.[28] The influx of skilled labor was heavily regulated; in several cases, guild masters emphasized the cultural uniqueness of their crafts and expressed fear of the arrival of "foreign hands" from neighboring cities.[29] When unemployment rates rose, the declassing of laborers incited fear of social conflict and occasional violence within all layers of the urban bourgeoisie. Even the first generation of Patriot bourgeois authors of pamphlets and belles-lettres, nonplussed by the sudden vexed reactions of the lower classes, viewed the corporative hierarchy as necessary to keep the demands of proletarianized workers at bay.[30] Obstreperous workers were less deterred by the disciplinary practices of municipal lawmakers.

In the eighteenth century, merchants and the rural bourgeoisie outside city walls were unhindered by the respective corporative regulations and could profit from the policy changes of central governments. These policies pursued an economy of scale that mobilized populations, wealth, and resources to the benefit of state-building abilities. The sovereign—emperor, king, or prince—relentlessly tried to curb or at least actively steer the obstinate behavior of the protectionist cities. The bourgeoisie had already been involved in extensive trade networks between provincial villages and major cities—commercial activities with the household economy or ground speculation. They seized the opportunity to control a more constant supply of cheap goods—textile, ceramics, ironworks, paper—through the establishment of manufactures and rural workshops.

Although these manufactures could generate a significant profit, the chances of commercial survival after the initial start-up and first cycles of expansion were almost nonexistent.[31] Along with the volatile nature of the loan-capital market and the unstable political framework, merchants swiftly became aware that the absence of a labor market prevented them from finding a permanently motivated workforce. The disciplinary regime of the manufactures was imposed for two main reasons: first, to create a new vertical hierarchy with oversight techniques to ensure workers' compliance with the instructions of the merchant-owner and overlookers-master craftsmen and second, to implement a chain of quality control.

But both skilled and unskilled laborers rejected this regime because similar to the British case, they adhered to the pre-modern social identity of independent producers. In most cases, these laborers did not fear the employer's authority. When rejecting a wage cut or deplorable labor conditions, workers one-sidedly terminated their employment without giving notice—individually or collectively—by actively sabotaging machinery or deliberately delivering faulty goods. The merchants sought the coercive assistance of local officials, whose interests lay elsewhere (the social peace of the village community prevailed over specific labor conflicts).[32] Without legal coercive means—as in the British case—these employers had little means to incite fear in the hearts of resisting workers.

THE EARLY FACTORIES: INDUSTRIAL HIERARCHIES, SOCIALISM, RELIGIOUS CONFLICTS, COMMUNAL IDENTITIES, AND POPULAR ANXIETY FOR THE OTHER

The French occupational regime, supported by Jacobin comities, abolished the corporative structures. Whether this policy was supported by the local population depended on numerous reasons: local political affinities, communal rivalries, the degree of equality and social mobility in the guild community, rent-seeking and occupational opportunities, and the general degree of aversion or sympathy toward a foreign occupier in a time of competing embryonic and un-crystallized ideological factions.[33] Furthermore, the degree of success guilds had in obstructing forced self-dissolution depended on whether their acts were perceived as merely economic protection of their livelihoods or as political subversion against the new regime.[34]

After Napoleon's defeat, both the upper bourgeoisie and the nobility legally reaffirmed the institutionalization of a modern labor market. In the buildup to its ideological class project, the bourgeoisie sought to align its interests with other elites while creating an economic and political space to stimulate its industrial and financial activities. A significant proletarianized group of formally free laborers provided cheap labor. But between 1830 and 1880, an uneven development of industrial activities existed between the Netherlands and Belgium. Belgium quickly started to produce cheap textiles, ironwork supplies, and coal for international markets, but the Netherlands still relied on financial services and trade.

In small, provincial Dutch towns, traditional craftsmen remained a part of middle-income groups. For example, grounded in local communal networks, a coppersmith in a small rural town in the province of Groningen passed his working days repairing the items of local customers or frequently lent pots and pans he had produced to families celebrating religious holidays. The rates of remuneration were fixed, but he doubled his rates when items came from outside his town.[35] This coppersmith resembled the Smithian model of the tranquil life of the independent producer whose conduct is guided by a sense of individual and communal duty that flourishes in the absence of fear for the corruptive self-love of the elites. In Delft, a few prominent *rentier* families, diversifying their investments, failed to build small glassmaking and textile workshops. They lacked the necessary technical knowledge and experience, and they realized that managing a small factory was rather different from earlier rent-seeking activities.[36]

Early industrial success in the Netherlands is found on the periphery of the country, in Maastricht. In the 1840s, Petrus Regout, the son of middle-class merchants, made his fortune by producing ceramics and glasswork. The old and impoverished garrison town provided him with the cheap, willing hands he needed for his factory; low property prices and political networks provided him with the room he needed for continual expansion. With Liege stretching to the south, Maastricht became part of the industrial axis of the Walloon region, which provided Regout with the necessary coal and other basic materials he needed. Maastricht became the first industrialized city of the Netherlands.[37]

In contrast to the hesitant attempts in the north, Regout combined these favorable conditions with new management techniques. He recruited skilled independent craft workers from the western German kingdoms and Liege. In an effort to obtain advanced British factory secrets, he offered generous contracts to their engineers and imported new machinery. Regout's administrative personnel could plan production in part with the use of a full-cost accounting system.

An analysis of the Regout factory hierarchy should avoid the false dichotomy of the feared patriarchal-conservative and the liberal technocratic-humanist factory owner. Regout and his offspring used discursive elements of the moral economy of the factory as a communal system to defend their rigid disciplinary practices. These practices entailed not only the attempt to control the worker's attitude and behavior within factory walls but also his communal and family life in the city.[38] First, Petrus Regout presented himself as a "father among his sons" to the outer world.[39] The factory was the social and material assurance of job security and the general well-being of the workers and their families. Without the father figure, Maastricht would be in economic decline and moral decay. Second, Regout and his sons heralded their acquired wealth as a gift to Maastricht's communal life. Labor had to be disciplined according to the general and daily demands of the factory as a system of output of commodities. Otherwise, the total worth of factory capital and thus "social wealth" would diminish.[40]

Regout was liberal in the sense that he redesigned his old factory building according to modern German blueprints. Cell-like production departments were efficiently arranged according to the logical sequence of the production process. This spatial creation of a microcosmic setting of power enhanced the rational extraction of surplus labor power. It also expressed a desire for a general docility of workers through fear of ubiquitous, controlling eyes. Despotic-patriarchal and liberal measures were not mutually exclusive. Laborers were strictly forbidden to drink or eat, to move from one department to another without explicit authorization, or to talk to certain colleagues. Even outside factory walls, laborers could be intransigently punished when management caught them red-handedly working for another employer.[41] Regout preferred to hire extended families as a means of controlling workers. The *patres familias* were held accountable for production irregularities caused by their workmen. Regout paid overlookers commissions or complete wages according to output rates. A few foremen were sanctioned to recurrently abuse laborers both physically and verbally, but management's main concern was the ability to increase labor productivity. Overseers had to prevent sabotage by implementing a system of fines for the production of faulty goods. More than once, these fines were used as the preferred means of creating a fear-suffused environment without giving a satisfactory justification for the penalization.

The company grew rapidly in terms of both output and labor force. This growth generated an intricate hierarchy between labor tasks.[42] The factory had to employ perhaps the most hated and feared employees: foreign craftsmen and engineers. On the work floor and in the community, these specialists were culturally alienated from the workers. Several reasons can be discerned why these employees were comprehended as the "other." Their different languages were apprehended as a secretive code; they had better housing; their fixed, high wages demoted the status of local skilled laborers; and their technical assistance appeared to be very intrusive. Whereas overlookers had to function within the communal ties of their neighborhoods, foreigners could only be related to their economic ties with management and the factory owner.

Local laborers were forced to go to the factory by pure economic necessity. During a session of a government commission on social conflicts, a laborer testified that children twelve years of age and even younger had to work in constant fear. If they had a choice, "they would prefer to become a metal smith or a cabinetmaker... because there exists a great difference between being an independent craftsman or being a factory-worker. The craftsman presents himself with more decency and is more civilized."[43] In the 1890s, after a first failed strike, relatively well-paid crafts-men decided to break the chain of fear and organize themselves in a secretive labor union. At the same time, the Dutch social democratic political movement had finally been unified and rapidly gained influence among a countrywide industrial proletariat. In a few years, local craftsmen, with the support of social democratic politicians, acted openly against management with a first successful strike. Initially, the board of directors tried to ignore this conflict, but when even the invited inter-vention of local Catholic priests proved fruitless, fear of more socialist agitation gained the upper hand. Although these workers initially had only very concrete and specific corporative demands on issues such as salaries, commissions, and job security, Maastricht gradually became a well-known bulwark of the organized labor movement.[44] Fear would remain a constant factor among workers. Management, in accord with Catholic-steered labor organizations, was able to postpone union recognition until after World War I.

CONCLUSION

The British market society had been determined by both the Smithian paradigm of freedom and the Steuartian paradigm of fear. So long as someone remained an independent producer and fulfilled duties in the exchange of goods, that person still belonged economically and culturally to the middle class. The huddle of wage laborers—especially casual laborers—consisted of judicial outcasts, whom the gov-ernment tried to discipline with severe punishment. These workers had to condone the misconduct of employers who were eager to reach for the tawse. Socially and communally, the status and reputations of these workers had been sullied by their exertion in low-valued labor tasks. Smith hoped legal reforms would engender a freer exchange between producing individuals through the proscription of institu-tionalized antediluvian practices. His hope was that the unequal relations between casual laborers and well-off masters could be remedied. After all, Smith asserted, in the main, inequality had been cast in the mold of exclusive corporative rights. But at the same time, these corporative rights protected the interests of smaller mas-ters against the exploitative tendencies of rich merchants. Smith, in a subtle way, ignored remarks about the positive effects of guild restrictions. He warned, in an inextricable but perspicacious line of reasoning, that the sudden creation of a legal framework based on impartiality would not fundamentally change the behavior of some avaricious and tyrannizing masters. Workers still did not possess the pecuniary means to redress the injustices inflicted upon them.

Steuart, in contrast, depicted these unequal relations as a necessary means to elevate British society onto a plane of riches for the few, accompanied by the abundant circulation of goods. Fear of the debased (but abstemious) classes and the incessant reminder of the social existence of the other, outside bourgeois culture lingered in the minds of all individuals endowed with property incomes. With money came suspicions and jaundiced views of the subaltern classes. During the eighteenth and nineteenth centuries, in the main, the long and seemingly endless transition toward a modern capitalist society was affected by the inability of apprehensive legislatures to extirpate social conflicts. Conservative polemists and political economists failed to insinuate their fatalistic precepts into the persistent moral economy of laborers and paupers. These laborers supported the exhortations of progressive reformers to decant Smith's support for the idea of an impartial law into a new set of judicial measures that would ensure their political rights.

In the Low Countries, corporative regulations protected the status and social welfare of guild members. But these members also feared the possibility of "declassation" in downward economic cycles. They tried to extort trade protections against unaffiliated entrants or monopolizing merchants from municipal and central authorities. Smaller craftsmen were apprehensive of the steady decline of their monetary means of subsistence within the context of growing income polarization. Wage laborers were among the declassed individuals, and they could easily shift ideologically between supporting the master craftsmen to rallying for the abolishment of corporative restrictions.

Public opinion vacillated. The public sympathized with guild members' lamentations about unfair competition and intrusions on their old corporative rights. But in contrast, the public was also considering the newfangled discourse about the general interest and the abolishment of legal prerogatives. In nineteenth-century factories, a relationship of fear existed between employers and workers, but factory hierarchies also induced fear among different categories of wage laborers. The factory as a place of complex coordination between labor tasks required an enhanced system of institutionalized disciplinary measures. Thus management used an intermediary layer of engineers, skilled foreign workers, and staff personnel to inculcate a culture of subordination. Contrary to eighteenth-century corporative antagonisms among social groups, the nineteenth-century factory was indeed an assemblage of, in the Foucauldian sense, a disciplinary *dispositive*—a coherent set of power relations and regulatory devices.

NOTES

1. Palliser, *Tudor York*, 209–280.
2. Arrighi, *Long Twentieth Century*, 188–194.
3. Lis and Soly, *Poverty and Capitalism*, 118–137.
4. Peil, *Adam Smith*, 10–23.
5. Dobb, *Theories of Value*, 54–55.
6. Griswold, *Virtues of Enlightenment*, 128.
7. Fleischacker, *On Adam Smith's Wealth of Nations*, 99.
8. Werhane, *Modern Capitalism*, 78–86.
9. Smith, *Inquiry*, 74–75.
10. See Stone, "The English Revolution," 99. Charles I imposed corporative regulations on numerous crafts and trades in an attempt to recentralize government control over the sphere of goods circulation. The king gave extensive powers to a few rich merchants and master craftsmen, which disturbed a balance of collective interests of the moral economy within local communities. This decision from above reflected negatively on the reputations of the respective guilds because they became associated with corruption, coercion, and despotic practices.
11. Pack, *Capitalism as a Moral System*, 141–150.
12. Karayiannis, "Sir James Steuart," 38–41.
13. Finkelstein, *Harmony and the Balance*, 247–252.
14. Marx, *Theories of Surplus Value*, 41–43.
15. Perelman, *Classical Political Economy*, 77–84.
16. Steuart, *Inquiry*, 166–169.
17. Biernacki, *Fabrication of Labor*, 217.
18. Biernacki, *Fabrication of Labor*, 22.
19. Lindert, *Growing Public*, 39.
20. See Robson, *On Higher than Commercial Grounds*, 17–48; Deakin and Wilkinson, *Law of the Labour Market*, 62–78; Gray, "Factory Reform in Britain."
21. De Jong, "Sociale verandering in de neergaande Republiek."
22. Leeb, *Ideological Origins of the Batavian Revolution*, 109.
23. For example, de Keyzer, "Opportunisme, corporatisme en progressiviteit."
24. For the late medieval southern Low Countries, see Dumolyn, "Political and Symbolic Economy"; for France, see Heller, "The Longue Durée."
25. For Antwerp, see Van Damme, *Verleiden en verkopen*, 164–169.
26. Stabel, "Temps de travail, temps de métier."
27. See Lis and Soly, *Worthy Efforts*, 538–539. As a reaction to their precarious social status, journeymen decided to create parallel corporative organizations.
28. Burstin, "Unskilled Labor," 64–68.

29. Raad van Brabant, *Processen van de ambachten en naties*, 331, 346.

30. Prak, *Republikeinse veelheid, democratische enkelvoud*, 111–112.

31. See Van Aken-Fehmers et al., *Delfts aardewerk*. Regarding the ceramic industry in the region of Delft, only one of more than thirty manufactures and workshops still existed during the Dutch industrial takeoff in the third quarter of the nineteenth century.

32. For an exemplary case in the southern Low Countries, see Lis and Soly, *Een groot bedrijf in een kleine stad*, 78–97.

33. Versieren, "The Perception of Labour."

34. For an economic and ideological comparison between Brugge and Maastricht, see Vanden Berghe, *Jacobijnen en traditionalisten*, 206–360; Spiertz, *Maastricht in het vierde kwart van de achttiende eeuw*, 165–172.

35. Koperslagerij Weduwe Lankhorst 1802–1840, 788.

36. De Jonge, "Delft in de negentiende eeuw," 156–163.

37. Brugmans, *De arbeidende klasse in Nederland*, 65.

38. Van Iterson, "Vader, raadgever en beschermer Petrus Regout en zijn arbeiders 1834–1870," 26–27.

39. Letter from Petrus Regout to city court concerning a labor dispute, 1852 (case: Karl Böhrer), NV Kristal-, glasen aardewerkfabrieken De Sphinx voorheen Petrus Regout & Co en voorgangers 1834–1958.

40. Letter from Petrus Regout to city court concerning a labor dispute, 1852, 858.

41. Letter from Petrus Regout to city court concerning factory rules, 1870–1884, 868.

42. See also, Lefebvre, *L'invention de la grande*, 126–135.

43. Giele, *Een kwaad leven*, 108.

44. De Vries, "Gebroken Stakingsgolven," 78–84; Perry, *Roomsche kinine tegen roode koorts*, 104–134.

BIBLIOGRAPHY

Arrighi, Giovanni. *The Long Twentieth Century: Money, Power, and the Origins of Our Times*. London: Verso, 1994.

Biernacki, Richard. *The Fabrication of Labor: Germany and Britain, 1640–1914*. Berkeley: University of California Press, 1995.

Brugmans, Izaak Johannes. *De arbeidende klasse in Nederland in de 19e eeuw, 1813–1870*. Amsterdam: Aula-boeken, 1967.

Burstin, Haim. "Unskilled Labor in Paris at the End of the Eighteenth Century." In *The Workplace before the Factory: Artisans and Proletarians 1500–1800*, ed. Thomas Max Safley and Leonard N. Rosenband, 63–72. Ithaca, NY: Cornell University Press, 1993.

Deakin, Simon, and Frank Wilkinson. *The Law of the Labour Market: Industrialization, Employment, and Legal Evolution*. Oxford: Oxford University Press, 2005.

De Jong, Theo P.M. "Sociale verandering in de neergaande Republiek." *Economisch- en sociaal-historisch jaarboek* 35 (1972): 1–27.

De Jonge, Johan A. "Delft in de negentiende eeuw: Van 'stille nette' plaats tot centrum van industrie." *Economisch- en sociaal-historisch jaarboek* 37 (1974): 145–247.

De Keyzer, Maïka. "Opportunisme, corporatisme en progressiviteit: conflicten en vertogen van corporatieve belangengroepen in het stedelijk milieu van het achttiende-eeuwse Mechelen." *Tijdschrift voor Sociale en Economische Geschiedenis* 7, no. 4 (2010): 3–26.

De Vries, Rob. "Gebroken Stakingsgolven: Een analyse van de stakingen in de Maastrichtse glasen aardewerkindustrie 1880–1920." PhD dissertation, Universiteit Nijmegen, the Netherlands, 1986.

Dobb, Maurice. *Theories of Value and Distribution Since Adam Smith: Ideology and Economic Theory*. Cambridge: Cambridge University Press, 1973.

Dumolyn, Jan. "The Political and Symbolic Economy of State Feudalism: The Case of Late Medieval Flanders." *Historical Materialism* 15, no. 2 (2007): 105–131.

Finkelstein, Andrea. *Harmony and the Balance: An Intellectual History of Seventeenth-Century English Economic Thought*. Ann Arbor: University of Michigan Press, 2000.

Fleischacker, Samuel. *On Adam Smith's Wealth of Nations—a Philosophical Companion*. Princeton, NJ: Princeton University Press, 2004.

Giele, Jacques, ed. *Een kwaad leven: De arbeidsenquête van 1887*. Deel 2: Maastricht. Nijmegen, the Netherlands: Uitgeverij Link, 1981.

Gray, Robert. "The Languages of Factory Reform in Britain, c. 1830–1860." In *The Historical Meanings of Work*, ed. Patrick Joyce, 143–179. Cambridge: Cambridge University Press, 1987.

Griswold, Charles L., Jr. *Adam Smith and the Virtues of Enlightenment*. Cambridge: Cambridge University Press, 1999.

Heller, Henry. "The Longue Durée of the French Bourgeoisie." *Historical Materialism* 17, no. 1 (2009): 31–59.

Karayiannis, Anastassios. "Sir James Steuart on the Managed Market." *Economic Thought and Political Theory* 37 (1994): 37–61.

Koperslagerij Weduwe Lankhorst 1802–1840, 788. Groninger Archieven, Regionaal Historisch Centrum, the Netherlands.

Leeb, I. Leonard. *The Ideological Origins of the Batavian Revolution: History and Politics in the Dutch Republic 1747–1800*. The Hague: Martinus Nijhoff, 1973.

Lefebvre, Philippe. *L'invention de la grande entreprise: Travail, hiérarchie, marché*. France, fin XVIIIe–début XXe siècle. Paris: Presses Universitaires de France, 2003.

Lindert, Peter H. *Growing Public: Social Spending and Economic Growth Since the Eighteenth Century*. Vol. 1. Cambridge: Cambridge University Press, 2004.

Lis, Catharina, and Hugo Soly. *Een groot bedrijf in een kleine stad: De firma de Heyder en Co. Te Lier 1757–1834*. Lier, Belgium: Liers Genootschap voor Geschiedenis, 1987.

Lis, Catharina, and Hugo Soly. *Poverty and Capitalism in Pre-Industrial Europe*. Brighton, UK: Harvester, 1979.

Lis, Catharina, and Hugo Soly. *Worthy Efforts: Attitudes to Work and Workers in Pre-Industrial Europe*. Leiden: Brill, 2012.

Marx, Karl. *Theories of Surplus Value*. Part I. Moscow: Progress Publishers, 1963 [1863].

NV Kristal-, glas- en aardewerkfabrieken De Sphinx voorheen Petrus Regout & Co en voorgangers 1834–1958, EAN 1012. Het Sociaal Historisch Centrum voor Limburg, the Netherlands.

Pack, Spencer J. *Capitalism as a Moral System: Adam Smith's Critique of the Free Market Economy*. Aldershot, UK: Edward Elgar, 1991.

Palliser, David Michael. *Tudor York*. Oxford: Oxford University Press, 1979.

Peil, Jan. *Adam Smith and Economic Science: A Methodological Reinterpretation*. Cheltenham, UK: Edward Elgar, 1999.

Perelman, Michael. *Classical Political Economy: Primitive Accumulation and the Social Division of Labor*. London: Rowman and Allanheld, 1984.

Perry, Jos. *Roomsche kinine tegen roode koorts: Arbeidersbeweging en katholieke kerk in Maastricht 1880–1920*. Amsterdam: Van Gennep, 1983.

Prak, Maarten. *Republikeinse veelheid, democratische enkelvoud: Sociale verandering in het Revolutietijdvak 's-Hertogenbosch 1770–1820*. Nijmegen, the Netherlands: SUN, 1999.

Raad van Brabant. *Processen van de ambachten en naties: Procesdossiers in het archief van de Raad van Brabant 1540–1795*, T 36. Rijksarchief te Anderlecht, Belgium.

Robson, Ann Provost. *On Higher than Commercial Grounds: The Factory Controversy 1830–1853*. London: Garland, 1985.

Smith, Adam. *An Inquiry into the Nature and Causes of the Wealth of Nations*. Chicago: University of Chicago Press, 1976 [1776].

Spiertz, Mathieu G. *Maastricht in het vierde kwart van de achttiende eeuw*. Assen, the Netherlands: Van Gorcum, 1964.

Stabel, Peter. "Temps de travail, temps de métier? Le temps de travail dans la grande industrie drapière en Flandre, 13e–14e siècles." Lecture originally delivered at the Maison Européenne des Sciences de l'Homme et de la Société (MESHS), Université Lille 3, France, May 31 2013, in cooperation with Universiteit Gent, Belgium.

Steuart, James. *An Inquiry into the Principles of Political Economy*. Vol. I. Chicago: University of Chicago Press, 1966 [1767].

Stone, Lawrence. "The English Revolution." In *Preconditions of Revolution in Early Modern Europe*, ed. Robert Forster and J. P. Greene, 55–108. Baltimore: Johns Hopkins University Press, 1970.

Van Aken-Fehmers, Marion S., Loet A. Schledorn, and Titus M. Eliëns. *Delfts aardewerk: Geschiedenis van een nationaal product.* Deel I. Zwolle, the Netherlands: Waanders, 1999.

Van Damme, Ilja. *Verleiden en verkopen: Antwerpse kleinhandelaars en hun klanten in tijden van crisis (ca. 1648–ca. 1748).* Amsterdam: Aksant, 2007.

Vanden Berghe, Yvan. *Jacobijnen en traditionalisten: De reacties van de Bruggelingen in de revolutietijd (1780–1794)* (Twee delen). Brussels: Pro Civitate, 1972.

Van Iterson, Ad T.M. "Vader, raadgever en beschermer Petrus Regout en zijn arbeiders 1834–1870: Stijlen van werving, behoud en beheersing van arbeid in fabrieksregimes in de beginjaren van de Westeuropese Industriële Revolutie." PhD dissertation, Rijksuniversiteit Limburg, the Netherlands, 1992.

Versieren, Jelle. "The Perception of Labour and the Discursive Temporalities of Guild Organisations, Free Trade Ideologues, and Early Industrial Capitalists in Western Europe 1750–1850." Lecture originally delivered at the Maison Européenne des Sciences de l'Homme et de la Société (MESHS), Université Lille 3, France, on May 31, 2013, in cooperation with Universiteit Gent, Belgium.

Werhane, Patricia Hogue. *Adam Smith and His Legacy for Modern Capitalism.* Oxford: Oxford University Press, 1991.

10

Aliens, Enemy Aliens, and Minors

Anti-Radicalism and the Jewish Left

Jeffrey A. Johnson

On July 23, 1892, twenty-two-year-old Alexander Berkman, armed with a revolver and a handmade dagger, arrived at the Pittsburgh office of famed Carnegie Steel executive Henry Clay Frick. Berkman was on a self-imposed mission to assassinate Frick, not only to retaliate for the industrialist's role in cracking down on steelworkers in the recent Homestead Strike but also to get revenge against what Berkman perceived as American capitalism gone awry. In a scrum, Berkman managed to shoot and stab Frick. Frick survived the attack, and authorities quickly captured Berkman, who ultimately spent fourteen years in prison for the failed attempt on Frick's life. Berkman, who was just starting a long career of radicalism, proudly declared his action to be "the first terrorist act in America."

Of special note in the Frick-Berkman incident, though, is how Berkman's ethnicity (and the subsequent fear of similarly radical and violent Jews) was featured prominently in news accounts. The day after the attack, the *Pittsburg Dispatch* described Berkman, who was already in custody, as a "Russian Hebrew Nihilist." In addition, it portrayed him as a wild-eyed Jewish radical who "looked like a crank or a fanatic," with a "dull and stolid" face, "bordering on the verge of stupidity." This depiction is significant in how it associates Berkman's Jewishness with radical and undesirable qualities. Criminality and radicalism intersected here, too, fueling the willingness of some to further generalize about American Jews. The Berkman example came to symbolize what many presumed to be a typical and prevalent radical Jewish American agitator.[1]

DOI: 10.5876/9781646420025.c010

Alexander Berkman, of course, did not typify Jewish immigrants. Much is known about American immigration in the late nineteenth and early twentieth centuries and the unwelcoming receptions certain ethnic and cultural groups sometimes received. Scholars have examined reactions to so-called radicalism in the early twentieth century, particularly the instances of restricted freedoms during and following World War I. Yet remarkably little work focuses on the intersection of anti-Semitism and anti-radicalism during these eras. One can make the case that fear of Jews and radical immigrants promoted the unprecedented anti-radical persecution of the first Red Scare. It is easy to surmise this cause because many on the American political left were not just radical but also considered by some to be Jewish rabble-rousers. Fear of these groups supported and drove, implicitly and sometimes explicitly, the widespread and undemocratic crackdown on political dissent. This chapter is perhaps too episodic to explain the entire political climate of the times. What is important to know, though, is that fears concerning Jewish radicalism colored American attitudes prior to and during the World War I era, a high point in history for fear-driven intersections of anti-radicalism and anti-Semitism.

IMMIGRATION AND NATIVISM

The demographics of the United States changed dramatically during the Gilded Age (ca. 1877–1897). In the last thirty years of the nineteenth century, 11.7 million immigrants came to the United States. The wave of immigration from early in this period, when many of the newcomers came from northern and western Europe, gave way to a larger group of immigrants later in the period who increasingly came from southern and eastern Europe. These later immigrants brought languages, customs, and religions that differed dramatically from the traditions of white American Christians. Some people regarded these later immigrants and their languages, customs, and religions as threatening.

Still, the United States has long celebrated its image as a melting pot society. At the time, many people were quick to celebrate the age of the new American immigrant. Norman Hopgood, writing in the *Menorah Journal* in 1916, announced, "Democracy will be more productive if it has a tendency to encourage differences. Our dream of the United States ought not to be a dream of monotony." Hopgood was not alone. Leftist intellectuals such as Randolph Bourne and Horace Kallan echoed this sentiment, frequently celebrating the new American pluralism.[2]

Despite the positive sentiments expressed by some in support of immigration, anti-immigrant attitudes were becoming the rule in the United States. Since the mid-nineteenth century, American nativism, rooted in long-standing trepidation concerning the "other," had colored the reception of immigrants in the United

States. The Know-Nothing Party of this era stands as a prominent example of American nativism. Social scientist Richmond Mayo-Smith embodied a nativist attitude in his 1895 book on American immigration: "It is scarcely probable that by taking the dregs of Europe we shall produce a people of high social intelligence and morality." By 1916, like-minded minister Josiah Strong had sold 175,000 copies (a notable number for the time) of his book *Our Country: Its Possible Future and Its Present Crisis*, a Protestant polemic on the new American immigrant. "The typical immigrant is a European peasant," he wrote, "whose horizon has been narrow, whose moral and religious training has been meager or false, and whose ideas of life are low." Strong gave voice to the widely held belief that among these undesirable immigrants were criminals and radicals. He continued that Europe "not only furnishes the greatest portion of our criminals, it is also seriously affecting the morals of the native population ... Immigration complicates our moral and political problems by swelling our dangerous classes." The sentiments expressed by Mayo-Smith and Strong stood well within typical stances on immigration.[3]

AMERICAN ANTI-SEMITISM

One ethnic group of immigrants that especially felt the sting of racism and reactionism was Jewish immigrants. Anti-Semitism in the United States was not a new phenomenon in the decades before World War I. Despite the claims of noted historian Oscar Handlin, who in 1951 contended that American anti-Semitism was trivial in the twentieth century (mainstream American attitudes toward Jews held "no hostility, no negative judgment," he wrote), anti-Semitism was extraordinarily routine in the late nineteenth and early twentieth centuries.[4]

Far from unique to the American experience, anti-Semitism had been cultivating unease among European Jews for decades. France's notorious Dreyfus affair of 1894–1899 demonstrated not only how, even in fragilely liberal France, anti-Semitism was used as an acceptable tool of mass politics but also how hate-filled, anti-Jewish propaganda could alarmingly fill a nation's mass media. In the 1880s and 1890s, Europe witnessed the rise of anti-Semitism in the forms of Adolf Stoecker's crusade against a Jewish cultural conspiracy in Germany and Édouard Drumont's overtly anti-Jewish newspaper, *La Libre Parole*, in France.

Anti-Semitism proliferated in the United States in the late nineteenth century, following, as it often did, these earlier European models. Around 1896, the American Anti-Semitic Association formed in Brooklyn. Its leadership, F. J. Gross, E. Augustus Lehuermann, and others, followed the typical German structure for such organizations. Greek immigrant Telemachus Timayenis, hoping to be on the front end of a methodical American anti-Semitism, authored many works on "the

Jewish Question," most notably 1888's *The Original Mr. Jacobs: A Startling Expose*. An obvious Drumont devotee, Timayenis repeated the common refrain that the scheming Jew hoped not only to compromise the capitalist system through control but also to ultimately overthrow the system. Thus anti-Semitism came to American shores as soon as Jewish immigrants arrived; from the start, Jews experienced patterns of discrimination, both socially and politically.

Jewish immigrants to the United States tended to settle, as many ethnic groups did, in specific neighborhoods, often as a way to preserve their culture in a new land. In an urban environment such as New York or Chicago, it was not unusual for the Jewish quarter to be located near Chinatown or Greektown. Yet some suggested that Jews should be less "clannish."[5] At the same time, "the gentile majority" met these Jewish communities with institutionalized discrimination that included restriction of Jewish membership in certain clubs, resorts, employment, and even neighborhoods. Throughout a considerable period of US history, specifically the Gilded Age and the Progressive Era, Jews also faced exclusion from private colleges and universities, hotels, hospitals, and law firms. As historian Hasia Diner has reminded us, the nation's "Jewish problem" and explicit anti-Semitism remained "a centerpiece of the national conversation."[6]

There are countless examples of rank discrimination against Jews in the late nineteenth and early twentieth centuries, but most shocking is the vehement rhetoric and frankness voiced by some contemporary figures. In 1879, Austin Corbin, a head of banking, railroad, and hotel companies, publicly made it clear that Jews were not welcome as guests in his company's Manhattan Beach Hotel. "Personally, I am opposed to Jews. They are a pretentious class," he announced. Corbin made it plain how Jews hurt his business: "We must have a good place for society to patronize. I say we cannot do so and have Jews. They are a detestable and vulgar people." Jewish residents of New York's East Side complained for years about incidents of police violence. A 1902 *New York Times* story documented such grievances and a number of confrontations. In one instance, two young Jewish men were reciting poetry to three or four girls in Seward Park. A police officer told them the park was no place for public speaking. When the young men playfully pointed out the difference between poetry and a political speech, the police officer clubbed one of the young poets and took him to jail. Dr. Joseph Barsky reported seeing "many such attacks on Jews" on the East Side. In early 1902 he heard of a boy beaten "into insensibility" by an officer.[7]

The "conspicuousness of Jewish wealth" further fueled fears that "Europe's Shylocks" stood poised to take jobs and exploit American wage earners. After all, a "society of Jews and brokers," claimed noted American commentator Henry Adams in 1893, left "no place" for him. This stereotype was fed by other sources, too. Intellectuals supported the notion of the money-hungry Jew. The presidents of three prominent institutions of higher learning (the University of Virginia, Vassar College, and Harvard University) declared in letters and in print that Jewish immigrants had gained "unfair" economic advantage through "questionable" business practices. At American universities, considerable WASP uneasiness with the changing face of student bodies emerged as well. "The Jew sends his children to college a generation or two sooner than other stocks, and as a result there are in fact more dirty Jews and tactless Jews in college than dirty and tactless Italians, Armenians, or Slovaks," wrote one white Protestant.[8]

Not only were Jews considered to be shady and suspicious in business, they also were blatantly considered to be criminals. In August 1908, the *New York Sun* ran an article with the headline "Criminals among the Jews." The exposé highlighted how New York's Jews, most notably Russian immigrants, swelled crime statistics in the city. According to Police Commissioner Theodore Bingham, "Russian Jew criminals" consumed a majority of the police department's work. A year earlier, Bingham estimated that "60 per cent" of the city's criminals were Russian Jews. More "precise" data came from the deputy commissioner's office, which claimed that of the department's 189,202 arrests in 1906, "50 per cent [of those arrested] were of Jewish parentage."[9]

At various points in the prewar years, anti-Semitism led to violence against Jews. One of the more notorious cases was that of Leo Frank, a Jewish executive at Atlanta's Georgia Pencil Company who was charged and convicted of the murder of a thirteen-year-old girl, Mary Phagan, during the summer of 1913. After being condemned to death, Frank's sentence was commuted, and he was incarcerated in Milledgeville State Prison. A mob of twenty-eight kidnapped Frank from the prison and drove him 170 miles to Phagan's hometown, where he was viciously beaten and lynched. The State of Georgia ultimately pardoned Frank in 1986, but in 1915, the Frank case typified anti-Semitic sentiments. Authorities and the angry mob that killed Frank thought of him as a Jewish interloper from the North. Editors in the Jewish press, not surprisingly, vehemently condemned the mob's actions. "This crime stamps indelible obloquy upon the State of Georgia," wrote Felix Gerson, editor of the *Jewish Exponent*. "This lynching is one of the most deplorable episodes in the history of our nation."[10]

The patterns of distrust and the stereotypes applied to Jews, not surprisingly, drew resistance from members of the Jewish community. Dr. Stephen Wise, a rabbi for New York's Free Synagogue congregation, took a public stand against such discrimination. He had been invited to an international peace conference, to be held at Lake Mohonk, New York. The host resort there, however, closed its doors to Jews during the summer months. As a sign of protest, Wise refused his invitation and spoke out against this discrimination in a May 22, 1911, speech at Carnegie Hall. "Land hunger and territorial greed," Wise declared, paled in comparison to "religious and national hostility, of which anti-Semitism is a most persistent and Christless example." Beginning in 1916, other prominent Jewish Americans formally undertook efforts to ensure civil rights and equality. Supreme Court Justice Louis Brandeis and others planned to establish what they called the "Conference of National Jewish Organizations" (later known as the American Jewish Congress, established in 1918) to fight against the "radical discrimination against the Jews of America."[11]

WORLD WAR I AND ANTI-RADICALISM

By 1914, US involvement in World War I gave rise to a heightened sense of fear among immigrants, leftists, and radicals. Much of the 1916 presidential campaign between Woodrow Wilson and Charles Evans Hughes centered on national loyalty, or "Americanism," as it was called during the race. Both Democrats and Republicans used loaded language during the campaign to hint that those people on the other side may be weak in their patriotism. The phrases "100 percent Americanism" and "disloyal Americans" were used in the campaign, complete with the connotation that being anything other than a "loyal" patriotic American was suspect. As the United States moved from determined isolationism and neutrality to imminent involvement in the war in 1917, many Americans, according to historian Leonard Dinnerstein and other sources, grew suspicious of "anything that smacked of Germany and Germans." Not insignificant, of course, was the fact that many German immigrants to the United States at that time were Jewish. As a movement, anarchism arrived in the United States at the end of the nineteenth century. Johann Most, a German immigrant, and his journal *Die Freiheit* (*Freedom*) disembarked in New York in 1882. Most established the anarchist branch of the International Working People's Association, which proved exceedingly popular among other recent German immigrants. Dubbed "the prince of anarchists," Most openly advocated and justified the assassination of politicians and monarchs.[12]

The rise of this reactive brand of American anarchism in the prewar years was not surprising. At no other time in US history (i.e., before the first part of the twentieth century) had capital and labor come into such marked conflict. The nation had seen labor violence at every turn. Violent discontent seemed to be spreading—for instance, the bombings at the *Los Angeles Times* building in 1910 and the San Francisco Preparedness Day parade in 1916. The prewar years had been a time of very active leftist labor agitation; therefore federal, state, and local governments had begun to enact legislation and to act out of profound fear of this emerging radical left. The argument can be made that subtexts of ethnic and religious discrimination surrounded many of these anti-radical sentiments. The most commonly persecuted and singled-out group within the radical fringe was leftist Jewish Americans. The political climate of France's notorious Dreyfus affair from two decades earlier, it seemed, had moved to the United States. Alexander Berkman, Emma Goldman, and other prominent Jewish Americans on the political fringe, more than any other immigrant group, had been on the receiving end of a wave of anti-radicalism that was not so thinly enveloped in xenophobia.

Emma Goldman had long been one of the most recognizable faces of the radical Jewish left in the prewar years. She came from a Lithuanian Orthodox Jewish family. Her radicalism extended beyond mere talk. Authorities had arrested her in Chicago in 1901 for her alleged role in a conspiracy to assassinate President William McKinley. Labeled by the press as "the high priestess of anarchy," Goldman had come to symbolize the leftist Jewish agitator in the early twentieth century. The press happily reported that during her interrogation by police, Goldman showed weakness and "became a woman, pure and simple, and cried." Police ultimately released her because authorities could not connect her to anything beyond inspiring Leon Czolgosz to assassinate President McKinley. Goldman retreated briefly from her public life of radicalism. She founded *Mother Earth* magazine in 1906 and proceeded to crisscross the United States on speaking tours on behalf of anarchism and labor militancy. At each event, Goldman took the podium only after downing a routine shot of whiskey to settle her nerves. Once she was onstage, however, any anxieties she might have had quickly gave way to her espousals of anarchism.

Goldman's longtime political partner (and lover) was none other than the failed assassin and anarchist Alexander Berkman. Upon assuming the editor's chair of *Mother Earth* in 1907, Berkman began thinking of publishing a radical journal of his own. He "longed for something of his own making, something that would express his own self," Goldman recalled. By the winter of 1915, at the urging of friend Eric Morton, he acted on the longing and founded *The Blast* in San Francisco. He had been so enthusiastic about the project that he created a letterhead, which he shared with friends, well before securing funding for the periodical or officially launching it. *The Blast*, not surprisingly, became a key forum for the expression of leftists' antiwar positions.[13] The mainstream press not so subtly associated both Berkman and Goldman with the image of the money-hungry Jew when considering the publications each had launched. For the *New York Sun*, Berkman was a "jack-in-the box . . . who bobs up in every kind of radical movement that promises financial returns," and Goldman was described as a "shrewd [individual] . . . who for many years has made anarchy a well paying profession." The article spoke of the pair's "money grabbing proclivities."[14]

The social and political left, with which Jewish immigrants were often associated, felt the quick rebuke of pro-war forces. From the start of the war, American socialists objected to the conflict, as did their comrades worldwide. After all, they claimed, all wars were imperialist wars that benefited only capitalists; the working class would do the bulk of the fighting. Amid opposition to the war, the unfolding political situation in Russia, and the accompanying Red Scare in the United States, if a person were identified as part of the nation's left or in any way associated with the "radicalism" label, it could lead to disastrous political and personal implications.[15]

Jewish Socialists remained an important part of this leftist opposition to the war. Since 1901, the Socialist Party of America (SPA) had been a constant radical presence on the American political landscape. Established in July 1912, the Jewish Federation of the SPA organized dozens of branches, primarily on the East Coast. By the next year, it boasted 2,700 members. Leftist (specifically, Jewish) agitators spoke against US intervention in the affairs of Europe. Indeed, Jewish members of the American left stood in unyielding and vocal support of antiwar causes. In 1917, the Jewish Socialist Federation (JSF) Convention endorsed the larger SPA convention's war resolutions. "Participation of America in the war is unjustifiable," the JSF resolved during its five days of sessions. These types of public objections to the war, however, came at a heavy price, politically speaking. The government targeted radicals—in particular, the perceived disloyalty of immigrants—to halt antiwar agitation. The Espionage Act (1917), the Trading with the Enemy Act (1917), and the Sedition Act (1918) all combined to restrict speech and repress "disloyalty."[16]

Jews had long had a "radical" reputation, and the stereotypically restless and revolutionary Jew became something to be feared by the time World War I had begun. Association with "radical" Jewish organizations and other known Jewish agitators often drew a mistrustful eye. Take, for example, Dr. Max Goldfarb of the leftist paper the *Jewish Daily Forward*, who attended the 1917 Socialist Peace Conference in Stockholm, Sweden, reportedly without a passport. His attendance, documented in the press, raised suspicions because Goldfarb was a former secretary of the Jewish Workingman's Committee and, according to the *New York Tribune*, "was conspicuously connected with the celebrated Jewish revolutionary organization known as the Bund and was one of its most gifted spokesmen." He and a fellow delegate to the conference, David Davidovitch, were "well known in Jewish circles." Thus a distinctive feature, if not *the* distinctive feature, of Goldfarb's and Davidovitch's identities in this newspaper account was clearly their Jewish ethnicity as part of a radical ideology. Only a month earlier, Dr. Goldfarb had addressed the United Cloth Hat and Cap Makers of North America convention in New York. Well received with applause, Goldfarb delivered his speech, it was noted importantly in the convention minutes, "in Jewish." This is revealing for two reasons: first the ethno-religious identification was significant to the editors, and second, the identifier was inaccurate (the proceedings were often held in Yiddish, of course).[17]

When the first efforts to establish Marxism in Russia erupted in 1917, many on the American left praised the events. On March 20, 1917, at least 11,000 people from the Jewish Socialist Federation of America and other Jewish newspaper and trade associations filled Madison Square Garden. Organizers planned the event to celebrate the Russian Revolution and the toppling of the tsar. The *New York Times* headline, though, read, "10,000 Jews Here Laud Revolution," and the story described how the speakers' tone turned radical and called for a socialist revolution in the United States. New York socialist Morris Hillquit presided at the event and proclaimed how "the fall of Russian absolutism is the doom of political oppression all over the world." Perhaps more than even the war in Europe, according to historian Michael Dobkowski, "The Bolshevik Revolution . . . haunted Americans and intensified fears of an encroaching influence dedicated to the destruction of Western democratic life. In their search for a single, comprehensive explanation for these developments and in their desire to weed out the 'Red' from the 'true blue,' they converged upon the Jew, that symbol of ancient, hidden enemies."[18]

Abraham Cahan, a fixture among leftist Jewish socialists, similarly embraced the recent political upheaval in Russia. In a piece that originally appeared in the Yiddish paper the *Jewish Daily Forward* (and was translated into English for readers of the *New York Call*) titled "A Dream No Longer," Cahan celebrated the revolution. "The hope of seeing Socialism established all over the world is no longer a piece of remote idealism but something on the threshold of realization," he enthusiastically wrote. For skeptical onlookers, it would have undoubtedly been true to expected form for radical Jews in America to celebrate the anti-capitalist events in Russia with such praise. Speaking to the immediate negative reaction to Marxism in the United States, Cahan asked, "Is it not time for all of us to cast off our former bitterness and venom . . . and wish our victorious comrades in Russia further success and happiness?" Cahan's question represented the Jewish left's sympathy with fear-inducing international developments. The editor of Boston's *Revolutionary Age*, Nicholas Hourwich, also embraced the historic moment, which he called "the greatest of revolutions." Marxism, the editor wrote, had "stepped out of the bulky volumes [of ideology] and become realized in life."[19] Hourwich was the son of famed radical Jewish lawyer—and immigrant from tsarist Russia—Isaac Hourwich.

LEGISLATING AND CODIFYING FEAR

America's post-Bolshevik attitudes, according to immigration historian Roger Daniels, "helped push anti-immigrant sentiment to perhaps its highest peaks in American history." Of course, those in the United States who supported the Russian Revolution and its ideology faced criticism and suspicion. The *New York*

Sun ran a long wartime piece under the headline "Bolsheviki Here Are Anything But American in Spirit." Based on an extensive interview with Assistant US Attorney Harold Content, the piece aimed to profile and discredit "agitators." In addition to multiple insinuations that "Emma and Alex" (i.e., Goldman and Berkman) and other anarchists benefited financially from their political agitation, clear statements were made about the ethnic origins of such leftists. "These radicals . . . are not American. The majority of these people come from Eastern Europe," the newspaper revealed.[20]

Morris Hillquit, a Jew, ran for mayor of New York at possibly the most unfavorable time ever for a candidate who was both Jewish and socialist—at the height of wartime anti-Semitic and anti-radical paranoia, in November 1917. The *New York Tribune*, with sneering accusations, covered his platform and campaign through a lens of suspicion. Running "under the guise of socialism," the *Tribune* charged, Hillquit was the embodiment of the suspicious Jewish agitator. In its curt profile, the paper described him as "a Jew, born in Riga (the Milwaukee of Russia), forty-eight years ago. He is now rich and lives on Riverside Drive." First, Hillquit's Jewishness stood as a liability. At the same time, his opposition to the war marked him as a candidate to be feared. (Not by accident, this Hillquit profile also included a sketch of him wearing a Prussian helmet.) Running on what the paper called an "anti-war, anti-conscription, and quick peace platform," Hillquit was in accord with many of the left's standard positions at the time. Still, this exposé on "Comrade Hillquit" ran under the headline "Who's Who against America," which clearly spelled out how the *Tribune*'s editors viewed his patriotism. Derogatorily called the "Pacifist-Socialist Candidate" in newspapers, Hillquit was scrutinized again the following year by Dr. Harry Best. Best closely tracked the neighborhoods where Hillquit had enjoyed the most success and reported his findings. Hillquit received 22.1 percent of the vote in the mayoral race, a rather strong showing for a third-party candidate. His candidacy, however, was quickly marginalized. According to Best, Hillquit's party, after all, had adopted a platform that included a stance in opposition to the war that was inconsistent with "the nation as a whole." Hillquit and the socialists, the piece made clear, remained political outliers. "The Hillquit vote," Best explained, "was packed into certain . . . sections of the city. The population of these sections is predominantly alien in origin, and unassimilated." The piece made clear that any electoral success Hillquit enjoyed had rested on the popular support of undesirable immigrant voters. Russian, German, and Austrian voters led the way in the neighborhoods that backed Hillquit, and they supported the Socialist Party of America, an "alien organization on American soil." This depiction, in short, made clear that people it called the "unassimilable immigrants" were to be feared, particularly as an influential voice in politics.[21]

During the World War I era, the government unambiguously legislated anti-radicalism. The February 1917 immigration restriction bill, despite some previous protest from President Woodrow Wilson, now saw support, and the statute contained significant anti-radical elements. Jewish antiwar dissent—and a broader fear of "alien radicals"—was greeted firmly by anxious citizens and lawmakers. The darkest moments came with the passage of the Espionage Act (1917) and the Sedition Act (1918), both of which drastically restricted free-speech rights. Minnesota's *Labor World* documented restrictions of speech during the war. The paper cited seven attacks in ninety days on the "liberty of the working class press" in the United States. Authorities arrested Margaret Sanger for "misuse of the mails." The arrests of Elizabeth Gurley Flynn and Emma Goldman followed, as did the suppression of two radical papers, *Revolt* and the *Alarm*. Also suppressed was the "last issue" of Berkman's *The Blast*. For *Labor World*, this period marked "an era of commercial imperialism backed by the bayonets of 'preparedness.'" In April 1918, the secretary of the Washington State Socialist Party, Emil Herman, was arrested for sedition after police confiscated approximately 700 pieces of "disloyal" literature and seven cases of correspondence, mailing lists, stickers, and receipt books from his office. A federal grand jury in Seattle charged Herman with seven counts of sedition and claimed that he had "willfully and feloniously attempted to cause insubordination, disloyalty, mutiny, and refusal of duty." As wartime paranoia reached its apex, two Jewish socialists, Victor Berger and Louis Waldman, were refused installation in seats to which they had been elected in the US Congress and the New York State Assembly, respectively. The Red Scare of 1919–1920 culminated in hundreds of deportations, typified by the voyage of the *Buford* (nicknamed "the Soviet Ark") that left New York harbor on December 21, 1919, bound for Europe with 249 leftists aboard, including Berkman and Goldman.[22]

When one reads accounts produced during this time of heightened paranoia, it is easy to see how the terms *Jewish* and *radical* were often used interchangeably and with obvious negative connotations. When the *New York Times* announced a wartime meeting of the Jewish Socialist Federation of America in early 1918, for example, the headline referred to the event as a "great meeting of radicals." Some people within the Jewish community had tried to counter this reputation for radicalism. "Jews Not Bomb Throwers" was the headline of an essay that ran in the *New York Daily News*. The essay quoted a recent speech delivered by Rabbi Dr. Judah Magnes at Temple Emanu-El on New York's Fifth Avenue. Rabbi Magnes stated that "Jews, as a people, were the most ardent advocates of peace, industry, and love, and that there was no class of people who were so strongly opposed to violence." Even "radical Jews," he maintained, stood committed to peace, justice, and non-violence.[23]

During World War I, many Jewish Americans demonstrated a keen sense of loyalty to the United States and its role in the war. On March 22, 1918, for example, in the *New York Times*, the Jewish Socialist Federation of America called on its members to support the war effort "Now is the time," the group declared, "when all parties and all beliefs should be united with a common purpose in the defense of the world." Further, Jews served in the military during the war at rates higher than their proportional numbers in the US population. About 250,000 Jewish soldiers served during World War I, which constituted about 5 percent of the fighting force at a time when Jews numbered about 3 percent of the US population. The *New York Sun* covered a mass demonstration of Americanism on Manhattan's East Side, in "a quarter, which, of the whole city, needed it most." Upon the occasion of the government issuing its third Liberty Bond in April 1918, thousands took to the streets to show their support for the war effort. "Jewish patriarchs" and "Jewish women" participated, according to this report in the *New York Times*, because Jewish children in this usual "hotbed of Bolshevikism [*sic*]" had been teaching their parents and grandparents the virtues of "Americanism." The *Sun* rejoiced, reporting, true or not, that "the red flag of socialism and anarchy has been chucked into the garbage pails." In addition, the Anglicization of Jewish surnames during the war was celebrated. The paper reported a rush to "adopt the gentile system" by those with names such as Rosenthal, Greenberg, and Goldstein. "Dislike . . . for everything with a sauerkraut flavor" reportedly precipitated about one name change per day in New York County. An old name, after all, "made its wearer the object of ridicule" and "hinders the petitioner's business."[24]

CONCLUSION

In the end, this culture of fear had profound implications for the political left. Both the Socialist Party of America and the accompanying anarchist movements sputtered after the war as a consequence of the government crackdown on leftist speech. The mood of anti-radicalism and its interconnectedness with anti-Semitism offers powerful lessons about racism, discrimination, and unfounded alarm—and just how far fear can drive political reactions that restrict prized freedoms. Leftist agitators and opponents of US participation in World War I, particularly Jewish organizers, faced a climate of fear and condescension. In 1916, Emma Goldman chaired a gathering of what the *New York Times* dubbed "socialists, anarchists, and other 'ists.'" Words used to describe the meeting included some with negative connotations, such as "tumult," "contentious," and "belligerent." The meeting, attended by "eighty organizations, representing every radical party," featured two hours of speakers "in five different languages." The paper, which clearly played to anti-immigrant feelings, took special care to point out that some of the speakers, such as Bernard Seneken, "talked in Yiddish" as they spoke about the war and critiqued preparedness.[25]

This World War I era of paranoia and targeting of radicals ushered in what historian John Higham called a "new golden age of American anti-Semitism." The mind-set behind Europe's "Protocols of the Elders of Zion," which apocryphally outlined a Jewish plot of worldwide dominance, inspired the postwar fears of Jews that matriculated into disturbing trends, such as the "new" Ku Klux Klan and the anti-Semitic crusades of public figures such as Henry Ford.²⁶ Still, the image of the Jewish wild-eyed anarchist or leftist assassin, akin to Alexander Berkman in 1892, remained the exception to the rule. The broadly anti-radical and specifically anti-Jewish hysteria of the early twentieth century and the World War I era is a powerful reminder of how wartime anti-radicalism, often predicated on latent and outward anti-Semitism, can stereotype people and limit liberties.

NOTES

1. Avrich and Avrich, *Sasha and Emma*, 1; *Pittsburg Dispatch*, July 24, 1892.

2. Hopgood, "The Jews and American Democracy," 202.

3. Mayo-Smith, *Emigration and Immigration*, 77; Shea, *The Lion*, 67; Strong, *Our Country*, 40, 42, 44.

4. Higham, "Anti-Semitism," 561; Handlin, "American Views," 328.

5. Higham, "Anti-Semitism," 576, 570, 562; *New York Times*, December 19, 1904.

6. Dinnerstein et al., *Natives and Strangers*, 237; Diner, "The Encounter between Jews and America," 5.

7. *New York Sun*, July 23, 1879 (quotation); *New York Times*, August 13, 1902.

8. Higham, "Anti-Semitism," 567, 573 (Adams quotation); Dobkowski, "American Anti-Semitism," 177; Gilman and Katz, *Anti-Semitism in Times of Crisis*, 215 (second quotation).

9. Joselit, *Our Gang*, 186 (Bingham quotation); *New York Sun*, August 12, 1908, 5 (deputy commissioner quotation).

10. *Philadelphia Evening Ledger*, August 17, 1915, 2.

11. *Washington Times*, May 22, 1911; *Broad Ax* (Chicago), September 2, 1916.

12. Lukas, *Big Trouble*, 61; *Marshall Republican* (Marshall, MO), October 18, 1901.

13. *San Francisco Call*, September 11, 1901; Avrich and Avrich, *Sasha and Emma*, 136, 252–253.

14. *New York Sun*, January 6, 1918.

15. See Johnson, *They Are All Red*.

16. Salutsky, "Report of the Jewish Translator," 1; *New York Call*, May 31, 1917.

17. *New York Tribune*, June 21, 1917, 2.

18. *New York Tribune*, June 20, 1917, 2, June 21, 1917, 2; United Cloth Hat and Cap Makers of North America, *Headgear Worker*, 1, 4; "10,000 Jews Here Laud Revolution," *New York Times*, March 21, 1917, 3; Dobkowski, "American Anti-Semitism," 180.

19. *New York Call*, May 31, 1918; *Revolutionary Age* (Boston), December 7, 1918.

20. Daniels, *Guarding the Golden Door*, 47; *New York Sun*, January 6, 1918.

21. *New York Tribune* October 28, 1917, March 10, 1918.

22. *Labor World* (Duluth, MN), April 22, 1916; *Party Builder*, August 20, April 20, 1918; *Co-operative News*, May 9, June 13, 1918; Schwantes, *The Pacific Northwest*, 354; Daniels, *Guarding the Golden Door*, 46–47; Waldman, *Albany: The Crisis.*

23. *New York Times*, March 2, 1918; *New York Daily Tribune*, April 5, 1908.

24. Michael, *Concise History*, 101; *New York Times*, March 22, 1918; *New York Sun*, April 28, 1918.

25. *New York Times*, April 3, 1916.

26. Higham, "Anti-Semitism," 570.

BIBLIOGRAPHY

Avrich, Paul, and Karen Avrich, *Sasha and Emma: The Anarchist Odyssey of Alexander Berkman and Emma Goldman*. Cambridge, MA: Harvard University Press, 2012.

Daniels, Roger. *Guarding the Golden Door: American Immigration Policy and Immigrants Since 1882*. New York: Hill and Wang, 2004.

Diner, Hasia. "The Encounter between Jews and America in the Gilded Age and Progressive Era." *Journal of the Gilded Age and Progressive Era* 11 (January 2012): 3–25.

Dinnerstein, Leonard, David M. Reimers, and Roger L. Nichols, *Natives and Strangers: A History of Ethnic Americans*. New York: Oxford University Press, 1996.

Dobkowski, Michael N. "American Anti-Semitism: A Reinterpretation." *American Quarterly* 29 (Summer 1977): 166–181.

Gilman, Sander L., and Steven T. Katz, eds. *Anti-Semitism in Times of Crisis*. New York: New York University Press, 1991.

Handlin, Oscar. "American Views of the Jew at the Opening of the Twentieth Century." *Publications of [the] American Jewish Historical Society* 40 (June 1951): 323–344.

Higham, John. "Anti-Semitism in the Gilded Age: A Reinterpretation." *Mississippi Valley Historical Review* 43 (March 1957): 559–578.

Hopgood, Norman. "The Jews and American Democracy." *Menorah Journal* 2 (October 1916): 201–205.

Johnson, Jeffrey A. *They Are All Red Out Here: Socialist Politics in the Pacific Northwest, 1895–1925*. Norman: University of Oklahoma Press, 2008.

Joselit, Jenna Weissman. *Our Gang: Jewish Crime and the New York Jewish Community, 1900–1940*. Bloomington: Indiana University Press, 1983.

Kennedy, David. *Over Here: The First World War and American Society*. New York: Oxford University Press, 2004.

Lukas, J. Anthony. *Big Trouble: A Murder in a Small Western Town Sets Off a Struggle for the Soul of America*. New York: Simon and Schuster, 1997.

Mayo-Smith, Richmond. *Emigration and Immigration: A Study in Social Science*. New York: Charles Scribner and Sons, 1895.

Michael, Robert. *A Concise History of American Anti-Semitism*. Oxford: Rowman and Littlefield, 2005.

Salutsky, Jacob Benjamin. "Report of the Jewish Translator-Secretary of the National Committee of the Socialist Party of America, May 1913." (First published as a type-set leaflet by the Socialist Party, undated. Specimen in Tim Davenport Collection, Collection 344, Hoover Institution Archives, Stanford, CA 94305-6010.) http://www.marxisthistory.org/history/usa/parties/lfed/jewish/1913/0500-salutsky-reporttonc.pdf.

Schwantes, Carlos. *The Pacific Northwest: An Interpretive History*. Lincoln: University of Nebraska Press, 1989.

Shea, William M. *The Lion and the Lamb: Evangelicals and Catholics in America*. New York: Oxford University Press, 2004.

Strong, Josiah. *Our Country: Its Possible Future and Its Present Crisis*. New York: Baker and Taylor, 1885.

United Cloth Hat and Cap Makers of North America. *The Headgear Worker*. Volumes 1–2. New York: General Executive Board of the United Cloth Hat and Cap Makers of North America, 1918. https://books.google.com/books?id=oioeAAAAYAAJ&printsec=frontcover#v=onepage&q&f=false.

Waldman, Louis. *Albany: The Crisis in Government: The History of the Suspension, Trial, and Expulsion from the New York State Legislature in 1920 of the Five Socialist Assemblymen by Their Political Opponents*. New York: Boni and Liveright, 1920.

About the Contributors

QUAYLAN ALLEN is an associate professor in the Donna Ford Attallah College of Educational Studies at Chapman University. His research addresses educational equity by critically examining the implications of social and educational policy and practice on culturally diverse populations. In particular, his research focuses on black male educational success, black masculinities in school, and participant visual methodologies with youth populations.

MELANIE ARMSTRONG is a faculty member in the Master of Environmental Management Program at Western Colorado University. Her research on biopolitics and the historical formations of nature explores how nature coalesces with fear to transform social relations. Her 2017 book, *Germ Wars: The Politics of Nature and America's Landscape of Fear*, examines the politics enabled by the belief that nature—in this case, microbes—can be managed through cultural practices. By studying how people incorporate knowledge of nature into their daily lives, she aims to show how securing the nation against disease binds citizenship and governance to new scientific knowledge of germs, body, and risk. She also coauthored *Environmental Realism: Challenging Solutions*, arguing for new approaches in the language and practice of environmental management, work that emerged from her fifteen-year career with the National Park Service.

TRAVIS D. BOYCE is an associate professor of Africana studies at the University of Northern Colorado. His research interests are in contemporary African American history and popular culture (the intersection of race, fashion, and social media in the sporting world). He is guest editing special issues (Fashion, Style, Aesthetics, and Black Lives Matter) of the *Fashion, Style, and Popular Culture Journal* as well as the *Journal of Asia-Pacific Pop Culture* (Race and Whiteness Studies). He is also completing his second book that will probe hash tags, memes, images, and commentary on social media related to the fashion of activist athletes with the context of history and contemporary life.

WINSOME M. CHUNNU is the director of Multicultural Programs at Ohio University. She holds a PhD in cultural studies from Ohio University. Her areas of expertise are educational policy, policy implementation, race and politics, and popular culture. She is guest editing a special issue (Fashion, Style, Aesthetics, and Black Lives Matter) of the *Fashion, Style, and Popular Culture Journal* and working on a book on educational policy implantation in Jamaica.

BRECHT DE SMET is a senior postdoctoral researcher in the Department of Conflict and Development Studies at Ghent University, Belgium. He teaches Politics of Development and Contemporary Politics of the Middle East. His research interests entail Gramscian theory, the dynamics of class struggle, the history of socialism, and Middle East politics. De Smet is the author of two monographs: "Gramsci, Vygotsky, and the Egyptian Revolution" (2015, Brill; 2016, Haymarket) and "Gramsci on Tahrir" (2016, Pluto Press) and is preparing a book on the socialism of Henri De Man.

KIRSTEN DYCK is the author of *Reichsrock: The International Web of White-Power and Neo-Nazi Hate Music* (Rutgers University Press, 2017). She holds a PhD in American Studies from Washington State University and has had fellowships with the US Holocaust Memorial Museum, the German-American Fulbright Commission, and the Auschwitz Jewish Center. She taught for James Madison University from 2012–2017 and has recently completed a 2017–2019 US Peace Corps term teaching English at Poltava V.G. Korolenko National Pedagogical University in Poltava, Ukraine.

ADAM C. FONG is a tenured professor of history at Merced College. He has previously taught at the University of Northern Colorado and holds a doctorate from the University of Hawaii at Manoa. His primary field of research is Tang dynasty China. He focuses mainly on issues such as urbanization, maritime trade, local identity, and cross-cultural interactions in southern China. He is also very interested in the links between East and Southeast Asia and tracing connections—for example, by researching immigrant networks—between regional histories and world history.

JEFFREY A. JOHNSON is a professor of history and director of the Graduate Program at Providence College in Rhode Island, where he teaches courses on the Gilded Age / Progressive Era, labor history, and the American West. He is the author of *They Are All Red Out Here: Socialist Politics in the Pacific Northwest, 1895–1925* (University of Oklahoma Press, 2008), the edited collection *Reforming America: A Thematic Encyclopedia and Document Collection of the Progressive Era* (ABC-Clio, 2017), and *The 1916 Preparedness Day Bombing: Anarchists and Terrorism in Progressive Era America* (Routledge, 2018).

ŁUKASZ KAMIEŃSKI is a university professor on the Faculty of International and Political Studies of Jagiellonian University in Krakow, Poland. His work concentrates on military technology and military transformation, the history and future of war and the military profession, and strategic issues of international relations. He has published three books in Polish. His recent study is *Shooting Up: A History of Drugs in Warfare* (Oxford University Press, 2016) also published in French, Italian, and Spanish. He is currently working on the project on neuroscience and neuroengineering and war.

GUY LANCASTER is the editor of the online Encyclopedia of Arkansas, a project of the Central Arkansas Library System, as well as an adjunct professor at the University of Arkansas Clinton School for Public Service and an occasional contributor to the *Arkansas Times*. He is the author of *Racial Cleansing in Arkansas, 1883–1924: Politics, Land, Labor, and Criminality* (2014), co-editor of *To Can the Kaiser: Arkansas and the Great War* (2015), and editor of *Bullets and Fire: Lynching and Authority in Arkansas, 1840–1950* (2018) and *The Elaine Massacre and Arkansas: A Century of Atrocity and Resistance, 1819–1919* (2018). His books have received awards from the Arkansas Historical Association and the Booker Worthen Literary Prize.

HENRY SANTOS METCALF holds a PhD in Education with an emphasis in Cross-Cultural Studies from Chapman University in Orange, California, where he also serves as a faculty member in the Wilkinson College of Arts, Humanities, and Social Sciences teaching LGBTQ Studies. In addition, he is an administrator for the Office of Accessible Education and Counseling Services at Brandman University, a member of the Chapman University System, where he supports non-traditional students, adult learners, and a large student-veteran and military population. He is a board member for the World Rehabilitation and Disability Conference (WRDC), where he has presented at their events held at various international locations and serves as the editor and scholarly resource consultant for The International Institute of Knowledge Management (TIIKM) organization. His recent research interests have focused on student-veterans navigating higher education, diversity and inclusion efforts, and queer discourse.

JULIE M. POWELL is a PhD candidate in History at The Ohio State University and a Mellon/ACLS Dissertation Completion Fellow. She is the author of "Shock Troupe: Medical Film and the Performance of 'Shell Shock' for the British Nation at War" (*Social History of Medicine*, 2017) and "About-Face: Gender, Disfigurement and the Politics of French Reconstruction, 1918–1924" (*Gender & History*, 2016). She is the recipient of numerous grants and fellowships, including funds from the Centre International de Recherche de l'Historial de la Grande Guerre, the American Historical Association, The New York Academy of Medicine, and the Social Sciences Research Council.

JELLE VERSIEREN is a postdoctoral researcher at the University of Antwerp. Affiliated with the Centre for Urban History, he examines labor concepts and the discourses of labor value in the Low Countries' economic transition to capitalism. He is a consulting editor for *History of Intellectual Culture* (University of Calgary) and a guest lecturer at Ghent University (on the histories and epistemologies of economic thought). He has recently published essays on Karl Marx, Michel Foucault, Antonio Gramsci, Adam Smith, Rosa Luxemburg, Thomas Sekine, GWF Hegel, French structuralism, the history of the Belgian labor movement, and state formations and economic transitions in early modern western Europe.

Index

Adams, Henry, 197

"addicted army," 12, 157–75; as myth, 163–65, 169; as scapegoats, 165, 168, 170–71

addiction, 168–69

Africa, smallpox eradication in, *60*, 60–61, *61*, *63*, 64

African Americans: depicted as lazy, 138–39; in elected office, 134–39; fear of, 7, 11–12; Redeemers portraying, 123–25, 127–28, 131–33, 137–38, 139; and wealth gap, 83. *See also* black masculinities

Alabama, Reconstruction resentment in, 133

alcohol use, 161, *162*

Aldama, Arturo J., 3, 4, 8

Alexander, Jeffrey C., 142

Allen, Quaylan, 9

Alsop, Stewart, 164

"Americanism," 199

American Jewish Congress, 199

"American labor," 114, *115*

Amherst, Jeffrey, 55

amphetamines, 157; heroin mixed with, 158–59; Vietnam War use of, 160–61, *162*; World War II use of, 158, 160

anarchism, 109–10, *110*, 111, 199–200

Andean soldiers, drug use by, 158

Anger Within, 78

An Lushan Rebellion, 43

anticommunism, 11, 13, 102–21, 204; American identity and, 116–17; as anti-labor tactic, 103–5, 107–8, 116–18; civil liberties eroded by, 113, 116; deportation and, 115–16; devil imagery in, 111–12; as "hysteria," 103, 104; immigrants and, 104, 108–18; Jewish victims of, 195, 204; in newspapers, 102, 108–16, *110*, *113*, *115*, *117*; as racist, 105; "Red" language of, 110–12; state repression of, 112–16

anti-Semitism, 13, 74–78, 194–208; and non-Jewish racial Others, 77–78; *Protocols of the Elders of Zion* and, 74–75, 206; ZOG theory and, 75–78

Arkansas, 10–11, 88–101; murders in, 132; railroad work in, 91, 92–93

Armstrong, Melanie, 9–10

Asia, smallpox eradication in, 59, 62, *62*, 63

Asians, stereotypes of, 106, 109, 111, 114

assassination, political, 128, 194, 200

Austin, Algernon, 5

Australia, white-power music in, 78

Austria, the far right in, 5–6

Al-Awadi, Abdul Rahman, 64

Banner-Haley, Charles Pete T., 144

Barreto, Matt, 5

Barsky, Joseph, 197

Bartlett, Billy, 80

Baton Rouge police shooting, 4, 5

Battlefront, 76–77, 79

Beck, Glenn, 139

www.ingramcontent.com/pod-product-compliance
Lightning Source LLC
Chambersburg PA
CBHW020252030426
42336CB00010B/732